CITIZENSHIP AND THE ETHICS OF CARE

Feminist considerations on justice,
morality and politics

Selma Sevenhuijsen

Translated from Dutch by Liz Savage

London and New York

First published 1998
by Routledge
11 New Fetter Lane, London EC4P 4EE

Simultaneously published in the USA and Canada
by Routledge
29 West 35th Street, New York, NY 10001

© 1998 Selma Sevenhuijsen
© 1996 Selma Sevenhuijsen, Amsterdam *Oordelen met zorg: Feministische
beschouwingen over recht, moraal en politiek*
Published by Uitgeverij Boom, Amsterdam
Translated from Dutch by Liz Savage
The translation of the Dutch edition was supported by a grant from the
Dutch Organisation for Scientific Research (NWO)

Typeset in Baskerville by
BC Typesetting
Printed and bound in Great Britain by
Creative Print and Design (Wales), Ebbw Vale

British Library Cataloguing in Publication Data
A catalogue record for this book is available from the British Library

Library of Congress Cataloguing in Publication Data
Sevenhuijsen, Selma.
[Ordelen met zorg. English]
Citizenship and the ethics of care: feminist considerations on
justice, morality and politics/Selma Sevenhuijsen.
p. cm.
Includes bibliographical references and index.
1. Human services–Moral and ethical aspects. 2. Caregivers.
3. Feminist ethics. 4. Feminist theory. 5. Justice. I. Title.
HV41.S38813 1998
362'.0425–dc21 97-42947
CIP

ISBN 0–415–17081–8 (hbk)
ISBN 0–415–17082–6 (pbk)

CONTENTS

PREFACE

Care is important to everyone. Most of us would agree that adequate provision of care is a valuable social good. However, it is exactly this self-evident value of care which raises a problem. For a long time it seemed natural for women to be responsible for care, in families as well as in social services. The modern women's movement, however, has challenged the self-evidence of women's caring role. It has argued for a fairer distribution of tasks between men and women, and for a re-evaluation of care as an activity, identity and morality. But the way in which these two aims should be politically combined has not always been as clear. In Dutch government policy, emancipation has for a long time been interpreted simply as increased participation in the labour market, equal rights and autonomy for women. The idea underlying this was that women needed to free themselves from the world of care. In recent years, however, a change has begun to take place: care is now recognized as an important part of our existence, and the idea that care does not necessarily have to be opposed to independence and self-realization is becoming more widely accepted.

In this book, I contribute to this debate from the perspective of political philosophy and, in particular, from the approach to this field adopted in women's studies. Each chapter will elaborate on a particular aspect of the recent debate about care and justice which has been taking place in various academic disciplines. All the chapters, apart from the first, contain reworkings of earlier texts in which I argue for a re-evaluation of care from a feminist perspective; this implies not only a redistribution of paid labour and caring tasks between men and women, but also a new approach to justice, morality and politics. I argue for a political concept of an ethics of care which is able to embody insights from feminist ethics. The book thus documents a search for ways of placing care within conceptions of democratic citizenship, in the hope that this will enable us to 'judge with care'.

Many people have contributed to the thinking process which is laid down in this book. I have been encouraged, first of all, by the response I have received over the years at congresses and public discussions, in individual conversations and through publications, as well as by the reception of the feminist ethics of care in the public debate and the academic world. I am therefore grateful to all those who have involved me in discussions or invited me to come and speak. The first steps towards this book were taken in my work at the University of Amsterdam, where in 1998 I led a student group on the subject of the ethics of care when this subject was still taboo in women's studies. The seminar series on feminism and morality which I was enabled to set up with SISWO launched the subject further and attracted more interest. At the University of Utrecht, I was able to continue developing my interest in gender, care and ethics. Working with colleagues in and around the Department of Women's Studies in the Faculty of Social Sciences has been a great support in this, in many ways. Kathy Davis and Ine Gremmen with their research into the ethics of care, gender and power in the caring professions have contributed considerably to my own views on the ethics of care and its narrative approach. In the graduate research carried out by Myra Keizer, Corinne Bekker and Jeanine Suurmond, the ethics of care has emerged at unexpected as well as expected moments. Their work and my conversations with them have kept me thinking about the ethics of care. The work of other (former) graduate students has also been important for the development of my ideas about care and justice, in particular that of Lieke Werkman and Rikki Holtmaat. Rian Voet's work on feminism and citizenship has challenged me to consider the place of the ethics of care in conceptions of citizenship. Mineke Bosch has sharpened my ideas about gender and science in all kinds of ways. The cooperation with Renee Römkens, Nicolle Zeegers, Sietske Dijkstra, Stephan Cremer and Josee Rijnaarts has fuelled my thinking about gender, sexuality, law and morality and the ways in which textual analysis and narrative interviews can provide insights in this field. Dymphie van Berkel, Janneke van Mens-Verhulst and Elly Singer have made important contributions, in recent years, to the research programme 'Gender, morality and care'. Claar Parlevliet has cooperated with great enthusiasm and creativity to the project on 'Choices in health care'. She has shown me how well care and pleasure can go together. Sandera Krol has, from the beginning, shared my thought processes about the ethics of care and feminist ethics, first as student and later as colleague. Her contribution to the subject and her friendship have been continually important in helping me to persevere. Petra Schreurs has, in her own particular way as student, colleague and friend, fulfilled a role in the realization of this book. Conversations with Christien Brinkgreve continue to add extra colour and depth to the subject which interests us both so much.

Outside the University of Utrecht I have also worked in some way or thought aloud about care and politics with many different people. My colleagues in the inter-university research programme 'Gender and care' have all, in their own ways, contributed to the academic development of this subject. In particular, working with Joyce Outshoorn, Jeanne de Bruijn, Annemieke van Drenth and Francisca de Haan was an important stimulus.

Carol Smart has been an inspiring friend and colleague from the start. Her work is a continual challenge to feminist legal theory. Visits to Utrecht by Nancy Fraser, Kari Wearness, Lorraine Code, Jane Flax and Herta Nagl-Docekal laid the basis for many good things. Through her original line of thinking and her personality, Iris Young has played an important role for me. At decisive moments she gave me the friendship and support I needed. Carol Gilligan was prepared to come to Utrecht and reflect on the reactions to her work: my talks with her were a source of support and new insights for me in several respects. Working with a number of colleagues in the University of Humanistics provided an inspiring climate for discussion. The graduate course 'Care as a moral and political concept', which I gave with Henk Manschot, Marian Verkerk, Douwe van Houten and Joan Tronto, was an exceptional meeting between different ways of thinking about care and ethics. The participants on the course together provided the ideal combination of creative and critical thinking, and curiosity, which proves so stimulating to academic work. It gave me the chance and the challenge to develop further a number of aspects of the feminist ethics of care. The cooperation and friendship shown to me by Joan Tronto was from the very first moment a continual source of creative ideas and intellectual pleasure. Her ideas have played a decisive role at a number of points in my thought process. I hope to be able to continue talking with her for many years to come about the relation between care and politics, and about the question of whether Machiavelli and the ethics of care can ever be reconciled.

Ine Gremmen translated the articles that were originally published in English into Dutch in an extremely skilful and careful way. I thank her for the attentiveness and imagination with which she did this. Catelijne Akkermans has painstakingly assisted me in the compilation of the bibliography, looking up of material and the editing of the manuscript. Marja van Nieuwkerk was a dedicated and stimulating editor. Liz Savage translated the text of the Dutch edition of this book in a most competent, careful and communicative manner into English. By supporting me in establishing what needed clarification she acted in many respects as an editor. It was a pleasure working with her. The English translation was made possible by a grant from the Dutch Foundation of Scientific Research (NWO). Chapter 5, 'Feminist ethics and public health-care policies: a case study on the Netherlands' also appears in DiQuinzio and Young (eds) (1997) *Feminist Ethics and Social Policy*, Bloomington: Indiana University Press.

Wibo Koole, Teun Oosterbaan and Arjen Oosterbaan have each in their own particular way shared in and contributed to the realization of this book. Without their presence in my life and their love it would all have been quite different. Henk van Nieuwenhuijzen was, through his unique style of entertaining friendship, a special witness of many stories behind this book. The friendship which I experienced during recent years with members of my family was a special experience. Liesbeth Sevenhuijsen helped me in a thoughtful and effective way to find a fitting illustration for the cover of this book. I dedicate this book to my mother, Clementia Mantel, in the knowledge that much of what stands here is written in her spirit.

Finally, a note to the English edition. Although my analysis is situated in the socio-political context of the Netherlands, I hope nevertheless that my arguments speak to a wider audience. In this English edition I have added some extra clarification on the context in which I have written this book. I have also tried to complete several of the arguments that were present in the Dutch edition in a more condensed form. Although Dutch politics has its own peculiar traditions of speaking about care, I hope that the international philosophical literature that I bring to bear on the situation in this country adds something extra. In spite of my plea for a situated ethics of care, it might indeed be the unmistakably universal aspects of care and its moral dimensions that can offer us a more sophisticated international understanding of what care is all about.

1

'HAS HEAD, HANDS, FEET AND HEART'

The context: care and politics under discussion

This morning activity supervisor Moniek van den Heuvel (23) is 'shmoozing' with Mrs Geurlings, who, wearing a pink dressing-gown, and leans lopsidedly in her wheelchair. 'Just among the crowd, walking down the road, those everyday things . . .' sounds from the radio, which, like the lampshades, plastic roses and an old-fashioned teapot, forms part of the furnishings of the 'shmooze' room. Moniek van den Heuvel hums along with the tune. She goes and sits down close to Mrs Geurlings, strokes her thin white hair and holds her hand. Then she takes a marshmallow from a glass jar. 'Ummm, we're going to have a treat today, Mrs Geurlings', she says, as she pops a tiny piece of marshmallow in her mouth. Mrs Geurlings starts to mumble, inaudibly, but suddenly the word 'eat' can quite clearly be heard. Van den Heuvel: 'This is the first time I have ever heard her really say anything at all. That alone makes my morning worthwhile.' Meanwhile the radio plays 'On the wide, lonely dunes', and Mrs Geurlings continues to chew.

This arresting description of an everyday scene in a nursing home formed the closing lines of the leading article in the Saturday supplement of the Dutch newspaper *NRC Handelsblad* on 5 November 1995. For the cursory reader it is probably just an everyday scene, a story that you read without really stopping to think about it. Few would be likely to read it as a 'moral tale', except those who are more familiar with the moral dimensions of providing care. The description of Moniek van den Heuvel contains various elements which are commonly regarded as characteristic of 'good care': patience, empathy, attentiveness, intimacy and, not least, the ability to draw satisfaction from fulfilling what may seem to be insignificant needs. Many readers will feel admiration for Moniek van den Heuvel's actions, but at the same time be grateful that they are not in her shoes. The description of Mrs Geurlings also arouses ambivalent feelings: everyone would like to receive such dedicated care if they were dependent on it, but most people hope that they will never end up in such a position of dependency. The story about Mrs Geurlings evokes fear: fear of deterioration and futility, fear of the winding, grey, twilit path which leads from growing dementia finally to death. The presence of Moniek van den Heuvel provides some solace for the reader; not only solace for their own vulnerability and fear of dying, but also for their difficulty in dealing with the illness and finiteness of their own loved ones. Her caring presence also symbolizes the patience which is so difficult to achieve for those who have become drawn into our achievement-oriented culture and the often stressful labour process.

The headline of the article, 'At the limits of care', will be more likely to raise associations with ethical issues than the excerpt quoted. The first association will probably be the familiar question, at present frequently raised in public debate, of whether the provision of care should be limited now that medical science and medical technology can prolong life in unprecedented ways. In discussions about euthanasia and the possibility of ending the lives of severely handicapped babies this problem is discussed in terms of 'meaningful life'. The ethical issue is usually posed as a problem of authority and rights, and as the issue of who should decide what constitutes meaningful life and on what criteria. From the article it becomes clear, however, that the journalist is referring to something else: to the limits of people's capacity to care under difficult circumstances. This applies to the task of caring in difficult situations; situations which involve making tolerable a vulnerable and finite existence within relationships of extreme dependency, rather than the promotion of growth or recovery. The ethical aspects of the situation in the article centre then, not so much on the issue of whether physicians are authorized to end life, but on the moral burden placed on carers. The moral question, although it is not posed in terms of ethics, centres on whether care-providers can and should establish limits to their emotional involvement, intimacy and tenderness, those qualities, in fact, which are precisely what is needed in caring for old people suffering from senile dementia. The nursing home director sees the problem as a conflict between emotion and professionalism, or how carers can avoid 'personal feelings' getting in the way of a professional approach. However, in the rest of the article there is less emphasis on the conflict between emotion and professionalism. On the contrary, a professional attitude is presented as being a necessary requirement for learning to render feelings productive and keep them in perspective, for turning commitment into self-knowledge and for reflecting on useful caring relationships.

The issue of the active ending of life is not entirely absent from the article, however. The direct pretext for the article was the report, a month previously, that a nurse in Delfzijl had confessed to killing nine patients suffering from severe senile dementia out of a sense of pity. What is remarkable in the article is the understanding shown for the nurse in question. A social worker who is interviewed about the case lacks the customary arrogance of experts who

2

wonder how this nurse could ever have let herself go so far. She interprets the nurse's actions rather as a sign of her loneliness and stress, signals which should have been picked up more effectively by her team leaders. Because the journalist has chosen to write an 'inside' story from a nursing home, the 'killing nurse' incident is described in a different moral vocabulary than that used in ethical discussions about the authority to end life. While it would not have been at all difficult to depict the nurse as a 'murderess' (the associations with the stereotypical image of the female poisoner are obvious) and outrightly to condemn her behaviour, the reader is asked for understanding instead; understanding for the heavy burden carried by those who care for psycho-geriatric patients and for the joys and sorrows which are inseparably linked to their daily routines. The article provides no clearly defined ethical norms. Rather than establishing fixed boundaries by means of ethical norms, it points out the difficulty of marking 'boundaries' at all.

Seen from this perspective the article is less arbitrary and innocent than is at first suggested. The report about the 'killing nurse' must, after all, have aroused consternation in many circles. 'What guarantees can be offered for good institutional care for ourselves and our families?' is the thought which must have occurred to many people when the report first appeared. 'How far can we entrust ourselves to professional care?' And, conversely: 'How can nursing homes prevent their image of providing good care from being tarnished?' A realistic, sympathetic story from everyday life manages to quell this unease. It presents care as complicated but also touching: joys and burdens are depicted as inseparably linked aspects of care. In the article patient love and compassion lead to respect and wonder for the fragility of human existence, even though this same love and compassion can degenerate into active killing. The boundaries are sometimes flexible, but we can guard them by ensuring that care does not have to be given in isolation, that it is embedded in a professional framework. The fear of the 'female poisoner' can be transformed into understanding, if we are able to appreciate what a heavy toll patience and empathy exact on the endurance of carers. There is no mention of a legal norm; a more professional system of care is presented as offering the necessary guarantee against such a deplorable act.

Although the words 'morality' and 'ethics' are not specifically mentioned, the contents of the article point in many ways to moral questions: the question of how to deal with dependency, responsibility, vulnerability and trust; the importance, but also the fragility of intimacy and connectedness; the ever-recurring problem of establishing boundaries between the self and others. This would suggest that the invisibility of the moral dimensions of care stems from the limitations of the vocabulary with which ethics is usually discussed: in the public debate ethical issues are mainly posed in terms of rights and duties, obedience and authority, and in the question of who has the competency to decide what is right and wrong, or good and bad. It is thus difficult to recognize many everyday questions as ethical issues. The protagonists in the public debate on ethical issues are lawyers, medical professionals, psychologists, theologians and moral philosophers, who rarely, if ever, mention nurses and carers, let alone marshmallow-chewing senile women and the daily moral interactions in the care of the elderly. Their judgement about the killing nurse would probably be unequivocal: punishable behaviour, which at best can be accorded some compassion if the nurse can be considered by the court as having acted from a condition of 'unsound mind'. This, then, is the importance of the article: it establishes different moral principles than that of conviction and punishment. It does not of course condone the nurse's actions, but it does invite the public to look more closely at the conditions under which care is provided in nursing homes and to show understanding for care-givers, for their loving, professional relationships with those for whom they care and for the heavy burden which this form of care can entail.

In short, the newspaper article invites 'judging with care' in more than one sense.[1] The audience is addressed in terms of those of its mental attitudes which indicate caringness: empathy, practical knowledge and compassion. This appeal to careful judgement at the same time brings care as a form of human agency within the arena of judgement. It makes it possible to consider care as an element of human existence. An obvious legal judgement on the nurse's actions is, even if only for a moment, suspended. Our attention is drawn away from the courtroom and directed instead towards the dayroom of the nursing home, which is conjured up for us by the familiar image of the teapot, lampshade and plastic roses. Thus, care enters into the story in two senses, as an attitude and as a form of action. Judging with care points then also to the necessity of viewing care as a form of social agency, which at the same time can inspire careful judgement. The importance of this double meaning of 'judging with care' is, however, broader, and this brings me to a third meaning of this phrase. To understand its wider importance we need to place the scene in the nursing home in a broader context of time and place. I am referring here to the public debate in which the newspaper readers are involved at this historical juncture, as citizens in a democratic political system in which the content and meaning of 'care' and 'justice' are continually under discussion, particularly in the context of the restructuring of the welfare state and the revision of the legal system. The nursing home can be seen as a microcosm of a wider *political* community, in which, as citizens, we are continually invited to pass political judgements on the quality of public and private care provision and many different aspects of human social existence.

But this is exactly where the problem lies, however: which normative vocabularies do we have at our disposal for judging *with* and *about* care in political contexts? We have become used to conceiving of citizenship issues in the terminology of enforceable authority, rights and duties, the language which seems pre-eminently designed for the expression of our manifestation in the public sphere. The problem of 'judging with care' lies not only in the fact that political judgement mainly proceeds in terms of rights and justice, but also in the cognitive attitudes that are supposed to guide judgements in these terms. Judgements in the public sphere are usually associated with distance and impartiality, and with the ability to transcend the individual point of view in order to reach a 'general viewpoint'. The virtues associated with care, such as compassion, attentiveness, empathy and attention to detail, in contrast, are depicted as belonging to a different sphere, that of interpersonal and private relationships. The modern ideal of citizenship demands that citizens free themselves from dependencies and loyalties in their political judgement in order to arrive at free and autonomous choices. As the American political theorist Joan Tronto has so aptly put it, modern political theory locates care both 'above and below' politics (Tronto 1995b).

Feminism and care: an uneasy relationship

This problem seems even more complex when we consider care as a political issue from the perspective of modern feminism. Feminism, in the form in which it arose at the end of the 1960s, can quite clearly be seen as a rebellion against a supposedly 'female' nature of care and the associated subordination of women to men.[2] Feminists demanded public space and made it abundantly clear that they no longer wished to be tied to a 'woman's destiny', to the life which their mothers before them had led. Caring was depicted as dull, monotonous and traditional, and thus as an obstacle to self-fulfilment; it could certainly not provide an identity for modern women in search of independence. By defining care as domestic labour feminists made it clear that necessary care could just as well be provided on a professional basis and that it was high time that men finally fulfilled their duties in that respect.

For politically engaged women of my generation, political alliance with liberal socialism seemed obvious; of all the political movements, it offered the clearest promise of emancipation, through its proposed combination of the liberal freedom rights and strong public services. This also meant that feminism could quite easily associate itself with the political idiom of modern citizenship: the language of freedom and equality, redistribution, autonomy and individualism. The vocabulary of rights thus seemed a logical normative partner for feminism. The paradoxical fact that this also led to an appeal for strong government was less easily recognized. In fact, it was compatible with the feminist objective of calling on official authorities to convince the public that 'sexual difference' should be abolished. It also tied in with the general feminist idea that the personal was political, which in turn implied that politics had the 'right', and in many respects even an obligation, to interfere in all aspects of human existence.

As a result, in those first years the figure of Moniek van den Heuvel would have been difficult to recognize as an example for feminist judgement. Even though feminism had also adopted the slogan 'We want to be strong without losing our tenderness' as one of its mottos, her patience and satisfaction with such insignificant details could hardly serve as an example for feminist political judgement, which remained imbued with the normativity of power, militance, justice, autonomy and liberation. The image of the conscientious carer belonged more to the political idiom of the Dutch Christian Democrats, for whom, in the 1980s, she was the symbol of the 'caring society'. This certainly did not provide an attractive image for feminists. The ideal of the caring society was accompanied by public pleas for an ethical revival, traditional family values, the naturalness of the heterosexual order and a revival of care as the willingness to make sacrifices. This meant that not only care but also morality seemed tainted to feminists. Together they symbolized normalization and paternalism, the antithesis of the ideals of freedom and self-determination.

Nevertheless, care remained an urgent question for feminists. In the practice of daily life the problem of care presented itself in countless different ways: from the care needed by children, friends and elderly parents, to women's own need for care and the way in which the health service treated women's complaints. In fact, feminist women were actively involved in the issue of care in many different ways: within private relationships, the health service and women's care organizations, as well as in political contexts. Here they struggled for the redistribution of paid labour and care, and new forms of valuation for what increasingly came to be called 'care labour'. The moral dimensions of care, however, remained controversial, not least because care as a political concept remained the property of the Christian Democrats. The media have always been happy to see themselves as the guardians of these divisions between political parties. Thus 'caring has a Christian Democrat feel to it', wrote Pauline Sinnema in Dutch newspaper *Het Parool* at the presentation of the National Care Plan by Jeanne de Bruijn in 1993, 'while the professor is actually a member of the Labour Party'. According to the journalist, De Bruijn should have called the plan 'National Work Plan' instead. The message is clear: care doesn't belong in a progressive person's framework. Progressives should either stick to the language of labour or join another party.

In this short introduction I have tried to convey the complex political relations within which the essays brought together in this collection have come into being over the past years. Since 1975 I have been actively involved in what, in retrospect, could be interpreted as a search for an appropriate vocabulary for making care into a political issue from a feminist perspective, and in so doing 'to think what we do', as Hannah Arendt has described the task laid out for political theory. My first approach started from the relation between domestic labour and the welfare state, and I tried to link care to Marxism, the dominant political vocabulary for left-wing feminists in the 1970s (Sevenhuijsen 1978). This approach enabled feminist theorists to raise a number of important themes. It became possible to describe care as

6

'labour', thus freeing it from its self-evidence. This also meant focusing more attention on the relation between family and state, propelled by the idea that throughout history there have been repeated shifts between what women do at home and what the state organizes in the form of public services. The relation between paid and unpaid labour is still an important issue. In this vein, feminists have managed to develop an original perspective on the restructuring of the welfare state, a debate which remains as relevant today as ever.

In political theory the overtures between feminism and Marxism did not last long, however. In retrospect, feminism played an important role in the downfall of Marxism as a political theory. The Marxist idiom distorted the complex experiences of intimate life, which feminists wanted to bring out into the open and the reduction of care and gender identity to 'labour' soon became problematic. This became clear definitively when subjects related to sexuality and motherhood began to occupy more space in women's studies, and when psychology and culture, as well as language and history, became subjects of feminist research. It also became clear that there are many ways in which 'gender' does not correspond to 'class' as a political factor, so that comparisons with class, from which feminism derived its legitimacy within Marxism, soon came adrift (Withuis 1990, 1995). And, at least as important, feminists levelled criticism at the forms of political engagement adopted in left-wing circles. Feminists proceeded from the ideal of a 'broad' politics and active political participation by women, which was in direct opposition to the political hierarchies and political intolerance in many groups of the radical left, which, as many only later realized, was susceptible to dogmatic, totalitarian forms of politics.

On the other hand, there are also problems to be found in feminism's approach to politics and democracy. The 'broad' conception assumes that politics, in the sense of power relations, is present 'everywhere'. This idea is also contained in the well-known slogan that the 'personal is political'. Although I too was enthusiastic about this slogan at the start, my doubts grew over the years. The slogan was initially used in a creative sense, to make clear that various 'women's problems' were not individual or psycho-logical in nature, but should be seen as social problems. It thus enabled all kinds of new issues to be put on the political agenda. However, the statement was also used in a descriptive sense, to make it clear that public life reaches into all aspects of intimate life. This gave the slogan an ambiguous normative load. Although it produced a moment of resistance (against the 'public check-ing of toothbrushes'), the slogan tended to serve as a justification for the ever-growing politicization of private life and the political regulation of human behaviour. The slogan obstructed questions about the specific natures of the private sphere and politics, and the desirability of a boundary between these two spheres. It gradually became clear to me that feminism lacked not only a theory of political action and political judgement, but also a satisfactory form of reflection on its own ethical stance and the moral dimensions of human agency.

This relative blindness to normativity undoubtedly has complex causes and it is certainly not as simple and straightforward as I have suggested here. During the past ten years many valuable publications have appeared in which moral issues are discussed and developed from a feminist perspective. Indeed, according to some American authors, feminist ethics has even become a 'booming industry' during the past few years (Jaggar 1991). Certainly, in Anglo-Saxon scholarship there has already been extensive debate about feminism and ethics, and feminist theory has been reasonably integrated into the field of political philosophy. This development is not so advanced in the Netherlands. The study of ethics here is, and has traditionally been, marked to a greater degree by religion. Political science has an overwhelmingly empirical, behaviourist and institutional slant. The discipline of 'ethics' was discovered comparatively late by feminists and its study is still relatively separate from thinking about politics. It is – also for feminists – still always easier to imagine morality in philosophical texts, literature, poetry, popular culture and, traditionally, drama, than in a political setting. One finds more food for thought about gender and morality from an hour of zapping through soaps like *New York Police*, *Chicago Hope* or *Star Trek* than from reading the average political document of Dutch feminist authorship. Religion and pedagogics have now also been discovered as ethically relevant subjects within women's studies. Within political feminism, however, certainly in the Netherlands, a certain prickliness has continued to dominate discussions of ethics and normative issues, and relatively few approaches have been developed in response to the recent revival of interest in public morality. In many respects social-scientific empiricism is more influential on ideas about gender politics and public policy than is thinking in terms of normative orientations or reflection on the values which can guide individual and collective action.

Motherhood: a source of inspiration for the ethics of care?

For me, motherhood has been an important means of approaching the evaluation of political idioms in regard to their capacity to talk about care in a meaningful way; in this respect my experiences as a mother and daughter have been influential on my intellectual work. I had my children at the beginning of my university career, when it was still quite unusual for women to combine these two paths of life. At first I had no intention of paying attention to this fact in my academic work: what did it matter? However, it soon became clear to me that the social and historical knowledge I encountered had almost nothing to say about the living conditions and the moral and political dilemmas of women in my situation. No information was presented about the historical genealogy of gender issues or the historical background to the complex relationship between gender and academic learning (Bosch

1994). The women's movement was absent from overviews of the political history of modern states and from the histories of political ideas. Academic study was thus an alienating experience for women of my generation. It compressed our world of ideas and political images into concepts and theories which were miles away from our daily experience. As we now know this fact was the impetus for the emergence of modern women's studies. This field of academic study attempts to make women's social experiences, and the diversity of images and representations of gender, productive as a source of knowledge and political judgement. As a result, the dearth of written texts about the 'feminine condition' has now been transformed into a dizzying array of feminist literature on the most diverse subjects.

Meanwhile motherhood, as an experience and social institution, has become a richly documented subject as well. The link between motherhood and (feminist) ethics, however, is still controversial. The concept of motherhood easily evokes, certainly in the context of morality, romantic associations with a space which is far removed from the political arena. The 'moral mother' has indeed for centuries been a powerful cultural symbol of moral goodness. Her image is frequently invoked to protect us from the corrupting effects of power. In the 1970s, feminists denounced this image. They pointed out that the way in which women mother and the meanings attached to motherhood and (sexual) identity are determined to an important degree in the public sphere (Rich 1976; Chodorow 1978; Sevenhuijsen and De Vries 1980). This idea was partly what impelled me to look more deeply into family law. At that time family law was under a great deal of political pressure due to the claims made by divorced fathers for the legal right to parental access. The relation between gender and care seemed to play no part in the political deliberations, in which politicians considered the claims made by the 'fathers' rights movement' as legitimate.

The dominant viewpoint was that men and women in a modern emancipated society were equal to one another, which therefore meant that the government should make this equality the guideline for legislation. The ease with which this norm was accepted led me to question the logic by which feminists had embraced the principle of equal rights: it could also, it seemed, strike back at women. The language of equal rights seemed so self-evident, but it continually struck me that within the feminist literature there was little space for open-minded reflection on the normative dimensions of legal strategies and principles of justice. Feminist aims were for many a seamless continuation of the equal rights idiom. Apparently, the idea that the relationships between men and women, once the struggle for equal rights was over, could be happy and harmonious seemed an attractive prospect.

Against this background I carried out historical research into the views on family and affiliation law developed by feminists around the turn of the century and the political–intellectual landscape in which these were formed (Sevenhuijsen 1987, 1992b). It appeared that the principle of equal rights had not occupied nearly such a prominent position in feminist legal politics at that time as had often been supposed, and that the ideal of equality had also been described and justified in a variety of ways. But what was at least as important was that the rules of family law and the political discourses and strategies which they expressed appeared to embody images and norms about motherhood and fatherhood which could be traced back to political controversies surrounding the meaning of sexual difference and social representations of good parenthood. It gradually became clear to me that the idiom of family law embodies its own ethics and even now has a specific manner of naming, categorizing, judging and ordering social relations in gendered terms, which I characterized as a 'patriarchal legal ethics'. In this way I tried to show the logic by which fatherhood, authority and hierarchical power, even though they are regularly challenged and contested, continue to occupy a seemingly unassailable position in law and morality. It became clear to me that family law is an important discursive field where the symbolic Law of the Father is materialized in legal rules and regulations. The relationship between mothers and children remains an issue of secondary importance in this patriarchal logic. The issue of how motherhood and law could or should be linked continued to intrigue me and led me into further exploration of normative political theory.[3]

At the same time (the 1980s) American feminist philosophers were extensively debating motherhood as a source of moral and political reasoning. Their publications ran parallel with the feminist debate about care and justice, the most important angle from which ethics and morality have entered the feminist agenda during the last fifteen years. Besides this there also appeared a whole series of feminist publications about the pros and cons of liberal political theory and the central normative concepts within it (Okin 1979; Elshtain 1981; Coole 1988; Pateman 1988, 1989 and many others). These three lines of discussion provided me with a springboard for considering several controversial issues in feminist political thinking, particularly in relation to the political recognition of motherhood and care (Sevenhuijsen 1988a). This was the starting-point for a number of articles in which I discussed the possibilities and impossibilities of a feminist ethics of care and in which I tried to bring this issue – often in a polemical way and always in reference to current political issues – to public attention. This was also an attempt to develop the philosophical principles and sociological premises of the ethics of care and formulate its possible effects and applications. A number of these articles appear in this volume in a revised form.

During the period when I wrote these essays, the influence of postmodernism was making itself profoundly felt in women's studies; this had various implications for the debate about the ethics of care. The idea of an ethics of care, certainly at first, was all too often the target of attack by postmodernist feminists, who felt that it only confirmed women in a traditional, one-sided identity. The ethics of care had supposedly acquiesced in what postmodern philosophers have described as 'representational thinking': the illusion that thinking can reflect an actually existing reality. Care ethics was accused of bringing a general truth about women into the world, which could have a normative effect on their self-image and behaviour, and which, certainly in political contexts, could be counterproductive. In all these respects post-modern philosophy has offered an important warning against the risks and pitfalls inherent in a feminist ethics of care. Paradoxically, however, feminist postmodernism has also provided a number of philosophical considerations and methods of interpretation which have, in my view at least, helped to make the ethics of care productive for feminism. But, conversely, the feminist ethics of care can also make us aware of the limitations of postmodernism as a normative idiom for feminism. In the next section I will further elaborate on my ideas concerning these three dimensions in the relationship between the feminist ethics of care and feminist postmodernism in order to emphasize the philosophical background of the articles which form the basis for this book. This will also provide me with the opportunity to introduce more fully my proposed approach towards an ethics of care. As the starting-point of my discussion I will use a number of articles by the American philosopher Virginia Held, who, within moral philosophy, has most systematically set out the ideas arising from developmental psychology on the ethics of care.

Postmodernism, identity politics and foundationalism in the feminist ethics of care

Held's work can serve as an important source of inspiration for critics of an ethics of rights. This is also the way I shall draw on her work in this book. She formulates her ideas explicitly as a criticism of currents in moral philosophy which view moral problems solely as a conflict of rights between individuals. (Held 1987b, 1989b, 1990).[4] Held uses a feminine model, that of the mother-figure, as the basis for her criticism and alternative approach. This feminine model does not refer to females in a biological sense, nor to women's natural destiny or the actual lives of existing women. Instead, she prefers to talk about the 'mothering person', who can just as easily be of either sex. She conceives of the mother–child relationship, then, as a metaphor or as an 'ideal type' in the Weberian sense. Through this approach she intends to articulate a critical perspective on dominant moral discourses, which will enable her to draw on a neglected form of moral knowledge and make it explicit as a philosophical principle. Against this background she asks what society would be like if the paradigm of economic man, the prototypical individual in moral philosophy, was replaced by the paradigm of mother and child. Feminist ethics could then find its basis in women's morality.

The essence of Held's criticism of an ethics of rights is that it presumes an atomistic view of human nature. Her main line of reasoning is that arguments made on the basis of this ethics, certainly if they arise from the liberal tradition

11

of the social contract, generally presuppose a detached, self-sufficient, independent or atomistic individual, primarily engaged in pursuing his self-interest; a being who is fundamentally egocentric, living in competition with and in fear of other individuals. Held's criticism of the ethics of rights is directed against the assumption that possession of rights is the primary factor transforming individuals into human 'persons'. Personhood, in contractarian thinking, is directly linked to the possession of rights. Individuals can claim respect from others because they have the possibility of knowing and exercising their rights, such as the right to property or the right to freedom from intrusion in personal life. Moral dilemmas then take the form of conflicts – actual, potential or hypothetical – between different rights claims. The task of ethics is thus to discover the highest principle, in order to determine which claim should take precedence.

As stated above Held takes the bond between mother and child as the starting-point for an alternative model of moral reasoning. First, she argues that concepts of equality based on the model of the possessive individual need to be rethought: the relationship between mothering persons and their children is characterized after all by dependence and nurturing. Mutual respect and equality of moral worth between people are of more importance, she argues, than contractual principles based on equal legal rights. The moral repertoire also needs to encompass notions of cooperation, intimacy and trust. Connection, compassion and affectivity should be recognized as important sources of moral reasoning. Second, she argues that the principle of non-intrusion is unsatisfactory as a primary moral principle, because it precludes the possibility of dependent people's needs becoming the focus for moral deliberation. And third, she argues that the perspective offered by the mother–child relationship throws a different light on privacy and personhood. Instead of taking as its premiss self-sufficient, atomistic individuals, ethics should start from processes of connection and individuation. This would lend weight to what have now become widely supported pleas for moral reasoning to be regarded as a contextual activity, directed at the evaluation of different ways of understanding and judging.

One can hardly accuse Held's approach of essentialism, that is, of suggesting that there is a natural link between women's identity and motherhood, which should count as the norm for women's destiny in life. She is quite explicit about the fact that the mother–child bond provides a *model of reasoning*, and that the moral reasoning she values can be derived from all practices of child care. However, there are a number of problems associated with Held's formulation of this 'motherly' metaphor and the way she presents it as the counterpart to the ideal of the atomistic 'economic man'. In the first place there is a philosophical problem. Since Held associates the mother-figure with values such as concreteness, care and compassion as opposed to abstraction and justice, she runs the risk of reproducing the mode of arguing in binary oppositions with which Western thinking is so thoroughly permeated.

Binary oppositions are nearly always loaded with meanings of gender: they are associated with symbolic, mutually exclusive concepts of masculinity and femininity which are also positioned in a hierarchical mode (Lloyd 1984; Hekman 1990; Jay 1991; Plumwood 1993). A strategy which reverses these oppositions, so that what was formerly denigrated is upgraded or cast in the opposite role remains trapped in an oppositional logic. It fails to undermine the existence of these oppositions or to open up innovative lines of thinking. If we follow this postmodernist line of thought, all forms of feminist ethics should engage in a continual process of deconstructing the meanings of gender inherent in various forms of thinking and search for new contents for moral concepts.

This philosophical problem repeats itself at the level of practical reasoning. Philosophical concepts and thought patterns have an inclusionary and exclusionary effect with regard to the question of what we can articulate in moral discussions and how we can do this; for this reason I consider them as discursive practices. Held's conceptual framework can easily lead to the (re)production of 'moral motherhood' in the way it deals with the expression of mothers' moral experiences. As long as such values as connection, empathy, consensus and protective love serve as the main goals of moral reasoning, the 'good mother' will remain the central subject position in the ethics of care (Mendus 1993). And when this image is also used as an example for feminist ethics in general, it becomes almost impossible to discount the 'shadow-side of virtue'; that is, the existence of conflict, aggression, ambivalence and discord in feelings and experiences related to care (Flax 1993). In fact, more attention needs to be paid to the reasons why feminism needs ethics and to the quality of moral identities and moral subject positions that feminists construct in their reasoning. At the same time these are *political* questions, because they raise the issue of which political context can best do justice to a feminist ethics of care. Too often, in my opinion, these political dimensions of moral reasoning are marginalized in discussions about the ethics of care, as too is the idea that the relationship between gender, power, care and ethics is complex and multi-faceted, something that cannot be 'solved' by taking a simple stance for or against the idea of a 'female' morality. In this book I try to overcome these problems by placing the discussion about the ethics of care, where possible, within the conceptual framework of politics and citizenship, thus striving for a combination of an empirical and political–philosophical approach to a feminist ethics of care. In this sense my work echoes recent pleas for a critical enquiry into the boundaries between moral and political philosophy (for example, Tronto 1993) and searches for a contextual and situated form of feminist ethics that can accommodate both care and justice arguments.

There is, all in all, little reason to give motherhood a privileged status in arguments about women's moral or political identity. The mere attempt to do this has led American feminists in recent years to formulate a whole range of alternative moral identities with corresponding forms of ethics, ranging from lesbian and Afro-American forms of ethics to Mestizo ethics. The importance of this development for feminist thinking about politics and morality should not be underestimated: it has put the issue of differences among women on the agenda of feminist ethics. It has also lent support to the aim of making diversity a guiding political principle and of recognizing the construction of multicultural societies as a crucial political task in the near future. However, this recognition of differences has also had its limitations: the issue of the relationship between identity and normativity has received scant attention. If we accept that diversity of identities, both between and within persons, can provide an adequate basis for making judgements, we are confronted with the question of whether it is still possible to arrive at forms of common judgement and reach decisions about shared values, and if so, how this should take place. The issue then arises of how far 'identity' can actually form a suitable basis for political action at all. In this sense questions about (political) identity become questions for political philosophy and for practical normative reasoning.

Here too, I would argue, we are confronted with the adverse effects of the slogan that 'the personal is political', certainly when this is combined with a one-sided embrace of a model of interest politics. In a radical model of identity politics, the public sphere easily comes to be seen as a sphere in which everyone – in accordance with the neo-liberal spirit of the times – can be 'themselves', and on the basis of this can assert claims with regard to others. The public sphere becomes an arena for a search for authenticity and for claims for recognition of 'authentic identities' by others. The political scientist Rian Voet has demonstrated the disadvantages attached to such a model of identity politics: boundaries are continually being drawn between 'us' and 'them' and people are assigned to a group membership which is often not of their own choice. The dangers associated with a 'politics of indignation' which allows all manner of claims to moral truth are not simply a figment of the imagination (Voet 1994). A better source of inspiration – also from a feminist perspective – lies in a neo-republican idea of active citizenship. Here the public sphere is seen as a meeting ground where people shape identities through action and interaction, through the exchange of narratives and opinion, through deliberation and debate, and where, in so doing, they can continually revise and transcend their images of 'self' and 'other'. Here identity depends more on what you do than on what you are. Rather than being fixed, it remains open to change. The public sphere then enables people to act in the sense of 'starting something anew'. The nature of our presence in the public sphere should make it possible for us to take up different positions so that we are better able to decide what should be considered valuable and relevant collective aims (Dietz 1995; Bickford 1995, 1996; Sevenhuijsen 1997a).

This image of politics and citizenship also provides the basis for the goal of publicly deliberating on what are significant similarities and differences between people and deciding which values should be given the status of common values, even if this involves only shaky compromises and temporary forms of consensus. In this book I argue that a feminist ethics of care can have a place in such a conception of citizenship, because the ethics of care is based on a dual commitment: on the one hand it assumes that people recognize and treat others as different and take into account other people's individual view of the world and of their place within it (Tronto 1993: 12 ff.) while, on the other hand, needs and narratives are not taken as absolute but are interpreted and judged in specific contexts of action (Code 1991, 1995). This demonstrates the necessity of locating the ethics of care within notions of citizenship, if it is to acquire a significant political meaning without being slotted into a concept of identity politics or a one-dimensional idea of interest promotion, or indeed a nostalgic return to harmony and consensus. This would enrich the conceptual framework of 'judging with care'.[5] When the ethics of care is located within such a notion of citizenship, discursive space is created for carers to bring their expertise and moral considerations into public debates without this being associated with a fixed caring identity or with associated claims to moral truth or moral goodness.

I start from the premiss that 'judging' is a principle task of citizenship and thus of collective action within a democratic context. Democratic citizenship assumes that people are able to distinguish between good and bad in responsible ways and can therefore be held accountable for their actions. In the context of democratic citizenship judging always takes place at the intersection between equality and difference. Democratic judgements have to be capable of dealing with the radical alterity of human subjects, through recognizing their individuality and diversity while at the same time conceiving of them as equals. It also has to take into account group affiliations and specific life contexts, while at the same time treating all citizens fairly, without stereotyping them as 'different' or 'deviant'.[6] Because people can meet each other in the public sphere as different but equal, they can adopt a public identity, and at the same time question its desirability. If we integrate values derived from the ethics of care, such as attentiveness, responsiveness and responsibility, into concepts of citizenship this will produce a dual transformational effect: the concept of citizenship will be enriched and thus better able to cope with diversity and plurality, and care will be 'de-romanticized', enabling us to consider its values as political virtues. In addition, politics can take into account the importance of care as a social practice and acknowledge the diversity of values it embodies.

This has an effect on the political aims which can be expected of the ethics of care. For Held, as for most other philosophers concerned with motherhood, the aim of the feminist ethics of care is still predominantly the construction of moral consensus. In her version of the ethics of care, ethics should in fact be 'above power', as it is in the liberal ethics of rights and autonomy, with the important difference that it is now a *feminine* perspective which must accomplish this. Here too, dualism and the related image of human nature must be undermined in order to avoid remaining imperceptibly trapped within its patterns of thought. If we want to make the feminist ethics of care viable and useful as a source of political judgement then its objective should not be to formulate a moral truth which stands above power. That ignores what for many is precisely one of the characteristic objectives of the study of ethics: how to deal with conflict, disagreement and ambivalence as well as with moral and political dilemmas. The feminist ethics of care can contribute to this by illuminating more fully the sources of moral dilemmas and formulating meaningful epistemological strategies in order to deal with these dilemmas, even if only on a temporary basis (Billig, Condor and Edwards 1988; Shrage 1994; Davis 1995; Warnke 1995). I would particularly like to emphasize the temporary aspect. Only attention to specificity and contextuality can keep us from expecting ethics to be a source of absolute normative truth. This is also the importance of the postmodernist warning against over-eagerly embracing an ethics of care in which women's identity is based on motherhood.

Within the work of Virginia Held and others with similar approaches there lies a problem which has been exposed in detail by postmodern philosophers: Held attempts to ground 'good' ethics in a subject ideal, which is then regarded as a normative image for moral reasoning and political action in general. According to postmodernist philosophers, we should bid a final farewell to foundationalism and the grand narrative of human progress. In their place we should accept the fragmented, ambiguous and contingent nature of the human condition. Every attempt to describe a homogeneous and unambiguous image of human nature contributes to the maintenance of an illusion which, at best, is counterproductive and at worst leads to a politics of uniformity and totalitarianism, which attempts to manage or eradicate every difference between individuals (Lyotard 1987). However, it would certainly not be justified to equate Held's ideas with the type of thinking which forms the target of attack for postmodern philosophy; her work provides too many occasions where traditional ideas about homogeneity are undermined. Nevertheless, Held's attempt to link the ethics of care to an unequivocal image of 'women' still displays too many traces of foundationalism.

The 'motherly metaphor', which should offer a counterbalance to the essentialist approach to the ethics of care is not helpful in this respect (Mendus 1993). It still relies too heavily on the mythical image of 'Woman', which has persisted for too long in various moral texts and which fails to do justice to the diversity of moral experiences of actual women. There is no fixed reference-point marked 'Woman', which can serve as a criteria for judging the quality of morality. In this respect a feminist ethics of care would be well advised to remain at a critical distance from the idea of a 'feminine' morality (Tong 1993). Paradoxically, this step can actually be helpful in evaluating more accurately the moral experiences of real-life women and their considerations about care, which emerge, for example, in their relationships with and responsibility for children and the life experiences linked to this. A feminist ethics which finds *no* connection to the concrete practices, aims and dilemmas of women would quickly become an empty shell anyway.

This points to the necessity of developing 'alternative moral epistemologies' for an ethics of care (Walker 1989), in which lived moral experience and lived moral considerations can be expressed. The English social theorist Zygmunt Bauman has argued in his book *Postmodern Ethics* that the postmodern demise of foundationalism does not necessarily bring us into a moral vacuum in which we can only live in accordance with an attitude of 'anything goes'. On the contrary, the postmodern condition gives us the possibility of becoming 'truly moral'. Bauman argues that under the reign of the modernist urge to bring moral life under a universalist law-oriented ethics, morality has been replaced by the finding of universal principles and legal codes and is thus shaped after the pattern of Law. 'Individual responsibility is then translated (again, in practice, even if not in theory) as the responsibility for following or breaching the socially endorsed, ethical legal rules' (Bauman 1992: 29). Modernity thus thrives in Bauman's analysis of an 'expropriation of the moral'. Modernity is fuelled by a deep-seated mistrust of the moral capabilities of its (non-enlightened) subjects and thus continuously aims at legislating its moral truth claims by laying them down in legal imperatives, which are then used to 'educate' those who are constructed as 'not-yet-moral'. Bauman talks about rational Law-oriented ethics as a 'control desk of society', which aims at taming moral impulses, smothering differences and eliminating 'all "wild" – autonomous, obstreporous, and uncontrolled – sources of moral judgment' (ibid.: 12). Modernity is thus built on a mistrust of human spontaneity, drives, impulses and inclinations; it tries to replace these with the universalizing gaze of unemotional calculating reason. In Bauman's view this leaves out precisely that which is properly moral in morality. 'It shifts moral phenomena from the realm of personal autonomy into that of power-assisted heteronomy. It substitutes the learnable knowledge of rules for the moral self constituted by responsibility' (ibid.: 11).

Under postmodern conditions we may, in Bauman's view, have a renewed hope of reclaiming truly human forms of moral agency, based on a recognition of ambiguity and responsibility. This attitude can make us understand that dilemmas are indeed dilemmas, and not as he says 'temporary and rectifiable effects of human weakness, ignorance or blunders [. . . .] Human reality is messy and ambiguous [. . .] and so moral decisions, unlike abstract moral principles, are ambivalent. It is in this sort of world that we must live' (ibid.: 32). In his view postmodernity boils down to 'modernism without illusions'. Bauman looks for an alternative approach in renewed concepts of moral responsibility, based on 'being with' and 'being for the Other'. It is striking, though, that care is almost absent in his thinking about this new postmodern form of being 'truly moral'. Although his book also contains passages in which he talks about care in a light-hearted spirit, Bauman tends to equate care in a more outspoken sense with dominating love, a kind of affection that 'smothers its object'. He thus locates it in the tradition of *agape*, the Christian ideal of self-sacrificing love (or at least a Nietzschean reading of this concept), that is characterized by this peculiar mixture of dedication to suffering and normative self-assertion of 'the' moral subject. Here he fabricates his own version of Foucault's concept of pastoral power, by labelling care for the other and 'love motives' as 'one of the most insidious of the many shapes of domination, as it blackmails its objects into obedience' (ibid.: 103). This, however, is a rather one-sided conceptualization of care, which in several respects echoes a (male) urge to suppress our dependence on the mother, and on women's care, for being in this world at all. There is indeed a strange contradiction between, on the one hand, Bauman's plea for ambiguity and a farewell to fixed systems of meanings and, on the other hand, the solid and determinate way in which he locates care in only one of the many possible discursive registers in which we can talk about it.

So while I can sympathize with Bauman's diagnosis of the 'moral poverty' of modernity and with the need to look for alternative conceptions of moral responsibility, based on a postmodern acceptance of spontaneity, ambiguity and wonder, our paths diverge when searching for sources of inspiration for alternative moral epistemologies. It is my contention in this book that a plea for simply 'being with and for the Other' is not a sufficient means for restoring 'lost moral capacities'. This remedy is certainly not radical enough to transform outworn configurations between the One and the Other. Bauman is correct in saying that modernist ethics has placed the Other in the shady background of our collective moral conscience, where it represents the repressed 'other sides' of ourselves, which, as Bauman states, is the 'animal', and – he does not say this but since Simone the Beauvoir we should know it – the feminine. If we really want to change this state of affairs, we need radically to alter the configuration of foreground and background; but this can only be done by attributing subjectivity to that which hitherto has been backgrounded. This calls for what feminist theorists have called a 'decentering of the subject'. In my view this would imply that we consider care as a normal aspect of human existence, not hiding it under the deceiving veils which male philosophers have woven around gendered patterns of dependency and love. For women it is certainly hard to identify with the idea of a subject striving after 'being with and for the Other', since it is *she* who has been – and still is – continuously pushed into the position of a voiceless Other, who is supposed to care about and take care of the One. Only by acknowledging women's 'truly moral voices' (in the plural) can we transform the intricate configurations around otherness with which modernity has left us and strive after, what I would describe as, 'being a self while being with each other'. Otherwise moral philosophy runs the risk of reproducing a state of affairs in which 'the other' unwillingly remains a mirror or a projection-screen for 'the' moral subject, the generic being that has truly inhabited modernity's phantasmagoric world for too long. By uncoupling care from symbolic forms of femininity, and at the same time listening to women's multiple voices in social practices of caring, we might come nearer to the forms of moral responsibility without illusions, that Bauman argues for.[7]

The 'lost moral capacities' might be closer to home than we would imagine after having read Bauman's book. We could pose the question of how 'truly moral subjects' could practice the responsibility that he is looking for, without caring about and taking caring of the concrete others with whom they share their 'being-in-the-world'. In fact, what we could demand of 'the' moral subject is for him to unlearn his denial of dependency and to fill the void between self and other with the living voices of those with whom he mingles within networks of care, while at the same time listening to his own 'caring voice'. Even Foucault's concept of 'care for the self', which he developed in his later work as an alternative ethos for the manifestations of both pastoral and disciplinary power, still contains too many echoes of the (male) solipsistic subject, who cannot fully acknowledge the interrelatedness of human existence and thus the inherently relational dimensions of care. Looked at from this angle, the feminist ethics of care is truly political in both the broad and the narrow sense of the word. It is political in the broad sense because it wants to break with the patterns of domination that have surrounded caring activities and moral feelings for too long and to establish new modes of being 'truly moral', both for women and for men. It is political in the narrow sense, since it wants to transform systems of instrumental and bureaucratic rationality, which aim at banishing the unexpected and the uncontrollable – the symbolically feminine – and argue instead for new forms of creative power – a power to act together in concert, to borrow Arendt's terminology – and thus for renewed forms of political agency, political judgement and social justice. And it is feminist since it argues for a full acknowledgment of women's moral agency, not because women are 'morally better' or more caring than men, but because their everyday moral voices and moral deliberations – with all the 'messiness' that may sound through them – deserve attention when we are looking for ways of being 'truly moral'. Only then can we reach a situation where both 'women' and 'care' are no longer above or below politics, or above or below moral life, but can be a part of what human life and human coexistence are all about.

Care and ethics as social practice

Against this background I view care in this book as a social practice, in which different sorts of moral considerations and moral vocabularies can be expressed. The concept of care as social practice fits in with a plea which has been put forward by several feminist thinkers from diverse backgrounds: the plea for situated thinking and a situated ethics (Rich 1985; Haraway 1988;

Walker 1989; Young 1990a). In order to make this idea productive for think-ing about the ethics of care I would like to consider in greater depth the concept of social practice. In philosophical texts this concept is described in different ways and is made to serve a variety of epistemological and political aims. The American philosopher Sarah Ruddick has introduced thinking in terms of social practices into the feminist debate about the ethics of care. Her aim in doing this was to develop in a systematic way the concept of maternal thinking and to apply this to feminist anti-militarism.

Ruddick defines a practice as 'collective human activities distinguished by the aims that identify them and by the consequent demands made on the practitioners committed to those aims' (Ruddick 1989: 13). Horse-riding and biochemical research require different attitudes and cognitive virtues than caring for young children or elderly Alzheimer patients. Ruddick finds that claims to truth in relation to social experience correspond to the perspec-tive from which actions are performed and differ according to the practice involved. In her view, the practice of maternal care is chiefly determined by the need for preservation, growth and social acceptability. Children are dependent and vulnerable and this evokes a 'caring response'. In her view, the practice of motherhood begins with the recognition of this vulnerability as a relevant social factor and as a phenomenon which makes care necessary. Care thus begins with the recognition that others need our attention, energy and commitment. The way in which this process takes place is dependent on social interpretations and conflicting notions of what constitutes good care.

More than Ruddick, I stress the existence of conflicting and contested notions of care. Even if care is to a certain extent generated by dependency and attentiveness, the concrete motives in social practices of care cannot always be derived from the urge to protect dependent people from vulner-ability. Caring for others can also stem from less noble motives, such as the urge to meddle or to control others. It can also simply follow from one's love or involvement with others, or from concern for their well-being. Care can also figure as an element in power strategies which are directed towards the construction of specific forms of gendered identity and subjectivity.[8] In Western societies there exists a long tradition in which the caring response is associated with a Christian sense of guilt and the resultant identification with the suffering of the other. This means that care in many situations takes the form of a literal commiseration or 'com-passion' in the sight of God.[9] The ethics of care is often conceived – and not only in connection with Chris-tian sources of inspiration – as the product of a caring response to human suffering (see, for example, Noddings 1984; Verkerk 1994). However, the motives behind care, and our judgement of these motives, is certainly not the only factor determining the quality of the caring activities themselves. For this we also need to look at the result. 'Bad' motives can also lead to 'good' care, just as a 'good' motive, such as attentiveness to vulnerability, is no guar-antee of good care: it can also lead to paternalism or undue protection. However, it would not be justified *not* to speak of care in these situations simply because they fail to satisfy the definition of 'protection of vulnerability'.

Ruddick's notion of social practice displays similarities with the political theory of communitarianism, in particular with the work of Alisdair MacIntyre (1981). Communitarians assume that people arrive at moral considerations because they belong to a community, within which they develop values which are important for their identity, their concept of self and political behaviour. However, there exist considerable differences between communitarian authors in both the degree to which and the way in which they consider this should lead to normative conclusions (Frazer and Lacey 1993). According to MacIntyre's version of communitarianism, we can improve our moral judgement by examining moral traditions and assessing their worth; his approach is thus strongly biased towards conservatism. In his view, the practice of ethics is a matter of cultivating and practising moral virtues. That is also the context of his definition of social practices, which he considers to be a form of human cooperation in which qualities and virtues are realized which meet the standard of excellence belonging to these practices (MacIntyre 1981: 187). It is striking that MacIntyre puts such high moral demands on social practices. His concern is not only 'excellence' – whereby he obviously seems to assume that people always aim for the highest achievements, as if it were a part of human nature to always want to be a top athlete or the smartest girl in the class – but also the premiss that practices *in themselves* set goals and demand virtues. This means in effect that he separates morality from its bearers, the people involved in the social practices concerned, who have the task of solving the moral dilemmas with which they are confronted. In this sense his notion of social practices and moral virtues demonstrates characteristics of a teleological image of human nature or the idea that forms of social life have an intrinsic purpose, separate from the considerations of those who participate in them.

Ruddick's work also shows signs of the influence of teleological thinking, even though her definition of social practice is less strict than MacIntyre's; the agents who actually take part in a practice are more visible in her definition. My view, however, is that it is not the practice itself which sets aims, but that these aims are embodied in the way human agents who are engaged in these practices perceive and interpret them. Here I follow Elizabeth Frazer and Nicola Lacey, who state that '"practice" refers to human action which is socially based and organised, underpinned by formal or informal institutions, usually a combination of these' (Frazer and Lacey 1993: 17). They stress the fact that practices are bound up by discourse which is both produced by and produces a practice. Practices and discourses exist independently of particular social subjects, yet they are also constituted by constellations of human action and behaviour (see also Fairclough 1992). Practices, thus conceived, are directed by formal and informal rules and habits, by interpretative conventions and by implicit or explicit normative frameworks.

These rules and norms are not fixed, however, but subject to dispute: they are the object of (re)signification, interpretation, negotiation and conflict. Against this background, care can be seen as a mode of acting in which participants perceive and interpret care needs and act upon these needs. How their interpretation and acting proceeds varies according to the situation and social and institutional contexts, and depends on a variety of factors, such as norms and rules about good caring and the relational dynamics between the actors concerned. This approach makes it possible to acknowledge that care takes place in all kinds of contexts, from child-rearing practices and intimate relations, to social services, education and political deliberation. It also means that, by acknowledging the flexible and contested nature of gender and care, care can be 'saved' from associations with traditional and fixed gendered identities, an association which continues to lurk within most versions of communitarian thought.

Thus, although this conception of an ethics of care, by linking care with social practices, may at first sight display similarities with communitarianism, I would rather stress the need for a social-constructivist and hermeneutical way of interpreting care, to counter the functionalism and the tendencies towards homogeneity inherent in communitarian thought (see also Warnke 1993, 1995; Frazer and Lacey 1993).[10] This allows us to foreground aspects of perception and interpretation in studies of the ethics of care and to investigate the constructions of meanings of care and human agency in this field. Perceptions of people's need of care are not directly determined by those needs themselves or by any 'necessity'. They are mediated by the language in which we talk about them and by the vocabularies deemed applicable to care practices.[11] They are also marked by the psychological and emotional dispositions of those involved and by their psychodynamic interaction patterns (Benjamin 1988; Flax 1993). Ruddick's notion of care and maternal thinking, although she presents it as universally valid, is in fact a notion of *good* care, or, as she sees it, care which responds adequately to dependency and vulnerability, and which aims at protecting vulnerable subjects. There is nothing wrong in itself with a definition of care inspired by moral considerations about its quality, except that this is better made explicit. Acknowledging that nearly all definitions of care contain normative dimensions and several 'interpretative moments' in fact strengthens the moral and political discussion and makes it possible to take different perspectives on care into account (Code 1995: 103 ff.). Applying normative descriptions in terms of values and virtues to the ethics of care means that it can provide standards for judging various practices according to whether they are considered to be sufficiently caring or not. Since this definition of social practice is characterized by agency and judgement, it may remind us on a day-to-day basis that caring is a form of acting, and that an ethics of care – by the very nature of values and virtues such as attentiveness and responsiveness – is rooted in a mixture of caring about and taking care of. Caring thus conceived is a form of 'real-life' responsibility and may indeed be a road to being 'truly moral', by caring 'as well as possible', to quote the both modest and ambitious goal that Berenice Fisher and Joan Tronto (1990) have posed for care as a social practice. There inheres indeed a deeper wisdom in the idea that we cannot understand care unless we practise it, but that our practising of care can also be improved in quality by trying to understand it as well as possible.

The notion of 'care as social practice' can provide useful points of departure, provided the practice of care is not exclusively sought in that which is generally thought of as care: the relations between 'caring' and 'dependent' people in situations of child-rearing, sickness and social need. In fact, practically all human behaviour carries aspects or dimensions of care, even though there is certainly not always an official vocabulary for expressing this.[12] Care is, and this cannot be stressed enough, not only directed at 'others' (those in need of care) but also at the self and the physical environment, as well as the interrelations between these. Even horse-riding and bio-chemical research can be carried out with greater or lesser degrees of care and attentiveness, and more or less involvement with the vulnerability and dependency of horses and biochemical organisms (Keller 1983). Too frequently houses and buildings, for instance, are designed without the needs and well-being of those who will use them being taken into account. The degree of attention paid to human needs and associated relational values in the labour process, economic science, medical science and policy-processes shows whether the dominant paradigms in these areas are able to take account of care in meaningful ways (Ferguson 1984; Tronto 1993; Folbre 1995; Hoek 1994). More generally, scientific practices can differ greatly in their care and empathy for the objects of study. This can vary from inconsiderate or enforced appropriation by the knowing subject, to the pursuit of empathetic knowledge and the practice of trying to see and value situations from different perspectives, giving others the room to speak for themselves. Several authors have contributed to the debate about responsibility in academic study and the social effects of epistemic practices from the perspective of a feminist ethics of care (see, for example Code 1987, 1991, 1995; Collins 1991; Krol 1992; Everts 1993; Rose 1994).

So, if we want to gain more insight into the moral dimensions of care and care as a source of moral and political judgement, we should develop a broad and diverse perspective on care as a form of human agency. This is one of the reasons why an empirical approach from the social sciences is indispensable in thinking about the ethics of care. In social practices people act on the basis of resources such as money, influence, expertise, competence and knowledge. Without wanting to contribute to a reification of care, I would say that the ability to provide and receive care could be seen as a resource, too. Access to these resources is determined by social relations and power processes of a social, economic and political nature. Social divisions in care are strongly marked by gender, class and ethnicity, and the power processes which inform these. People with power are more often in a position to receive or demand care than to provide it, and, conversely, people with less social power find themselves more often on the 'underside' of care; that is, in situations in which they provide care without much power over the conditions and the means, and often in positions of invisibility and voicelessness (Morée and Oldersma 1991). Care for others is more readily associated with a feminine than a masculine sexual identity (Knijn, Nunen and Van der Avort 1994; Duindam and Vroon 1995; Duindam, 1996, 1997). But even in relationships of relative powerlessness people can develop effective and adequate modes of behaviour, just as they are able to manage moral dilemmas and find ways of solving complex moral questions (Gremmen 1995; Davis 1995). So if we want to learn something from the moral experiences related to care in larger social contexts, such as academic study or public debate, it would be better to approach these from the perspectives of the care-givers and care-receivers, and to try and create rhetorical and discursive space for moral narratives of care, which are marginalized in dominant discourses. In this way we can also reflect on the question of how to revalue care in a more general sense (Sevenhuijsen 1993b).

From this perspective, the fact that women's narratives can play an important role might have less to do with their author's gender than with the social positions in which women find themselves, partly because of their gender. It is striking that women's gendered identities in this respect are so often seen as an admission of weakness and set against the idea of liberation through employment and 'equal rights'. We could also see the dilemmas around care and labour market participation as a social condition in which women are, at this point, trying to find their way and from which we can learn a political lesson. Women with children are confronted in all sorts of ways with the contradictions involved in combining work and motherhood, not only in the way they spend their time and in the social support they do or do not receive, but also because the attitude and moral orientations which each practice brings with it tend to conflict (this of course also applies to the experience of working fathers who share in the care of their children). On a daily basis these people have to deal with moral dilemmas and find solutions which can be justified to themselves and to those with whom they are engaged in social and political interactions. Seen from a historical perspective women as a social group stand at a crossroads. Individually and collectively they are confronted on different occasions with the question of whether they want to transcend the world of care on the way to 'true' individuality or whether they can make their experiences and considerations in relation to care productive in their view of a 'good society'.

This situation of rapid social change can be made productive by adopting the position of a 'stranger within'.[13] This implies realizing that one is a newcomer in an established culture; the distance which this brings can then be utilized by turning the clash between different values, cultures and identities into a source of creative judgement. Participating in the established world of labour and political power means that women acquire new capacities and sources of power. Keeping a distance from this world allows them to retain a sense of relativity and permits them to adopt a position of moral curiosity in situations which, for others, invite a morality of certainty and unambiguity. In this sense it might be worthwhile to consider care as a virtue, in spite of the feminist criticism which may be levelled at male traditions of virtue-ethics. This of course assumes that the formulation of virtues and moral feelings is not taken at face value (well-meaning care can, for instance, conceal shame, guilt or aggression), and that we continue to think about which aspects of care can be considered virtuous and which not, and in which contexts that is important, for whom and why (Spelman 1991).

The feminist ethics of care: a postmodern form of humanism?

I would conclude that it is precisely because social practices of care are undergoing such far-reaching changes at this historical moment that so many new notions about care and the ethics of care are now emerging in public debate. In the postmodern condition people take part in a variety of social practices, adopt different identities and come into contact with a variety of positions and social or political aims. Demographic changes and the enormous speed of globalization and different forms of mobility cause ruptures and sudden changes in patterns of 'caring about' and 'caring for'. The conflicts and dilemmas arising from this form fruitful starting-points for considering the values that can be seen as relevant for future society and for political decision-making about the direction of social change. The society of the near future will, in one way or another, have to adjust to a plurality of lifestyles and moral orientations and the resultant social and political frictions. It is more productive to use this fact as a constructive starting-point for reflecting on current value systems than it is to fall back on old and secure patterns or, conversely, to fear that a positive evaluation of care will carry women back into tradition.

This is why it would be such a historical mistake to neglect the meaning of motherhood and care for women or, from a postmodern fear of the notion of fixed identities, to dismiss it as normative. The feminist discussion about an ethics of care is too heavily weighted towards questions of identity rather than questions of agency and morality. If we read the work of feminist thinkers such as Gilligan, Ruddick and Held as arising from a wish for transformative views about the value both of care and maternity at this juncture, and thus as crucial building blocks in the search for meaningful vocabularies in this respect, the historical value of their ideas cannot be overestimated. As Robin May Schott has argued, if we leap from a Platonic transcendence of the human body, and women's bodies in particular, to a postmodern deconstruction of human bodies, and women's bodies in particular, then we will reiterate the devaluation of birthing and motherhood that has marked the ascetic tradition in Western philosophy (Schott 1993: 180). The fact that the 'motherly metaphor' is outdated should not make us forgetful of the moral relevance of maternity and the fact that we are all 'of woman born', nor of the fact that the moral responsibilities of motherhood can be sources of the ambiguities of pleasure, anger and grief and, thus, of both moral tornness and moral wisdom for women who mother. We could even say that the responsibility of the mother is an example of a caring responsibility for living beings that are completely dependent on others. The moral responsibility of the mother is a form of morality that is literally unthinkable without affection and emotion. From a feminist perspective we thus need new examples, and also new metaphors and symbols, to deal with maternity in women-friendly ways.[14] We can perhaps best conceptualize motherhood under postmodern conditions as a series of changing social practices. Motherhood, both as a social institution and as an experience, is expressed in various settings: cultural representations, ideals of child-rearing, legal discourses, medical–technological inventions, the regulation of labour and care, norms of professionalism and the possibility of being able to combine these with care, a new canon of novels about the relation between mothers and daughters (and daughters and fathers) and, last but not least, the way in which care is valued as an aspect of the human condition (DiQuinzio 1993; Everingham 1994; Keizer 1997; Mann 1994). Within such practices women with children have to find a way of giving shape to their relationship with and responsibility for their children, as well as their changing patterns of relationships with men. Here too it holds that motherhood should not be seen simply as an identity, but as a series of relationships within which identity and commitment are expressed.

From the perspective of women's lives the problem of care has long since ceased to be merely the dilemma between paid work and motherhood, or 'the combination'. Adults are confronted with care in work situations, in friendships and in relationships with children, parents and relatives. A common issue is the balance between care for oneself and responsibility for others. Children are no longer, as a rule, born and raised in a life-long relationship between a man and a woman. We have to relate to issues such as test-tube babies, artificial insemination, egg donation, surrogate motherhood and pre-natal screening, and the way in which the modern reproductive technologies influence kinship cultures. Upbringing and care take place in the most diverse family and kinship relations, and in the public debate we are continually challenged for our opinions on such issues. It has become apparent that the family and the sphere of intimate relationships do not – to be sure – always live up to the image of the 'haven in a heartless world', which countless philosophers, social theorists and politicians over the ages have had us believe in. Modern citizens in both private contexts and in their political judgement have to find a way of dealing with physical violence and abuse in family and other human relationships. Marital rape and sexual abuse have attained the status of 'citizenship questions', but for a long time these issues were either ignored or repressed by liberal political philosophy or had a discreet veil drawn over them (Pateman 1989; Vega 1986; Slotboom 1994; Zeegers 1996). Some observers feel that this public interest in the dislocated family may in fact reflect concern about the 'ordinary' family and its importance for a democratic society, and that this should also be a matter for consideration. We encounter these sorts of contests about care every day in newspaper articles, talk shows on TV and in our confrontations with such problems as poverty and insecurity.

This diversity of experiences and moral questions relating to the quality of care has far outgrown the traditional dividing-line between the private and public spheres, the line which has for so long marked the separation between care and politics and which in fact is continually being disputed and redrawn. The argument that we now find ourselves in a 'heterogeneity of public spheres' provides a more satisfactory starting-point for characterizing the postmodern condition in general and also with regard to the social organization of care (Young 1990a). This description does justice to the fragmented nature of the public sphere and to the fact that there are many different locations in which people shape their political agency and social involvement, just as there are many locations in which we have to deal with decision-making and authority. This description also makes it clear that in postmodern existence there are few aspects of life that can be kept private and legitimately protected from any form of public control. Against this background we are continually confronted with the task of reflecting on the meaning of liberal freedom rights, such as the protection of privacy and intimacy. Here too the ethics of care can offer new points of departure, through its plea for intimacy and close relationships to be counted as important humanitarian values (Blustein 1991; see also Nussbaum 1990, 1992, 1995).

This plea for consideration of a diversity of social practices and situations from the perspective of the ethics of care prevents care from being too firmly linked to a fixed division of roles between care-givers and care-receivers, whatever gender these roles may assume. It also ensures that the ethics of care is not framed solely in terms of the care-giver's experience and motivation (as in Noddings 1984 and Manning 1992). At some point in their lives, almost everyone will assume the role of receiver as well as provider of care, although the extent to which each of these roles is fulfilled may vary greatly during a lifetime. Thinking in terms of a fixed pattern quickly reproduces the mechanism whereby vulnerability and needs are located in the so-called 'needy', and not in 'normal' moral subjects themselves. This can lead to complicated patterns of interaction, such as projection or displacement of needs and responsibilities (Römkens 1991, 1992). It also reproduces a one-sided image of human nature, enshrined in the idea that the self-sufficient individual should be the basis of moral existence and political regulation. Patterns in which care needs are located in 'others' can actually have a harmful effect on the practising of morality, since this contributes to an 'externalization' of morality and to a rather thin conception of what moral subjectivity is all about.

In this respect I have always found the objective of government policy of ensuring that every citizen should in principle be able to look after themselves – an aim which was laid down in Dutch emancipation policies in the 1980s – to be paradoxical.[15] This norm of self-sufficiency and the related view of human nature assumes each citizen to be a detached individual, whose aim is autonomous behaviour, who needs nobody and who recognizes dependency and vulnerability only in others. It means that care figures in politics as a handicap, as a burden or as a 'necessary evil' (Zwinkels 1990; Tronto 1993; Werkman 1994). This image expresses a one-sided and, in a certain sense, harmful subject ideal because it encourages citizens also, in the exercise of their citizenship, to look for needs and problems in others rather than in themselves. Because citizenship is a normative concept, this slogan can contribute to patterns of 'objectifying otherness', and thus to an inability to feel connected with others and to deal with difference (Young 1990a; Tronto 1993). The ideal of abstract autonomy in fact overlooks what it is that makes care an element of the human condition, i.e., the recognition that all people are vulnerable, dependent and finite, and that we all have to find ways of dealing with this in our daily existence and in the values which guide our individual and collective behaviour.[16] This idea is one of the main themes of this book. In this respect my argument for a feminist ethics of care can be seen as a plea for a postmodern form of humanism.[17]

Care and ethics as textual practice

With this plea to regard care and the ethics of care as a social practice, I have, in a certain sense, contributed to a long-standing questioning in feminist philosophy of the elevated position of ethics as an academic discipline (see also Braidotti 1986). This points to another theme in the essays collected here, the exhortation to see argument and deliberation as integral parts of political agency. In the previous section I referred on several occasions to 'narratives' in relation to the question of how we can make women's experiences visible and valued in the practice of care. I thus see the practice of ethics as a narrative and textual practice (Prins 1989). Social practices of moral deliberation can be interpreted as forms of 'story-telling', in which signification, evaluation and judgement are intertwined.

My conception of care as a social and moral practice has been inspired partly by feminist pleas for dialogue and open forms of interpretative and communicative ethics, for an ethics, in fact, which provides space for situated forms of political action and judgement (Fraser 1989; Frazer and Lacey

1993; Shrage 1994; Haber 1994; Meehan 1995; Code 1995; Bickford 1996), and thus for a politics of 'small narratives'.[18] Moral stories about care can be seen as a means of interpretation and communication, in which people from a diversity of positions and perspectives exchange values and aims relating to care. We meet these stories in all kinds of interaction in daily life. They are also laid down in written texts, varying from newspaper articles, first-person narratives and novels to political and philosophical texts. In research and journalism we can generate moral stories by interviewing people about their moral experiences in relation to care or by observing situations in which judgements are made about care and ethics, such as medical–ethical committees, or in the practices of nursing and daily care (Gremmen 1995). Such texts can guide our thinking on normative questions concerning care, even if that is not their explicit goal; the Dutch newspaper article quoted at the beginning of this chapter is a striking example of this.

I interpret such texts about care and ethics, following Michel Foucault, as moral discourses: specific ways of constructing a moral problem and distinguishing between true and false, valid and invalid, good and evil (Foucault 1988; Dreyfuss and Rabinow 1982). In women's studies the 'Foucauldian turn' has had a productive influence on research. We now know a lot more about the manifold and subtle ways in which gender is constructed in discourse. I have difficulty with this approach, however, when it leads to a neglect of interest in active agency and thus to an institutionalized forgetfulness that normativity and judgement are necessary, and that we make judgements in our everyday practices. The postmodern turn in women's studies has obscured the idea that there are countless moments in which the necessity for judging is inherent in the situation and the position from which we act. Overlooking this can only lead to a lack of (self-)reflexivity, which feminist theorists argue for in many other respects. Under the influence of postmodern feminism, one of the classic aims of politics, the taking of binding decisions and the bearing of responsibility for these, has been marginalized in many knowledge practices of women's studies.

The postmodern influence, as argued above, tends to lead to an excess of attention for the construction of identities as shaped by outside forces, which is reflected in the passive phrasing of the question 'how is gender constructed?' Normative questions relating to individual and collective behaviour, or the specificity of *political* action, can thus hardly be posed (Voet 1995). The endless attention to identity seems to underlie recent pleas for a restoration of agency in social and political theory. In that light gender can indeed be made productive in active terms, as something which we can make, fantasize, think and do, and which we can value in different modes and, not least, something which we can dispute. This active dimension of gender is of importance not only at the individual or group level (the way in which people acquire gender identities and find their way through gendered cultures), it is also expressed in political contexts at the level of acting together in concert.

29

There it continues to have an effect on the way people can manifest them-selves and on the values which they (can) call on in doing so.[19] However, in political contexts the question of agency far outweighs that of identity. Politics after all is concerned with the shaping of collective responsibility and productive use of the tension between difference and equality. This raises the question of when gender identity is actually relevant for the networks in which we live our lives and for the contexts in which we express our political involvement. In politics we have to judge between good and evil. In post-modernity we lack solid foundations for making such judgements: the need to live with contingency and ambiguity, and 'without illusions', leaves us with no other option than to trust a will to be 'truly moral', to be found in a human ability for autonomous judgement based on our being-in-the-world with others. In order to practise such forms of political judgement we have to be able to separate ourselves from self-proclaimed identities and to meet the other in ourself. Or as Zygmunt Bauman (1992) concludes, moral responsi-bility is the most personal and inalienable of human possessions and the most precious of human rights.

Against this background I argue that the methods which have been developed for discourse and textual analysis should be applied to policy and legal texts, in order to analyse the ways in which these texts assign meaning to gender, care and sexual difference.[20] Policy texts and legal texts are, after all, 'stories in themselves': they include patterns of dealing with things which are often the result of political compromises and discursive traditions. They often contain fixed patterns of speaking and judging, but they can also open up unexpected discursive spaces, where new forms of thinking and judging can start. The law can be seen as the body which has the highest or greatest 'authority to speak'. It contains terms and rules for speaking which are not easy to change, but which can certainly have far-reaching consequences for the distribution of resources and social positions, for the way in which author-itative 'social diagnoses' come about, and for the speaking positions from which this happens. The law is, to use the British sociologist Carol Smart's term, an important discursive apparatus and, notable in this context, a 'gen-dering machine' (Smart 1992, 1995). An analysis in terms of power, discourse and gender makes it possible to assess political and legal texts for their inclu-sionary and exclusionary effect, analysing which and whose perspective can be expressed and with which normative message. In this respect texts have a selective effect, which I try to capture with terms such as 'discursive space' and 'legitimate speaking position'. In this way gender can function openly and also in more hidden ways, both through explicit references to sexual dif-ference and through the symbolic meanings of traditional patterns of thought in relation to sexual difference. This is the approach which is taken in Chapters 4 and 5 of this book.

I start from the premiss that political and legal texts harbour many aspects which have enabling and/or constraining effects on human agency and which provide parameters for the way in which people can profile themselves in the public sphere and politics. In their political practices, feminists use diverse normative frameworks, both in a critical and a creative sense. Sometimes this happens unconsciously or as a matter of course, because these thinking traditions have a common-sense status. It then becomes almost impossible to see that there are other claims to truth and other normative considerations which may also be worth noting as guidelines for action. Political philosophy can thus contribute to a more detailed reflection on the normative frameworks that guide and justify political action. Thus, I find one of the most productive branches of women's studies to be the rereading of the canon: the still-growing project in which feminist philosophers examine the work of major thinkers for the meanings of sexual difference their work contains and its usefulness for normative reasoning from a feminist perspective. In this book I use the work of these feminist philosophers as a source of inspiration for finding links between the ideas which are embodied in it and a number of current political issues, in which care, ethics and judgement are interwoven. To make this possible I take specific arguments and texts as the starting-point of my discussion. My aim is to analyse – in an illustrative fashion – characteristic modes of argument in the field of care, in terms of power, discourse and gender. In this way I will try to find out which modes and positions of speaking are productive for feminist objectives and how we can further give shape to the idea of 'judging with care'.

Now that the grand narrative about 'the' moral objectives of human society and 'the' moral subject has been toppled from its pedestal by postmodernism and the diminishing belief in the malleability of society, we are better able to evaluate the meaning and contribution of different traditions of thought. This means that we can ask ourselves which elements are worth keeping and which are now worn out and need replacing. We can also view the ethics of care in this light. Various authors have already found sources of inspiration for an ethics of care, responsibility, connection and friendship in the philosophical tradition. They draw on the work of classical philosophers such as Aristotle, early Christian thinkers in the tradition of Stoa, eighteenth-century thinkers such as David Hume and Adam Smith, or twentieth-century thinkers such as Martin Heidegger, Simone Weil, Hannah Arendt and Emmanuel Levinas, or postmodern philosophers such as Michel Foucault, François Lyotard and Paul Ricoeur, or on literary work such as that by Iris Murdoch, even though these thinkers have not themselves necessarily been proponents of a (post)modern ethics of care. In many respects, the ethics of care thus intersects with other attempts to think about morality and normativity in a new way. Where possible these various approaches have been incorporated into the text of this book or referred to in the notes. Thinking in terms of moral traditions does not necessarily imply that one's view is by definition turned towards the past or that one is led by a desire to return to bygone conditions and certainties. Future utopias can also be a source of inspiration, whether they come to us from the nineteenth century or whether we make and consume them via science fiction novels, television series, Internet communications or policy-oriented future scenarios. From these too emerge images of gender, care and ethics which we can use in our moral deliberations about care.

A number of thinkers have become involved in a discussion about the epistemological premises and central values and concepts of the ethics of care. They have elaborated on the suitable contexts of application and characteristic social practices for an ethics of care. I see this project as an attempt, situated in time and different socio-political contexts, to 'think care', to make it visible as a cognitive, reflective and moral practice. This also means that the political importance of care emerges: the issue of how far we can see the ethics of care as a political virtue, and whether this enables us to perceive and judge political problems in an innovative way (Tronto 1995b; Jones 1993). I consider the essays in this book to form a contribution to this collective project. My own judgement about the content and worth of the ethics of care has developed over the years. It has often come into being through detours, for example by thinking through the arguments against it or by comparing the ethics of care with other moral vocabularies. On balance, my judgement is positive, though without any plea for the ethics of care to be granted a superior status in the practice of ethics. The forming of moral judgements should be seen as a complex task, rather than a stroll through a supermarket, where a pre-packaged moral idiom can be picked off the shelf. To use a medical metaphor, there is no simple prescription for the treatment of moral experiences.

My route to this book

This book reflects the gradual strengthening of my opinion on the ethics of care and my increasing acceptance of it. In my first exploratory article on the work of Carol Gilligan, Sarah Ruddick and Jean Elshtain, which in fact is not included in this collection, I was still quite tentative and reserved about the possibilities of an ethics of care (Sevenhuijsen 1988a). After this I wrote a number of articles about family law, in which I drew attention to the absence of care as a social practice and moral consideration within that domain (Sevenhuijsen 1991b, 1992a). Here I argued more directly that the ethics of care should be taken seriously as a moral and normative idiom. I persevered along this path in the speech entitled 'The morality of feminism', which I presented at my inauguration as Professor of Women's Studies at the University of Utrecht, a post which I took up in 1990. This has been included here in a thoroughly reworked version as Chapter 2. The reworking of the text of this speech gave me the chance to clarify a number of issues and further to develop my vision on the contribution to be made by an ethics of care. Together with Chapter 3, 'Paradoxes of gender', in which I frame my critique of the paradigm of distributive justice, and which has undergone less drastic revision, it presents a fairly complete picture of the intellectual bases of my current thinking about the feminist ethics of care. This has made it possible to weld the two articles about family law mentioned above into one chapter, Chapter 4, and to argue more forcefully than in the earlier versions for the innovative contribution to be made by the feminist ethics of care to the public debate about parental rights.

My development towards a more solid elaboration and defence of the ethics of care has been supported by a number of intervening developments. In the first place there has been what can be described as a breakthrough in the public debate about labour and care in the Netherlands. This demonstrates the fact that women's organizations and women's studies, in spite of the rift which grew between them in the 1980s, now seem to be moving closer together again. I do not treat the political developments surrounding labour and care separately – that would merit a book in itself – but in various chapters I show what the contribution of an ethics of care could be to thinking on this subject. In the second place, the recent public debate about the Dutch government's publication, *Choices in Health Care*, offered me the opportunity to give the feminist ethics of care 'hands and feet' in a public debate, and to investigate in cooperation with women's organizations what this could lead to. The result of this has been published on several occasions (Parlevliet and Sevenhuijsen 1993; Meinen *et al.* 1994; Sevenhuijsen 1993b). In Chapter 5 of this book I present the most systematic treatment of this issue in terms of feminist political theory.

Here, I have developed my vision of the political meaning of a feminist ethics of care beyond that of my earlier publications. This emerges in my plea to integrate care into conceptions of democratic citizenship and social justice, and to look for suitable moral epistemologies and forms of public debate which make this possible. The issue of which approach to politics and ethics forms the best context for the ethics of care is integrated into the different chapters. This has resulted in a repetitive effect, which may seem tiresome, but which, in my opinion, is necessary because the value of the ethics of care can only be argued in context. Moreover, this approach makes it possible to read each chapter on its own.

As my thoughts have developed I have begun to describe the ethics of care more and more as a moral vocabulary. This makes it possible, I hope, to formulate its content more systematically and to assess more effectively its capacity to expose and express social problems and to make them available for judgement. A vocabulary is of course always a construction of those who speak it. In the attempt to make the vocabulary of the ethics of care visible and contrast it with other political idioms, the concept has been systematized in a way which, on the one hand, can prove elucidating, but which can also have a simplifying effect. In this sense the articulation of a system of thought can best be seen as a heuristic device, an attempt to illuminate and bring to the fore, in a meaningful way, specific experiences and considerations. In reality, discussions about care and ethics are of course much more complex, many-sided and fragmented, encompassing a host of various different combinations of elements from different moral vocabularies. In this respect it is perhaps more appropriate to see the public debate as a series of language games, in which the participants employ fragments from different vocabularies in order to achieve specific rhetorical effects.[21] The example at the beginning of this chapter hopefully makes it clear that there is a considerable difference between the story of the nurse who killed a number of elderly patients as told from a strictly legal point of view or from the perspective of an ethics of care.[22] In this sense the different vocabularies can be used in order to articulate moral problems or talk in different ways about the problems which need political judgement.

The philosophical discussion about care and justice in this book takes place in a way which may suggest that neatly defined moral idioms are involved, or alternative and mutually exclusive modes of thinking about morality and ethics. The question of the relationship between each of these vocabularies is, however, also from a philosophical perspective, much more complex. The answer depends to a certain extent on the particular variety of the theory of justice and particular version of the ethics of care which are being employed.[23] However, in spite of this it seems clear that in a number of respects the feminist ethics of care offers a radical alternative to the liberal justice idiom. The manner in which moral subjectivity and moral situations are considered in the ethics of care leads to a relational image of human nature which is incompatible with the atomistic, individualized subject of liberal political philosophy. In my opinion, the feminist ethics of care employs a moral epistemology which forms a radical break with epistemic rules of liberal political philosophy. On the other hand, this does not imply that I argue for a definitive farewell to liberal concepts such as equality, justice and autonomy, or deny their value for gender politics; on the contrary, it simply means that they need to be rethought from the perspective of the ethics of care. My ideas on this point are most clearly expressed in Chapters 2, 3 and 5.

Finally, although it is quite possible to conceptualize the ethics of care without attaching the adjective 'feminist' to it, I still prefer to add this word wherever possible. In the first place it shows the source of my inspiration and aims: further reflection on the feminist attitude to care and ethics, and the decoding of the gender-load inherent in established moral and political philosophy. Both care and ethics are indeed so interwoven with gender that we cannot do without continuous reflection on feminist interpretations and feminist points of view. But I also include the adjective 'feminist' for the sake of historical accuracy. *Feminist* thinkers, after all, have, since the 1980s, most clearly drawn attention to an ethics of care and responsibility. In doing this they had a political objective: to expose the sexism and gender-blindness in moral philosophy and to give space to the moral considerations of women, and 'feminine' moral voices and considerations. They thus strive to expose and transform institutionalized forms of dominance and the discursive patterns inherent in them. None of this has led to any agreement about the value, sources and content of the ethics of care. When we accept the idea that care is not unproblematically present in social and intellectual life, but that we have to put effort into developing our understanding of care, we can appreciate that this disagreement has in itself been fruitful. It has made it possible to articulate and develop the moral, political and epistemological dimensions of a feminist ethics of care in a more consistent way, so that a point has now been reached when its central concepts can be applied to different areas and issues. Precisely in a period in which the term 'feminism', in some circles at least, seems to be falling into discredit, it is important to continue to recognize how much we owe to it. The feminist adage about the combination of tenderness and strength can thus continue to direct thinking about care, so that people like Moniek van den Heuvel can assume their rightful place in political ethics.

2

THE MORALITY OF FEMINISM

The uneasy relationship between feminism and ethics[1]

The relationship between feminism and morality has recently been one of unease and suspicion. Many modern feminists see morality as one of the phenomena from which women should be liberated, and they easily associate it with paternalism, restrictive regulation of women's lives, and conservatism. It seems to be an obstacle between tradition and freedom, between subordination and equal rights. When viewed in this way, there could be no connection between morality and feminism. The title of this chapter could at most refer to an argument in which revelations were made about the norms and regulations which are imposed within feminism itself until, freed from moralistic prejudices, the scientific discipline of women's studies can really get under way. This would herald a new phase in which subjective judgements could be replaced by objective knowledge about gender relations and those elements which need to be changed.

The term 'morality' in my view, however, does not refer to restrictive regulations or absolute value judgements. That is a description which is better applied to the concept of moralism.[2] I use morality in the sociological sense to refer to the totality of rules, codes, values and norms which are used to justify behaviour by labelling it 'right' or 'wrong'. Seen in this light, feminism without morality is inconceivable. Like every other social and political movement, feminism has its judgements, objectives, collective modes of behaviour and principles. These are inscribed in feminist knowledge practices and thereby in the issues, theories and methodologies of women's studies. I start from the premiss that every knowledge practice embodies normative elements and normative objectives. Scientific practices are motivated by a will to know and a will to change, which leave their mark on the concepts and modes of thought employed. By the same token, systems of knowledge have a structuring effect on the ways in which change can be conceived with regard to method and content.

The title 'The morality of feminism' is thus meant as an invitation to consider the moral dimensions of feminist knowledge practices and the basic principles of feminist judgement. The study of these moral dimensions brings ethical questions into the domain of women's studies. Ethics provides theoretical reflection on dominant values, moral codes and moral convictions. It studies 'how morality works' and makes claims about the bases and sources of moral judgement as well as discussing values and concepts which can guide complex judgements. It is almost impossible to give a single unambiguous definition of ethics, since the way ethicists define their discipline is closely tied to the philosophical school of thought in which their work is situated. Against this background I define ethics as the systematic and critical reflection on human action in the light of good and bad, and right and wrong.[3] The advantage of this definition is twofold. First, through the centrality of agency, it refers to moral reflection as a *social practice*. This practice is not limited to the domain of academic theory (which one might be inclined to think on reading many ethics texts), but takes place in all kinds of social practices. Second, when starting from this definition we can evaluate many different types of moral considerations. Even a branch of ethics which at first seems to have nothing to do with value judgements (such as the ethics of distributive justice) makes all kinds of claims – often implicit – about what constitute 'good' forms of judgement and behaviour.

Much of the feminist opposition to ethics is derived from the fact that in this type of thinking good and bad are thought of in absolute, metaphysical terms and that these absolute moral truths are not infrequently associated with normative images of a 'proper' femininity. Opposition to a specific type of ethics means that feminists are too often inclined to banish the subject as a whole, with the unfortunate result that we are deprived of the means for reflecting on our own distinctions between good and bad. The subject of ethics becomes more acceptable if we realize that in practically all contexts of behaviour we are confronted with questions of judgement and responsibility, which, in my view, are *the* central categories of a good ethics. Ethical issues arise in concrete situations, in the form of questions such as 'how to act?', or 'how to lead a good life?' Hence, the way in which a political movement like feminism justifies its actions can also be enriched by taking ethics seriously. Claims, observations and objectives are no longer self-evident, but become the object of (self-)reflexivity, through reflection on how to act. From this perspective issues of agency have everything to do with issues of knowledge and interpretation. A feminism that is conscious of its moral and normative dimensions no longer believes in a single truth, but continually questions its truth claims and reflects on their normative implications.

Although modern feminism may have had difficulty in expressing its normative dimensions and seeing its truth claims in that light, various forms of ethics are still quite clearly discernible in its practices and aims. The most influential political ethics of the second wave of feminism is the liberal ethics of equality, justice and autonomy. These values have become so self-evident in the normative framework of modern feminism that they are often no

37

longer recognized as part of an ethics at all. Thus, for many it is also difficult to think critically about the meaning and usefulness, and the advantages and disadvantages of liberal ethics. It is as if reflection on such matters would shake the security and the foundations of modern feminism. Nevertheless, liberal ethics has remained controversial within the women's movement, even though this has not always taken the shape of reflection about the value of different normative systems. The first manifestations of second-wave feminism drew on liberal values such as equality and self-determination to undermine traditional (political) patterns of thought about sexual difference, in particular the idea that sexual differences should have a place in a natural, hierarchically ordered social system. Feminists claimed that liberal values should be applied more consistently to women. Soon, however, in feminist circles there emerged a critique of the norm of equality between the sexes and in particular of the automatic way in which women, under this regime of the equality norm, continually had to adapt to 'masculine' values and lifestyles. It was felt that feminism should also orient itself towards a re-evaluation of women's voice in politics and culture.

In the 1970s this point of tension emerged as a conflict between liberal feminism and cultural feminism, although this opposition was not directly expressed in the terminology of political ethics. In the 1980s this changed. With the emergence of feminist ethics and feminist political philosophy as branches of academic learning, the terminology which had been used in the earlier debate was subjected to a thorough philosophical enquiry (Eisenstein 1981; Jaggar 1983). And, what was equally important, earlier ideas about a specifically feminine voice and feminine morality were discussed and systematized in the debate on the ethics of care, which really started to take off with the appearance of developmental psychologist Carol Gilligan's work around 1980 (Gilligan 1980, 1982). This launched the 'care–justice' debate, the discussion about the advantages and disadvantages of an ethics of care as opposed to an ethics of justice.[4] This debate caused quite a commotion among feminists. The *care* standpoint had to contend, at the start, with a whole series of reproaches from the *justice* supporters. The most serious point of criticism was that an ethics of care would confirm women in a traditional identity derived from motherhood. This would prevent them from overcoming their limited field of vision and becoming capable of 'genuine' moral judgement, in which universal and universally applicable values determine the nature of judgement. Moreover, it would confirm women in their 'otherness', and thus prevent them claiming access to the moral and political order on equal terms, as fully-fledged, independent individuals.

Although in the beginning I was inclined to share this opinion about the value of an ethics of care (see, for example, Sevenhuijsen 1986, 1988a), I became increasingly uneasy about the severity of the criticism which was levelled at it, and the refusal of the supporters of liberal ethics to pay serious attention to the motives and arguments of those in favour of an ethics of care.

Further examination of the debate showed me that condemnation of the ethics of care was often based on a superficial or inaccurate acquaintance with the work of its spokeswomen and a refusal openly to discuss one's own normative assumptions and truths, especially about care. Moreover the debate – as tends to occur with debates – became caught up in a repetition of arguments and unproductive polarizations (Davis 1992). If you were 'for' care ethics, for instance, then you *had* to be an adherent of natural sexual differences or – even worse – essentialism, and thus you were unable to think in terms of equality; this was of course an unattractive perspective to many.[5]

Recently, a great deal has been written about the possible relationship between the ethics of care and justice, and whether they could possibly be united in a single ethical system. In my opinion there is another question which should in fact precede this, the question of why the compatibility of the two moral orientations is of such overriding importance in the care–justice debate. Why should it be necessary to derive one from the other or to conceive of one in terms of the other? We need to look more closely at the question of why these ethical approaches have such an uneasy relationship to each other, before deciding on whether or not they can be reconciled. In this chapter I will argue that the philosophical assumptions of liberal ethics, with regard to universality, impartiality, rationality, and equality versus difference, almost inevitably lead to a negative evaluation of the ethics of care. These assumptions determine the way in which the ethics of care is perceived, interpreted and judged from a liberal normativity. I think we need to examine the critique made by a number of feminist philosophers of the central assumptions of liberalism in order to be able to offer a valid assessment of the value to be gained from an ethics of care.[6] To understand the steps of this argument more fully, I will first look at the relationship between feminism and universalism in this chapter.[7] This will allow a more explicit clarification of the contribution of the ethics of care to the debate about feminism and ethics, the subject of the third section.

I will begin by discussing a number of the chief characteristics of universalist ethics. Starting from an analysis of equality arguments, I will show that equality in universalism and in what I call the 'radical–liberal version of the distributive paradigm' is consistently defined as 'sameness', so that difference and equality appear to be irreconcilable opposites. The ethics of care, which is conceived of as 'different', is thus at a disadvantage from the start. I will show that the norm of equality-as-sameness goes together with a negative evaluation of difference, which in turn is related to the dualistic logic implied in universalism. A universalist ethics can only exist if differences (including those related to sexual difference) are reduced to categories of 'otherness', within which they are, as it were, enclosed and thus rendered harmless. In this way universalism situates factors such as embodiment and emotionality, partly because they are so easily associated with femininity, outside the moral domain.

Finally, I will discuss the implication of these ideas for a feminist assessment of the possibilities offered by an ethics of care and responsibility. I will argue that the ethics of care has an innovative view on a number of issues in moral epistemology and thinking about moral subjectivity and moral deliberation. In fact, the ethics of care presupposes that we rethink a number of the central notions of ethics. Because these notions also appear in other established scientific epistemologies, particularly with regard to notions of rationality, objectivity and impartiality, this has consequences for the way in which we are able to understand and judge care. My argument is that the debate about the relation between care and justice can only progress if we integrate these radical implications from the feminist ethics of care into thinking about justice in general.

Feminism and universalism

Equality and sameness as ethical principles

Since Kant, universalism in ethics has been conceived of as a totality of rules, norms and principles which are equally applicable to everyone, and which in principle should also be recognizable and acceptable to every rational thinking person. The task of ethics is to formulate higher principles in cases of conflicting interests, rights and opinions. This finds expression in the search for a normative basis for the 'general interest' and the establishment of priorities among basic human rights when making (political) judgements in complex situations, which would in turn make it possible to introduce a hierarchical distinction between claims and rights. Neutrality, impartiality, rationality, abstraction and objectivity are the most important requirements for acquiring insight into the correct criteria. Morality entails the finding and respecting of rules. Making morally just decisions thus involves arriving at the correct rules and applying them to specific cases in accordance with accepted procedures. Equality, autonomy and justice are the key concepts of modern universalist ethics, a fact which is borne out by the popular precept that justice consists of treating like cases alike.

Universalist ethics seems, at first sight, an attractive ally for feminism. The application of impartiality carries with it the promise of an end to stereotypical images and prejudices about women. Armed with objective knowledge about sexual difference, feminists can claim greater validity for their judgements and thus make a convincing and legitimate case for change. Universalist ethics is often invoked because it signifies a break with remaining forms of the double standard in morality whereby different and often arbitrary criteria are used to judge the behaviour, achievements and manifestations of men and women. Feminist objectives can thus quite clearly be linked to a universalist ethics and politics where feminism is principally linked to the goal of ensuring that liberal principles such as equality and freedom are

40

applied to women. However, if we examine the internal logic of the debate about equality in more detail, certain limitations become apparent in the liberal ideal of equality.

The norm of treating like cases in a like manner forces us to reflect on exactly when cases *are* alike. In recent public debates, this problem has mainly been framed within the context of legal issues relating to the 'gender' question. There are countless examples of this in a number of fields, and jurisprudence is permeated with arguments on this issue. Legal arguments in turn influence the content, direction and terminology of the public debate. The legal obligation to participate in the labour market, anti-discriminatory legislation, affirmative action, the redistribution of paid work and care, and the equal participation of girls in education are all issues in which the assumption that men and women are equal forms the mainstay of the argument. If differences in performance or behaviour are observed, then the reply is usually that they are the result of sex-stereotyped socialization and unequal treatment. The most important norm is to make no distinction between men and women and to treat them consistently either as equals or, failing that, as prospective equals.

This argument implies a specific application of the distinction between sex and gender as set forth in the first phase of modern feminist theory. The concept of gender was developed in the first instance to allow us to distinguish between innate and acquired characteristics. It was thus intended as a critical instrument in order to combat traditional ideas about women's 'natural' characteristics or 'natural' destiny, and in particular the idea that women were predestined to motherhood and care, and to the service of and subordination to men, on the basis of their biology (see Outshoorn 1989; Haraway 1991: 127–148; Oudshoorn 1991). Sexual difference thus refers to the biological or anatomical difference between the sexes, and gender to the socially constructed identities related to this sexual difference. The argument is that if women are involved to a greater degree in providing care for children, men and the elderly, and less active in the public world of paid labour, culture and politics, this is not because of any innate qualities, but because this role is ascribed to them and so they acquire it. The concept of gender fits in with the liberal idea that we are all born equal: deviations from this equality can be ascribed to the fact that during the course of their lives people acquire the dominant norms of their culture and assume them to be logical and self-evident.[8]

From this perspective, equality is used, in the first instance, as a descriptive concept: the claim that all people are born equal serves as the starting-point for this mode of reasoning. At the same time, the concept of equality also contains a highly speculative and normative element which is often overlooked, as Merle Thornton has argued in her analysis of what she calls 'dogmatic equality' (Thornton 1986). According to this version of the equality argument, because people are born equal, this means that they must also be treated as equals under all circumstances. This is then coupled with the expectation that equality in treatment will lead to equality in results. And because this equality exists, or will do so in the near future, men and women should also have equal rights and duties. The power of equality as a normative concept lies in the fact that its speculative empirical element has a logical counterpart in a political programme. Equality marks the boundary between unacceptable conditions and an ideal vision, and therefore it is equality which provides the correct criteria for making the right choices. The route to liberation can be reached only by eliminating inequalities and differences; achieving justice entails a collective effort to dismantle all mechanisms which maintain the division of humanity into two genders. From this point of view, feminism seems primarily to be a matter of redistribution. Inequality and difference become the crucial concepts for indicating what is wrong in gender relations.[9] Underlying this is often a positive norm of 'sameness': the idea that, in principle, people are identical to each other and that there also exists a uniform human subject which can serve as a starting-point for normative reasoning and political regulation.

It is neither an easy nor an inviting proposition for feminism to relinquish the norm of equality.[10] The idea that men and women do not differ systematically in their capacities is an indispensable element in a feminism whose principle objective is the fair treatment of men and women. The criterion of equal treatment remains an important corrective to arbitrary judgement, and thus functions as a norm which can be mobilized against ingrained thinking in terms of male superiority. The problems associated with the equality norm reside principally in its application and in the way in which this application is automatically traced back to an unprovable notion of original equality, and thus to a norm of sameness for human subjects. This mode of argument belongs to the dominant political paradigm in which the equality argument was applied during the 1980s, and which I will call here the 'radical–liberal' version of the distributive paradigm.[11] I will go on to outline three problems associated with this approach: the first on a logical and rhetorical level, the second on the level of political organization and moral judgement, and the third in relation to the thematization of gender and sexual difference in the light of (political) identity.

First, the logical and rhetorical aspects: although the argument that equal treatment will produce equal results sounds quite plausible, in fact this is a circular and speculative mode of reasoning. Since it is hard empirically to prove a natural or original equality, evidence of its existence is largely based on differences in treatment. The implication is that it is because people are treated differently that they depart from their natural sameness. The principles and objectives of equal treatment are thus conflated into an indivisible whole.[12] Because of this confusion, the public debate about gender issues repeatedly ends up in a vicious circle. If the expected equality in results fails to appear, this easily leads to assertions that people are 'obviously' not equal and their biology 'obviously' has an unavoidable effect. Currently this argument seems to be gaining prominence, particularly since the rapid increase in knowledge about the effect of genes and hormones. Supporters of the 'nurture' argument then counter this with ever more elaborate insights into the effects of nurture and culture.

The public debate about sexual difference thus remains trapped in a search for authenticity and in a logic of comparison, without attention being paid to the criteria for comparison or the moral or political relevance of the discussion. In fact, arguing for a norm of equality logically implies the existence of differences (Komter 1990). Moreover, if there were no differences, it would be pointless to take equality as an ideal. However, if it is never made explicit what acceptable criteria for equality are, then dominant or tacit norms will quickly fulfil this role. In a culture where comparisons between men and women are the order of the day and in which various traditions of male dominance persist, masculine norms easily come to be seen as the implicit standard for comparison. This is evident for instance in the oft-repeated question of whether women are different or act differently from men, and the corresponding infrequency with which the question is posed the other way around. The debate about the ethics of care also continues to centre around a question which, in my view, is both uninteresting and unrewarding, that of gender differences in moral reasoning. In this way women are continually grouped together as a single category, so that they can be presented as deviant from the masculine, which in turn is considered to be the general. And because people keep on looking for differences between women and men, there is a great risk that various phenomena which may have little or nothing to do with sexual difference will be attributed to it. In this way sexual difference continues to reverberate through the public debate, without its relevance always being clear.

Then the second point: the political implications. A universalist ethics which takes sameness as its basic principle and aim will have an effect on the aims, content and form of gender politics. The principle that equality in results should be the touchstone for politics and policy has the effect of marginalizing other moral questions, such as the question of how oppression, violence, vulnerability and plurality should be dealt with, or how quality of life can be improved. Issues like these are also difficult to objectify; this means that attempts to resolve them by means of the equality paradigm will be unable to pay sufficient attention to the associated moral dilemmas. The norm of equality as 'sameness' or 'prospective sameness' also leaves its mark on the legitimacy of different forms of political and moral deliberation, and on the manner in which women are supposed to organize themselves politically. A universalist ethics implies that women should conceive of themselves as little as possible in terms of sexual difference. Instead they should merge into the rational order and the political community as ungendered individuals, at most accompanied by a number of (temporary) specific interests.

If they make an appeal to moral judgement *as* women or on the basis of characteristics which are commonly labelled as 'feminine', they will quickly find themselves accused of traditionalism or reproached for their obvious belief in 'natural' human qualities or, whether intentionally or not, for strengthening this belief. In this way an opposition between equality and difference – and coupled with this, between nature and culture, and tradition and modernity – is elevated to the status of a criterion which can be used for judging all kinds of behaviour. The equality norm seems then to refer not only to the distribution of rights and obligations, but also to a more diffuse 'speech right'. I am referring here to the way in which people can manifest themselves in the public sphere, to the values and considerations to which they can appeal and to the voice in which they can speak.

This brings me to my third point, the question of identity and politics. The idea that the principal aim of feminism is redistribution and the standardization of identity is a rather oversimplified view of the feminist message about gender. In fact, the second wave of feminism has, right from the start, also fought for a re-evaluation of the characteristics commonly considered to be 'feminine', and a reshaping of the images which are commonly associated with sexual difference. However, when these aims are subsumed within a policy of redistribution, we are left with an oversimplified and often ambiguous idea of (sexual) identity. First there is the risk that processes of identification are continually reduced to upbringing and psychological mechanisms. This can be termed the 'psychologizing of identity': identity is brought under a regime of knowing and controlling, in which a combination of psychology and a politics of control is the norm. This view fits in well with a conception of politics as a medium of education or as a pedagogical instrument, often expressed in the notion that politics should stimulate people to behave in a certain way. This in turn is based on the assumption that a person should be thought of as a *tabula rasa*, so that politics is justified in making one of its goals the (trans)forming of identities. The issue of how people construct and value their identity and express it in their behaviour and negotiations is then eclipsed by the idea that the process of identity formation is concerned with how people 'are' or 'are made'.

Paradoxically enough the *content* of identity then has but little moral and political significance. In fact, what communitarian philosophy terms an empty, thin or unencumbered concept of personhood has become the norm for political judgement (Sandel 1982; Taylor 1989). It is as if the human person is a shell which society can fill as it pleases, without worrying too much about how the people concerned value their lives. Through this fusion of public and private identities, it becomes almost impossible to introduce another important dimension of the liberal tradition – the search for a normative balance between public authority and private responsibilities – as a fully-fledged element in judgements relating to sexual politics. And if sexual difference is conceptualized as a category of being rather than doing, as something that you 'are', then there is very little room for deliberating creatively and constructively about it or for discussing its agency aspects and relevance to other phenomena; it also becomes difficult to conceive of the public sphere as a suitable space for doing that.

If, on the other hand, we start from the premiss that (self-)images and conceptions of sexual identity have to do with questions about 'how to live', they actually become part of an ethics of the good life. While classical–liberal ethics has a tendency to ban such questions to the private sphere, labelling them as 'individual preferences', the radical–liberal version of the distributive paradigm is even more rigorous when it comes to sexual difference. It hardly grants any independent position to the moral dimensions of identity and to issues relating to the ethics of existence, as these are fitted into the political 'logic of identity' and the dismantling of the boundaries between the private and the public.[13] In this sense liberal-individualist feminism has aligned itself with what is aptly described as the 'attenuation of morality' (Reinders 1994: 88). This finds expression in the previously mentioned inability of many feminists to consider the normative dimensions of their own discourse, and in the difficulty of the radical–liberal version of the distributive paradigm to see moral motivations and moral orientations as a meaningful and worthwhile attribute of human beings and the networks of relationships within which they live.

The gender-load of impartiality, neutrality and rationality

In the preceding section I showed that the radical–liberal norm of sameness repeatedly leads to a negative evaluation of difference. Differences, whether speculative in nature or accompanied by convincing evidence, are always considered deviant and negative in relation to a universal norm. This means that not only is there a logic of comparison, but also a hierarchy in which various values and phenomena are ordered. Many of the dominant norms are thus defined in relation to their opposites. This issue has been extensively analysed in feminist philosophy in terms of the logic of identity and the critique of dualism.[14]

The American feminist philosopher Iris Marion Young has convincingly demonstrated the relationship between the logic of identity and impartiality. Following philosophers such as Adorno, Lyotard, Irigaray and Derrida, she states that

> the logic of identity expresses one construction of the meaning and operations of reason: an urge to think things together, to reduce them to unity. To give a rational account is to find the universal, the one principle, the law covering the phenomena to be accounted for. Reason seeks essence, a single formula that classifies concrete

particulars as inside or outside a category, something common to all things that belong in the category. The logic of identity tends to conceptualize entities in terms of substance rather than process or relation; substance is the self-same entity that underlies change, that can be identified, counted, measured.

(Young 1990a: 98)

The logic of identity is effective because it denies or represses difference. Thinking with this logic implies a denial of the difference between subject and object. Instead, a unity is pursued between the object and the subject. 'Through the logic of identity thought seeks to bring everything under control, to eliminate uncertainty and unpredictability, to spiritualise the bodily fact of sensuous immersion in a world that outruns the subject, to eliminate otherness' (ibid.: 99). In the logic of identity the subject is conceived as pure transcendental origin: it has no foundations outside itself, it is self-generating and autonomous. 'The logic of identity also seeks to reduce the plurality of particular subjects, their bodily, perspectival experience, to a unity, by measuring them against the unvarying standard of universal reason' (ibid: 99).

The logic of identity implies that difference is turned into otherness and deviance. This implies that variety, insecurity and changeability have to be reduced to unambiguous terms, which serve as standards of comparison against which so-called 'deviant' phenomena can be set off. However, the deviant only exists because it is defined in terms of the norm. Thus, normativity is hidden within scientific practices in many ways. The question: 'How can I best conceive or interpret a phenomenon?' is superseded by the question 'What is the nature of that phenomenon?' In other words, a question of interpretation and judgement is replaced by an ontological question, posed in universal terms. The situatedness and the behavioural context of the knowing, interpreting and judging subject are thus obscured as relevant factors for scientific research and for moral judgement (see also Code 1991, 1995).

This attempt to collapse differences into homogeneity implies that instability and unpredictability must be eliminated in order to be able to consider a phenomenon and maintain its universality and thus normativity. Normative and impartial reasoning, which employs universal standards and which abstracts as far as possible from the definition of particularity and context, is assigned an important role in confirming unity and homogeneity. Within this framework, impartiality can only be reached by separating reason from emotion. Because the logic of identity situates emotion in the body, abstract reasoning can only be realized by conceiving of desires, affectivity and embodiment as threats to universality and impartiality. And because these phenomena which need to be discarded are usually represented as 'feminine' characteristics, symbols and metaphors, sexual difference is in fact inscribed in that which passes for generality and impartiality.

The logic of identity is thus also linked to thinking in terms of binary oppositions. The essence of dualistic logic consists of constructing difference in terms of hierarchy. Under the influence of philosophers such as Plato and Descartes, Western culture has been permeated by thinking in terms of oppositions or mutually exclusive opposites. The most important of these are the oppositions between culture and nature, reason and emotion, spirit and body, rational and material, rational and emotional, fatherhood and motherhood, freedom and necessity, self and other, inner and outer, universality and particularity, public and private, Western and Eastern, civilization and primitiveness, and masculine and feminine, independence and dependence. What is important here is that these are not just individual distinctions, but that together they form a whole system of hierarchy, control and exclusion. They are discursive processes or, in other words, they are mechanisms of exclusion in which knowledge and power are interwoven. The first item in each pair, such as culture, rationality, freedom, universality, civilization and masculinity, derives its meaning from the fact that it is considered superior to its counterpart. The idea of superiority can only be maintained, however, by enforcing a strict demarcation between the opposites, and by continually labelling the 'inferior' item as 'Other' in contrast to the 'One', the dominant norm. The construction of categories of otherness accompanies a one-sided and unambiguous concept of the subject. True personhood is defined as the dominant norm and the 'other' can have no subjectivity of its own; this process is termed the 'objectifying of otherness'.

In order to understand the effect of binary oppositions in political culture, dualism can best be conceived as a series of thought figures which are embedded in cultural and political norms, and which explicitly and implicitly structure various kinds of representations and modes of thinking, acting and judging. These thought figures, in turn, are a part of academic philosophy, which, following Michel Foucault, I see as a discourse containing specific rules on how relevant knowledge can be acquired within a specific domain or discipline (Foucault 1988). A discourse always has both inclusionary and an exclusionary effects. Certain knowledge claims and methods of knowing are 'allowed to participate'; they have the status of accepted or acceptable knowledge. Others are excluded by being declared irrelevant or by being assigned a lesser status or degree of legitimacy. Arguments are more than merely ideas: they exert material power effects, which can vary from the ability to control resources to the manner in which people express their identity, present their bodies or realize cultural artefacts such as medical technology.

If we see universalism and dualism as interrelated discourses we can also see more clearly the role gender plays in universalist moral philosophy. Feminist philosophers have recently developed more sophisticated concepts and theories of gender than in the first phase of modern feminism, when gender was exclusively located at the level of psychology and subjective identity. They have indeed shown that gender is multi-layered in its power effects

(Harding 1986; Scott 1986). Gender works at the *symbolic level*, where images of femininity and masculinity attribute meaning to phenomena which at first sight seem to be separate from it; gender also works at the level of *individual and collective identity*, because the dualisms associated with it control the way in which men and women in our culture develop their self-image, manifest themselves and are judged. It also works on the level of *social structures* because access to (power) resources, social institutions and positions of power are marked by gender norms and gender symbols.

Let us look, for example, at the effects of norms and symbols in philosophical texts, in this case at the criteria by which universalism selects relevant knowledge and indicates privileged procedures of moral deliberations. The ideal moral agent who meets the demands of universalism places himself outside a concrete reality and decides, as an impartial observer, which claims legitimately satisfy the highest moral principles. Abstraction, distance and neutrality score highest on the list of characteristics which are deemed necessary for acceptable moral judgements in the universalist discourse. Embodiment, nature and emotions are represented as phenomena which need to be transcended and controlled in order to reach a 'true' judgement. The same philosophers who put forward this proposition also argued that these moral characteristics were reserved for men, since women were supposedly determined to a greater extent by their body and emotions, and therefore incapable of the transcendence necessary for being a moral subject.

A number of feminist philosophers have pointed out that the disembodied moral self corresponds to a male fiction of an individual who imagines himself free from particular relationships and living conditions as well as from his dependence on women and the existence of 'feminine' characteristics within himself.[15] This accounts for the sharp demarcations and separations which are so typical of dualism, and which, according to the Australian philosopher Val Plumwood, are maintained by discursive mechanisms such as hyperseparation, backgrounding, instrumentalizing, denial and stereotyping (Plumwood 1993: 41 ff.). Abstract universal reasoning can only be achieved by imposing a strict separation between body and mind, and passion and reason. The body and the emotions stand for that which diverts one from a distanced judgement. They continually threaten to draw the moral agent back into the sphere of particularist self-interest, which would stand in the way of a generalizable judgement. Embodiment and affectivity are thus better excluded from the domain of morality, because they are so easily associated with femininity. As long as a male-defined rationality is allotted the task of containing these 'different' characteristics, we will continue to be saddled with implicit or explicit cultural images of male superiority.

The public sphere of citizenship has a special role in this process, because it is supposed to enable the moral subject to transcend his private self. In the liberal tradition, politics means transcending the particular in order to recognize and guarantee a common will and a common good and interest. This makes it possible to imagine the 'sameness' of individuals. Abstract individualism is necessary in order to be able to postulate the existence of an identical subject, even when differences are quite clearly present. Moral deliberation consists then in the moral agent abstracting from differences, and standing as it were above them, thus placing himself in the position of a 'generalized other', characterized by a combination of observation, introspection and logical reasoning. The assumption accompanying this is that human subjects, in principle, have similar needs and moral perspectives. This means that a singular subject is representative of, and thus a standard for people in general; that is assuming that this subject keeps strictly to the requisite argumentational rules. This produces a monologic form of ethics, which, within critical social philosophy, is termed 'subject-centred' ethics.

This moral discourse has left its traces on the way in which women and their moral considerations are judged in various situations. Liberal conceptions of citizenship are constructed through a combination of excluding and 'homologizing' the feminine (Cavarero 1992). Women are either excluded, or admitted 'as men', or they are appointed to an inferior, special or subordinate position on account of their (capacity for) motherhood. Our culture is still permeated by a collective mistrust of women's moral capacities, so that they are confronted with false dilemmas and choices: it often seems as if women can only enter into the ranks of the moral community, the collection of people who are considered capable of true morality, if they are prepared to leave behind 'feminine' phenomena such as embodiment, affectivity and connection and consider themselves and their sex in general to be purely rational beings. A different route to moral acceptance is to fulfil the traditional image of womanhood in which women are attributed a specific morality of self-denial and dedication to others. If a woman fulfils the image of the self-sacrificing moral mother there will always be a pedestal waiting for her. Both solutions imply that women must sublimate their own interests and desires and subordinate themselves to something or someone else. Dualism thus harbours a split image of femininity in which desire and dedication, sexuality and motherhood are seen as contradictory and mutually threatening identities (Vegetti Finzi 1992; Hermsen 1993; Diprose 1994).

If sexual difference appears at all in universalist moral philosophy, it is located primarily with women and femininity. Apparently 'Woman' is the problem and has to be turned into an object of (moral) philosophy: she figures more often as deviance to the norm than as somebody with a moral subjectivity of her own. Thus, sexual difference appears as asymmetrical and almost irreversible. The fact that the prototypical moral subject is imagined as being generally representative for all human beings maintains both the mechanism by which women are marked as deviant from the norm and makes it almost impossible to talk about the male character of the 'general'. While women are continually seen and judged as representative of their sex, men are encouraged *not* to view themselves in terms of their sex, but to consider themselves as representative of humanity in general. This means that they lack the conceptual framework for thinking about the moral or political implications of their masculinity.

Viewed in this way, ethics in universalism is far from gender-neutral. It is a discipline which is loaded with gender symbolism.[16] Because gender dichotomies are inscribed in the descriptions and objectives of what are counted as 'good' forms of moral and political judgement, feminism cannot easily align itself with the universalist discourse and the associated moral epistemology. Making the primary aim of feminism women's participation in the dominant system of abstract rationality and equality-as-sameness is tantamount to incorporating women into a cultural and political sphere which is marked as masculine, and which achieves this by strictly separating the 'masculine' from the 'feminine' and marginalizing or inferiorizing the latter. Liberal feminists' standard answer to the exclusion of women from rational and moral capacities is that women are just as capable as men of abstract rationality. Relevant as this answer may be in confirming women's rational capacities, it also carries the risk of normative uniformity. If feminism limits itself to this answer, it can easily take on board other aspects of dualist thinking as well. The image of ethics as resting on the exclusion of everything which has to do with the particular or the embodied (the symbolically feminine) thus remains. And this in turn forms an obstacle to the development of an adequate normative feminist language for issues in the area of embodiment, sexuality, reproduction and care.

The feminist ethics of care and responsibility

If we follow the argument outlined above then the liberal ethics of 'equality-as-sameness' is hardly innocent with regard to the power effects of its norms; nor can it be united unproblematically with the aims of self-identification and self-determination for women (Van Heijst 1992; Werkman 1993). Instead, it is directed towards the levelling of subjects by bringing men and women together under a single heading of 'general human subject'. The urge to include women in a universal moral order also emerges in the debate about the ethics of care, especially in the negative reactions to the research carried out at the end of the 1970s, by the American psychologist Carol Gilligan, into the moral development of girls and women. In *In a Different Voice*, published in 1982, Gilligan claims that the standard picture of moral development and moral maturity, as described in the established developmental psychology of Piaget and Kohlberg, results from a male image of autonomy. Autonomy is seen as the defining characteristic of the 'detached' individual, who, cut off from connections and social contexts, practises moral deliberation and moral judgement. According to Gilligan, because Kohlberg interviewed only men and because he questioned them only about hypothetical moral dilemmas, his idea of general moral development and moral maturity actually masks a masculine ideal image of moral subjectivity. In addition, she also points out the similarities between this image and the normative views of justice and moral subjectivity, as these appear in the work of leading political philosophers such as John Rawls, the most important spokesman of the paradigm of distributive justice and rational choice.

On the basis of her interviews with women about their moral dilemmas Gilligan argued for the existence of a 'different moral voice'. While men tend to formulate moral problems as a conflict of abstract rights and rules, the women she interviewed almost always appeared to construe moral dilemmas first and foremost as conflicts of responsibilities in specific contexts. Moral dilemmas occurred for them in situations in which the norm of maintaining connections and caring for others conflicted with their own integrity. According to Gilligan, women reach the stage of moral maturity when they are able to transform this dilemma into an ethics of responsibility, where there is a balance between their own need for autonomy and caring about others. Thus, the ethics of care does not primarily concern collisions of rights, but is geared rather towards conflicts of responsibilities. This means that the ethics of care is a practice, a particular manner of perceiving and deliberating, rather than a matter of simply finding a series of rules or principles and applying them to clear-cut moral dilemmas.

In the years following the appearance of her work, Gilligan's ideas gave rise to fierce debate in more than one academic discipline: not only in developmental psychology and sociology, but also in moral philosophy, theology and legal studies. Criticism of her research methods was added to criticism of the way in which she linked sexual difference and morality, and the political conclusions to which this could lead. Because she distinguished two moral voices and linked these to sexual differences, she was accused of reinforcing women's traditional role.[17] I can agree with this criticism on a number of points. The way in which Gilligan presents two developmental psychological trajectories means that differences in moral orientations are perceived and interpreted in a dichotomous system. Her conclusions about a different type of moral maturity for women could have a normative effect, certainly when linked to common-sense notions of a 'feminine morality'. In these respects her claims should be treated with caution, and certainly so since subsequent empirical research has shown that styles of moral reasoning are not so neatly divided among men and women as Gilligan seems to suggest. There exist indeed considerable overlaps and similarities between the moral orientations of men and women.

However, at the same time it is important to realize that these adverse effects do not necessarily adhere to Gilligan's findings; they may have as much to do with the way her findings are interpreted and applied in the discourse of disciplines other than psychology. Moral philosophy and jurisprudence have discursive traditions, epistemologies and rules for deciding relevance which differ from those of developmental psychology. I cannot share the view that Gilligan's ethics of care necessarily encourages particularism or conservatism. What we are actually faced with is the traditional framework within which modern universalist ethics perceives and interprets sexual differences and assigns them a negative load. It seems more than likely that the sharpness of the criticism levelled at Gilligan was in part due to the fact that for many her message was far from welcome. Moreover, it could not be fitted into prevailing ideas about universalist ethics without referring to the doubtful place which this traditionally reserved for 'feminine' characteristics such as care and concern; in universalist ethics this is a moral attitude, which at best can be seen as socially functional or morally worthy, but which possesses no ethical relevance, because it cannot lead to generalizable judgements.[18]

In the reactions to Gilligan's work, norms inherent to the universalist discourse emerge in diverse ways. Thus, for example, it is argued that the sexual differences she finds are an expression of the subordination or powerlessness of women. These arguments call on the results of sociological research which indicate that oppressed groups tend to identify with the wishes and viewpoints of dominant groups and incorporate them into their self-image. This would not only occur in the case of white middle-class women (the group interviewed by Gilligan), but also with women *and* men from non-Western cultures. In short, the existence of concerns based on an ethics of care would not be related to sexual difference but to powerlessness. This criticism would be important, in my view, if it managed to open up a discussion about ethnocentric perspectives in the field of ethics. However, this is not generally the case in the argument outlined above, where the ethics of care is presented as a 'lesser morality' emerging from powerlessness and self-sacrifice. The idea that people should be free from determination by others is maintained as the standard norm for possession of a moral identity and for true moral agency. The Western male ideal of autonomy and non-connectedness influences the judging of 'others', who, by the same token, are imagined as backward and powerless. In this sense the argument confirms rather than undermines ethnocentrism in moral philosophy. Ethnocentrism can only be tackled by taking seriously the moral considerations of those who are represented as 'different' in Western thought and by exposing the mechanisms which continue to construe fixed categories of 'self' and 'other' (Flax 1993; Shrage 1994). This would also imply that moral considerations which people (male or female, black or white) derive from their connection to, involvement with and responsibility for others are no longer disqualified as different, lower or backward. Taken in this sense a feminist ethics of care can be seen as part of the current striving for the recognition of multiculturalism in politics and philosophy (Collins 1991; Tronto 1993).

A similar reaction to Gilligan's research is expressed by Kohlberg, who concludes that although Gilligan may indeed have found convincing evidence for the existence of sex-differences in moral reasoning, the ethics of care which she discovered can only apply in the private sphere, the domain of emotional bonds and relationships. In the public sphere a more detached and impersonal ethics would be necessary. According to this view, the fact that women pay more attention to care and responsibility has to do with the fact that their activities still take place more in the private sphere than men's. If women were emancipated, they would automatically be capable of the higher phases of morality. Here again we see that a morality expressed by women is explained by means of concepts associated with power relations and women's 'backwardness'. 'Masculine' morality remains the norm and is linked moreover to a dichotomy between private and public, which has all kinds of implicit and explicit gender connotations. The political theorist Joan Tronto has suggested that this argument demonstrates an attempt towards the 'containment' of care, whereby barriers are erected between the different spheres in which an ethics of care and responsibility could be relevant (Tronto 1993). Thus, once again women's concerns in relation to care are marginalized. In addition, the public sphere is viewed as a domain in which only moral considerations of rights and justice should apply, and in which, in our moral deliberations, we should abstract from who we are or want to be, and from the way in which interpersonal relations actually proceed.

The dismissive reactions to Gilligan's publications show that her research raises more than simply the question of whether empirically demonstrable sex-differences in moral reasoning exist. The question of why we search for sex-differences and, above all, how we interpret and value them cuts through this, and determines, to a large extent, the tone of the criticism and the normative intentions surrounding discussions about care. As long as sex-differences are ordered in a binary system and the phenomena associated with them are placed in a hierarchy in which 'masculine' values and characteristics are judged as more important, more high-minded, and more progressive, it is an uninviting and certainly complex task to bring 'feminine' characteristics to the fore. This might also be the reason why the question of the relationship between the ethics of care and the ethics of justice and their compatibility continues to attract so much interest. The issue, in fact, fits into a long historical tradition of discursive contests about sexual difference, the question of whether men and women actually differ from each other and how femininity is related to masculinity. The different answers to this question are clearly recognizable in the rhetorical strategies which are adopted in order to determine the relationship of the two moral orientations to each other.

Linking these two areas of ethics to different social spheres (Held 1987b) thus provides little satisfaction as a solution; as little as the idea that both forms of ethics, although perhaps different, are certainly equal and therefore complementary (Brabeck 1993). Rhetorical strategies which argue for a reversal in the binary hierarchy by positing 'women's' morality as superior (Noddings 1984) offer no more of a solution to the problem, even if only because they maintain an outmoded sexual division. Also, the attempts which have been made to fit certain elements of the ethics of care into other ethical systems, for example into the normative system of distributive justice (Okin 1989), into a (modified) universalist discourse (Benhabib 1987, 1992), into one or other version of the ethics of rights (O'Neill 1989; Nagl-Docekal 1992; Shrage 1994), into an ethics of charity (Den Hartogh 1995) or into a utilitarian injunction to optimally promote general utility and welfare (Dupuis 1995) can be seen as an unsatisfactory answer to the challenges posed by the feminist ethics of care to contemporary moral philosophy. These attempts at integration, whether pursued with positive or a negative intention, function in a certain sense as a safety-valve, which serves to defuse the radical implications of the ethics of care. None of them consider the possibility that the ethics of care cannot be reduced to the categories of liberal universalist ethics, but may instead best be considered as a moral perspective in its own right with a number of basic assumptions which are at odds with universalist ethics.

In order to make these radical implications visible it is necessary first of all to break with binary systems of perception, interpretation and appraisal of moral judgement, and with the norm of abstract rationality that goes with them. It then appears that the ideas about morality developed by Gilligan and other feminist authors can also be used to provide a critical perspective and an alternative for dominant discourses about ethics and morality. Some authors have even attached to this the claim of a paradigm change.[19] The feminist ethics of care embodies its own particular vision of moral subjectivity and the central issues and aims of moral deliberation. This means that it also has a specific view on the issue of where moral deliberation takes place and what is morally relevant knowledge. Moreover, the moral situation takes on a different form than in the liberal ethics of rights. The ethics of care has its own moral vocabulary, which is able to incorporate certain elements of liberal ethics, but which at heart has a different moral epistemology. This is why one cannot be derived from the other. I will go on to demonstrate a number of ways in which the feminist ethics of care can make an innovative contribution to the current practice of ethics. In doing this I will place the feminist ethics of care, as argued in the introductory chapter, within the framework of a postmodern moral and political philosophy, and link it to psychodynamic notions of moral subjectivity which are expressed within this framework (Flax 1993). I have chosen this point of departure because the conceptual framework of moral subjectivity – the issue of what it means to be a morally thinking and acting person – is the quintessential issue in moral theorizing: other issues in the debate about morality are connected with it.

New directions

Moral subjectivity

In the concepts of moral subjectivity in ethical approaches, images of human nature are expressed. These images contain answers to the question of what it means to be a moral subject and the necessary conditions for this. These claims are often presented as empirical observations, but it is more useful to interpret them as normative images that indicate the direction moral deliberation should take. In this sense every form of ethics also contains a meta-ethics, or a system of presuppositions (whether or not these are made explicit) about how moral judgement can best be orchestrated. In universalist ethics the ideal moral agent is represented as a detached subject. In Kantian ethics the moral subject is separate from and stands above empirical reality. In this way he can determine what constitute universal moral obligations. According to Kant's categorical imperative – 'I ought never to act except in such a way that I can also will that my maxim become a universal law' – a moral subject should be oriented towards duties which are recognizable and acceptable to everybody. The moral subject can only be held responsible for autonomous choices, whereby freedom is understood to mean being free of dependence and bodily and historical contingencies, as well as the ability to formulate an autonomous will (Mendus 1987; Hermsen 1993; Schott 1994). The moral subject is a detached and separate individual, whose central question is how best he can satisfy universal moral obligations. Obligations and rights are thus two sides of the same moral coin: satisfying one's moral obligations makes one eligible to be the bearer of rights. Rights, in turn, are seen as the cement of the social order, as the most important way in which people can engage in orderly social relations. Kant links this, following many other philosophers, with the idea of society as a contract, a series of legally determined agreements on the central aspects of human society. Being a moral person is thus, almost by definition, linked to the ability and the authority to exercise rights and fulfil obligations. Moral dilemmas take the form of conflicts between rights claims and are thus predominantly expressed in that register.

The feminist ethics of care opposes this with a radically different image of human nature and thus a different view of the objectives of moral deliberation; this view has more in common with social constructivism and some strands of communitarianism. In contrast to an atomistic view of human nature, the ethics of care posits the image of a 'relational self', a moral agent who is embedded in concrete relationships with other people and who acquires an individual moral identity through interactive patterns of behaviour, perceptions and interpretations (Addelson 1991). This means that the definition of identity and selfhood has shifted. Individuals are no longer seen as atomistic units with a pre-determined identity, who meet each other in the public sphere to create social ties. Identity, and with it the ability to engage in moral activity, is formed in specific cultural and historical situations, and thus it coincides with subjectivity, the ability to judge and to act. The self is not conceived as an entity, but as the 'protagonist in a biography' which can contain all kinds of ambiguities and unexpected turns. This implies a radical break with the idea of the pre-social self in liberal ethics. The feminist ethics of care has more to gain from the idea of a processual self, a self which is continually in the process of being formed; moral identity is continually being developed and revised through this process. The construing of moral identities is thus, in this sense, inherently a social practice, something which we do and make within human relations and within specific social and political contexts, and the narrative conventions reflected in these. In this sense, the relation between gender and morality is relevant, because both the attributing, as well as the experiencing and disputing, of sexual identities takes place in social practices; gender cannot thus be simply erased from these. Or, as Elizabeth Frazer and Nicola Lacey have argued, in a world in which gender is an important category of social differentiation, gender itself will always generate powerful discourses, so that it is an important dimension of all social practices in which subjects participate (Frazer and Lacey 1993: 201).

Moral issues and the objectives of moral philosophy

The fact that the feminist ethics of care starts out from a different view of moral subjectivity changes the objectives and central issues of moral philosophy. From the perspective of universal justice, the aim of ethics is for autonomous individuals to establish rules and principles. On the basis of these it would be possible to establish universal justice if laws and authority were legitimate and if people *therefore* had a duty to obey or, alternatively, if the situation justified it, to rebel. Duty and obedience are thus the principle moral categories. The crucial moral question is, then, 'what do I owe to others, in a general sense?' The feminist ethics of care replaces this with a different question, or rather, with several different questions. If the dualistic logic is followed, the alternative question would become, 'what do I owe my proximate others?' (those who deserve my care through the special relationship I have with them). This is an issue which, according to a number of authors, should indeed be central in the ethics of care. However, this question suffers from all the disadvantages of dualistic thinking, such as the separation of self and other, distance and closeness, familiarity and strangeness, public and private. A more adequate alternative is to replace questions surrounding duty with situated questions concerning responsibility, such as, 'how can I best express my caring responsibility?' (Tronto 1993); 'when is it justified for me to be held responsible?' or 'how can I best deal with vulnerability, suffering and dependency?' (Baier 1989, 1991; Manschot 1994; Verkerk 1994). And, if I pose these questions here in the first person form, I by no means wish to suggest that a feminist ethics of care is individualistic or private. Questions about dependency and responsibility occur in collective situations as well. A fixed boundary between public and private cannot be drawn; it is precisely the task of politics to concern itself with the question of where boundaries should be drawn between personal and collective responsibilities in relation to all kinds of different issues.

Moral dilemmas thus have a different location in the feminist ethics of care than in the liberal ethics of rights. They are no longer primarily conflicts between the legal claims of discrete, coherent persons; instead, the starting-point for moral deliberation lies in the experiencing of moral dilemmas in individual and collective contexts. Moral deliberation is not concerned primarily with solving or eradicating moral dilemmas, but with making them productive, by looking, for example, at an issue from different perspectives and taking conflicting moral reactions and moral idioms as sources of morally relevant knowledge (Billig, Condor and Edwards 1988; Code 1988a, 1988b; Shrage 1994; Davis 1995; Gremmen 1995). Because the starting-point is no longer a conflict between the rights of autonomously defined individuals, moral deliberation also includes the process by which claims are constructed. Moral dilemmas and moral deliberation also have to do with the question of how clashes between individual claims and responsibility for others can be solved or made 'liveable with'; they also have to do with the issue of how suffering and harm can be reduced or made tolerable. The question of when a translation of claims into rights is morally justified, and when rights can be enforced, then becomes an ethical issue in itself. Feminist political philosophers have already elaborated this approach in relation to various concrete questions, for example, in cases concerning parental authority, abortion, reproductive technology or pornography.[20]

Because the feminist ethics of care with its relational image of human nature rejects a radical separation between self and other, or subject and object, and replaces this with an interactive image of moral subjectivity, care and responsibility apply not only to 'others' but also to moral subjects themselves. In the ideal of the atomistic individual, the moral subject is primarily expected to pursue autonomy and independence. In this way vulnerability and dependency easily become separated from the ideal self and localized in, or projected onto others: weak or 'needy' people. A feminist ethics of care, through its image of human nature, is also better able to situate vulnerability, ambiguity and dependency within the moral subject. A care ethicist cannot think about these issues separately from the network of relations surrounding the moral subject, whether concrete interactions are concerned or the psychological images and fantasies (the internalized Other) within which people experience their subjectivity. The stable, complete and unlimited self of universal ethics makes place for a multiple and ambiguous moral self, who is aware of his or her own limitations, dependencies, vulnerability and finiteness, and who is prepared to accept responsibility for these things (Van

Heijst 1992; Flax 1993). Altruism and egoism are no longer situated in different registers of moral behaviour and moral reasoning, but are related to each other. They appear as a continually occurring moral dilemma, or alternate with each other as relevant moral considerations.

The relation between (the ethics of) care and self-sacrifice

From this perspective, equating the ethics of care with self-sacrifice, as is often done, is a rather simplistic notion. Of course too great a degree of dedication to others or a 'good cause' can lead to the risk of people losing themselves or the feeling that they can be 'a self'. The moral devotion to self-sacrifice, historically seen, has also frequently been associated with symbols of femininity or with conceptions of a typically feminine character structure. Care is all too often defined as servitude, so that it has become associated with subordination. However, the opposite can also be true. An excessive drawing of boundaries between the self and other can lead to a barricaded self, to psychological isolation or an inability to trust or confide in others. This psychological condition finds its moral–philosophical counterpart in the ideal of the isolated self, the moral subject who can reach moral judgements entirely on his own. When these psychological and philosophical views reinforce each other, this can lead to various forms of moral laziness, to the inability to understand the individuality of the other, and thus to an incapacity to deal with human plurality and difference. Those who equate the ethics of care with self-sacrifice often tacitly accept the view that ethics is chiefly to do with duty, and that 'giving' would only be justifiable if it were balanced by an equal degree of 'receiving'. The solution for servitude is then sought in the introduction of a morality based on equal exchange. If this is associated with the idea that caring is by definition a dutiful event (whether arising from an external or inner compulsion), then the ethics of care can indeed seem to be a heavy weight to bear, and it becomes difficult to imagine that people can derive a meaningful moral identity from disinterested giving or that caring can be a source of self-realization and a satisfying and pleasurable activity.

The equation of the ethics of care with self-sacrifice may also have to do with the opposition between dependency and autonomy with which the modern practice of ethics and Western moral culture are permeated. If the definition of personhood is exclusively marked by the ideal image of autonomy and independence, it is difficult to imagine that 'giving' can form part of a person's feeling of identity or moral ideals, or that 'giving' without getting anything in return is worth pursuing on moral grounds or, indeed, is justifiable under any circumstances. Women who make this their aim are quickly labelled as self-sacrificing or even masochistic (for example Withuis 1995: 14 ff.). If, as Ine Gremmen has argued, self-sufficiency, youthfulness and autonomy are more highly valued in a society, care easily comes to be seen as a 'necessary evil' and the ethics of care can only with great difficulty be perceived as a 'real' form of ethics. This appears, for example, in the social under-valuation of the ethical considerations of nurses and home-helps (Gremmen 1995: 232–233).

However, when the ethics of care is released from its ties with the ethics of rights and duties and is more appropriately expressed in the vocabulary of responsibility, then care is no longer by definition a burden; in addition a more open form of moral deliberation becomes possible, involving such questions as whether and how we can/want to give shape to responsibilities and how we can deal constructively with dependency and trust.[21] This does not exclude reasoning in terms of rights and duties, it simply means adopting a different point of departure. In this respect the ethics of care displays similarities with an Aristotelian virtue-ethics, particularly in relation to the moral virtue of friendship. The ability to form disinterested friendships with others is considered by Aristotle to be a virtue which not only benefits character and personality, but which also forms part of good community life: it has benefits for the judging which takes place in this context as well as the associated pursuit of political justice (Komter 1995; Tronto 1995b). In Aristotelian virtue-ethics the pursuit of human well-being and the pursuit of justice do not take place in different 'moral registers'; each is an extension of the other.

The importance of narrativity and context

The ideal moral agent of universalist ethics abstracts from specific circumstances in order to achieve responsible moral judgement. In contrast to this, the moral agent in the ethics of care stands with both feet in the real world. While the universalist ethicist will see this as a threat to his independence and impartiality, or as an obstacle to creating order in his moral imaginary, the care ethicist sees this precisely as a crucial condition for being able to judge well. In fact, moral issues surrounding care and responsibility rest on the assumption that it is possible to assess what is needed in order to enhance the quality of life in specific circumstances. The ethics of care demands reflection on the best course of action in specific circumstances and the best way to express and interpret moral problems. Situatedness in concrete social practices is not seen as a threat to independent judgement. On the contrary it is assumed that this is exactly what will raise the quality of judgment (Wallace 1993; Tronto 1995b). An abstract norm of impartiality can create an inability to understand moral situations and can lead to what Joan Tronto has termed 'privileged irresponsibility', the inability to see what people need to maintain life and the quality of life (Tronto 1993).

This can be made clear by comparing the ways in which needs are discussed in both the moral orientations under consideration here. Universalist ethics assumes an ambivalent attitude to needs. Because needs are easily associated with inclinations, emotions, preferences or desires (phenomena which need to be transcended to reach a 'good' ethics), they are distorted in the vocabulary of universalist ethics. If they figure in the practice of ethics at all, it is mostly in the form of discourses about 'general human needs'. In this way needs are separated from specific subjects.[22] The feminist ethics of care, on the other hand, argues for a narrative approach to moral subjectivity. A narrative approach refuses to separate needs from the people who are their subjects and takes as its starting-point the idea that people themselves (can) have knowledge about their own subjectivity; in principle they are competent to express who they are and what they need. It takes seriously people's stories about what they need to live well. In the ethics of care the crucial moral situations are those in which needs are interpreted. Nancy Fraser has made an important contribution to these issues through her development of the idea of a 'politics of needs-interpretation' (Fraser 1989).

Because a feminist ethics of care attaches value to understanding the needs and values of specific others (whether they are proximate or distant), it undermines the idea of an unambiguous homogeneous moral subject. The central values of the ethics of care, responsibility and communication lead to a commitment to deal with differences, not only between individuals and social groups, but also within the self (Tronto 1993). This is made possible because a definition of the self as multiple and unstable is no longer seen as a threat, but rather as a part of life, which can be made productive in order to improve the quality of moral interactions. While, in the unambiguous subject ideal of universalist ethics, the 'other' is separated from the self and projected onto 'Woman' or 'Foreign Cultures', the fragmented and multiple subject has more possibility of experiencing the other within the self, instead of conceiving of the 'other' as foreign to the 'self' (Young 1990a; Kristeva 1991; Graybeal 1993; McAfee 1993; Mullin 1995). This makes it possible, and in fact normal, not to assume that one's own values and world view are self-evident and to continually question the ability of one's moral framework to enhance the quality of life. A feminist ethics of care grafted on to postmodernism thus has the capacity to deal with diversity and alterity, with the fact that subjects are different and in this sense both 'strange' and 'knowable' to each other. Precisely because 'strangeness' and 'knowability' are related to each other, neither of them appears as an absolute, but rather as an attempt to span the oppositions between self and other.

Lines between feeling and thinking

Ethicists from the rationalist tradition are inclined to depict emotions as distractions from clear, calm and rational judgements. Emotions divert the attention of the moral actor, make him blind; they are either absolute or co-incidental, and *therefore* without moral content or moral relevance (Bordo 1986; Jaggar 1989; Pott 1992; Wallace 1993). They lead him to give priority to his self-interest instead of the 'general interest'. Overcoming and defeating the emotions would thus be a necessary condition for reaching an understand-

ing of the correct modes of behaviour. In the rationalist view, care is associated with emotionality and femininity, which are combined in the image of
'Romantic Love' and the 'Good Mother' (see, for example, Dupuis 1995). In
this way care, in fact, is romanticized and domesticated (Tronto 1993). This
provides plenty of pitfalls and traps for a feminist ethics which aims to make
traditional femininity the subject of critical discussion, as the association
between femininity, caring and emotionality is still powerful in our moral
culture. As I argued in the introductory chapter, a postmodern feminist
ethics of care can change this state of affairs, at least if it can succeed in exposing the effect of binary oppositions and if care is viewed as a social practice.
A key to this lies in the central values of the ethics of care: attentiveness and
responsibility. These can, after all, be seen as epistemological values, or
values concerned with the question of how we can know caring practices in
the best possible manner (Code 1987, 1991; Krol 1992). The question, 'how
can I best realize my responsibilities in this situation?', then implies the question, 'how can I best know this situation?'

Developments in women's studies have led to exploration of the concepts of
'the rationality of caring' and a 'sentient actor', and the question of how practical knowledge can contribute to the quality of human society (Waerness
1987; Code 1991; Rose 1994). The ethics of care implies being open to the
'other'; it thus attributes an important place to communication, interpretation and dialogue. In contrast to the tradition of abstract and instrumental
reasoning, a type of rationality in which the pursuit of knowledge goes hand
in hand with a pursuit of control, it appeals for the restitution of sensory
knowledge, symbolized by the unity of hand, head and heart. From this perspective knowing is a social and dialogic process. There is not just one way to
know a social situation; on the contrary, it is important to become acquainted
with the many ways in which different social agents interpret a situation and
act in it. Here, too, transcending the subject–object distinction has radical
implications. The care ethicist does not place herself outside and above the
practice of care and human interaction in order to observe and analyse, she
sees herself preferably as a participant within caring practices. The recipient
of care is, for her, not an 'object to be known', but someone to whom she
listens, whom she tries to understand, and with whom she communicates.[23]
Neither does she deny herself as a care-receiver; rather she reflects on the
dynamics of care-giving and care-receiving in several social practices.

This is also the reason why empathy, intuition, compassion, love, relation-
ality and commitment (the willingness to make connections) are important
epistemological values or 'epistemological virtues' in the feminist ethics of
care.[24] Subjects come to understand themselves to an important degree
through their relationships with others. Human subjects do not arrive in the
world as beings with a fully developed rational ability; they develop their
moral and rational capacities in connection and interaction with others,
in the first instance with those who care for them and on whom they are

dependent. Gender is an important factor here in various ways. Through the experience of receiving or providing care everyone has developed ways of dealing with care and dependency, of making it an element of their self-image, their emotional make-up and their manner of thinking about social reality; this is related to images of motherhood and fatherhood, 'daughter-hood' and 'sonhood'. These concepts are anchored in the way in which human subjects acquire knowledge and in the dynamics of autonomy and dependency expressed therein (Van Mens-Verhulst, Schreurs and Woertman 1993). The moral subjects in the ethics of care have not separated their experi-ence of these things from the way in which they wish to understand social reality; rather they use it as a source of morally relevant knowledge.

This holds not only for the emotions which are considered to be virtues, such as attentiveness and commitment to others, but also for the more com-plex emotions such as fear and aggression, shame, revulsion, suspicion and resentment, which are also encountered in the practice of human experience and moral reflection. Someone who cares for the self and for others cannot escape these emotions, because they present themselves in the daily inter-actions of care, whether one wants to acknowledge them or not. They often form the reverse side of moral virtuousness. This indicates once again the ambiguity and complexity of moral experience; considering the question of 'how to act well' means being prepared to examine the awkward aspects and ambivalences of human existence. An open moral attitude implies not assum-ing that one knows in advance what is right or wrong, or where the boundary between virtue and vice should be drawn. It may, for instance, sometimes be better to do the 'bad' thing in order to achieve the 'good'. And, whatever the rationalists among us may think, emotions do not allow themselves to be 'shut off' by reason. They will always be present in the way in which we inter-pret and value our moral experiences. If the practice of ethics does not make 'reasonable room' for this, then it will be saddled with repressed emotions, which can equally well assert absolute claims on moral interactions and moral judgements. This is also why the 'attentive reasoning' of the ethics of care offers a better starting-point for moral reflection than the universal reasoning of liberal ethics or the associated instrumental reasoning of many modern scientific practices.

Placing equality and autonomy in renewed conceptions of care, justice and politics

If we follow the basic premises of the feminist ethics of care and its assump-tions about moral epistemology and moral subjectivity, then a whole series of liberal moral concepts are in need of revision. It is certainly not my argu-ment that we should eliminate these concepts from our moral and political vocabulary; on the contrary, the ethics of care can provide the inspiration for giving them new meanings and applications. This project has been approached from different angles during recent years in feminist moral and political philosophy. I will go on to discuss a number of examples of this, and again I will stress the need to situate the discussion of the meaning of these concepts in a renewed vision of democratic citizenship.

Within the feminist ethics of care the concepts of moral equality and moral autonomy have undergone a change in meaning. They no longer refer primarily to a *sameness* in relation to an abstract rationality, but to an *equality* in the ability to display moral characteristics. Various feminist authors, inspired by the ethics of care, have linked this to an appeal for concepts such as moral respect and moral trust (Meyers 1987, 1989; Grimshaw 1988; Baier 1989, 1991; Jackson 1989).[25] The ability to be a moral agent implies the demand to be treated as morally responsible and reliable. This implies starting from the assumption that each person's aims and conceptions of what is good initially deserve respect, because they are important for determining a sense of self. The capacity for self-respect is a value which can be both nurtured and damaged in people's mutual relationships (Govier 1992, 1993). The ability and the space to form good intimate relationships can be seen as a crucial human value in this respect because it enables a fundamental recognition of the value of 'selfhood'.

This has implications for the way in which we think about autonomy and dependency. In the liberal framework, autonomy and independency tend to be conflated, and autonomy, in the sense of autonomous judgement, is linked to an ideal of independence as self-sufficiency and to marginalization or even repression of the dependent dimensions of the self. This leads to a philosophical denial of dependency and interdependence as aspects of the 'human condition', as I argue in this book, and to a conception of care in which care is easily denigrated or pictured as 'debilitating' because it would restrain both dependent people and those who care for and about them from true moral judgment (see also Kittay 1995, Young 1995). The feminist ethics of care exposes this version of the requirements for autonomous judgement and argues instead for a recognition of connection and dependence as part of human life and moral subjectivity without, on the other hand, reifying them as 'natural', or glorifying them as sources of moral goodness. In the ethics of care the quality of autonomous judgement can be regarded as enhanced, not only because the moral actors are better attuned to a diversity of moral considerations, but also because the illusion of a solipsistic subject is replaced by an idea of 'being in the world with each other', as described in Chapter 1 of this book. In such a vision, possessing an autonomous moral self does not rest on disputable assumptions about a uniform rationality, but rather on the norm of not approaching others in an objectifying or stereotyping manner (Code 1987, 1988a; Morgan 1988; Jackson 1989; McAfee 1993). This implies that women should be accepted as morally competent actors and as moral subjects, on their own terms, unaccompanied by the customary doubts as

63

to their moral reliability or dubious labels referring to 'fixed' female characteristics. And I want to underline that this remark refers to women in the plural, not to 'Women' as a unified category, but rather to many different women, with their diversity of experience, background and moral viewpoint. Although at several points in this book I use the metaphor of the 'voice of care', in fact we can only make sense of Gilligan's 'different voice' when we allow ourselves to hear this voice in the plural.

Reflections on justice can also receive new impulses from this source. The ethics of care's criticism of justice arguments is mostly directed towards a specific variety of it: the moral epistemology and the argumentational rules of the paradigm of distributive justice as expressed by John Rawls and other thinkers in the tradition of liberal individualism and rational choice.[26] A number of its objections, however, also apply to the theory of communicative discourse ethics of Jürgen Habermas (Fraser 1989; Young 1990a; Benhabib 1992; Meehan 1995). In my view the discussion about the compatibility of care and justice can be useful only if thinking about justice is freed from the parameters of the radical–liberal version of the distributive paradigm and the notions of universalism and impartiality contained within it; and if we aim towards achieving judgements in a situated way, proceeding from an interpretative, dialogic and communicative moral epistemology. But while a number of feminist discourse ethicists still prefer to conceive of this in the terminology of moral and political consensus and universal values based on this (Benhabib 1992), I prefer to assume that reaching consensus should not be the primary aim of political deliberation (Fraser 1989; Frazer and Lacey 1993). We have more to gain from conceptions of social justice and deliberation in the public sphere, in terms of heterogeneity and plurality (Young 1990a), and from the idea that politics is better served by compromise than by striving after consensus.

This point of view does not imply that we should abandon thinking in terms of universal values. On the contrary, it may assist us to tackle in a more solid way some of the thorny questions that have recurred in recent discussions about justice, and universal values and norms. This can become clear when we consider the problems that inhere in claims of epistemic universalism (Shrage 1994: 162 ff.). Epistemic universalism, in its strongest form, assumes that we can find and know rational and objective standards which will enable us to make decisions in situations of disagreement. As I argue here, this is an impossible and counterproductive exercise. The task of positing a 'sameness' of people in order to be able to decide on universal values quickly leads to abstract speculations which will always remain controversial, and which, at worst, can lead to what Iris Young has termed cultural imperialism (Young 1990a). Questions can also be raised, however, in relation to the weaker forms of epistemic universalism, for example the idea that an 'empathic dialogue' can lead to the establishing of general values. Laurie Shrage (1994), following Charles Taylor, has argued that a better starting-point is the idea that moral standards are always culturally and historically formed and that we should be restrained in our use of general standards. Moral identities and values are diverse, culturally formed and relevant to moral deliberation. They express what people care about, and what they find important and worthwhile for their individual and collective existence. According to Shrage, an interpretative ethics is pluralistic and does not let itself be swayed by fears of cultural relativism. It works on the basis of dialogue, ethnographic knowledge and the creation of discursive space for differing perspectives and forms of moral expression. This enables individuals not only to 'know about the other', but also to take distance from their own cultural values, and thus to 'other the self'. It leads people to recognize their own cultural assumptions and their own situatedness through exchange and dialogue, without having the obligation imposed on them to derive – in the end – something which is 'universally applicable'. As Shrage argues, no single moral critic can always consider all possibilities, so moral knowledge is always limited and tentative.

However, even this proposal supposes an (implicit) attitude of moral universalism which should be accounted for, not because it is a 'residue' of an objectionable moral universalism but rather because it refers to values that are crucial to our ability to engage in truly open forms of moral and political dialogue. Shrage's radical pluralism assumes that everyone has the opportunity to develop their moral capacities, that all moral perspectives in principle deserve attention and that, on the basis of moral pluralism, we can enter into a discussion of which moral values are worthwhile. They assume what Iris Young has called 'equality in access and voice', and what liberals would call democratic freedom rights: the freedom of opinion and freedom of association. I would argue more strongly than Shrage that moral pluralism is not opposed to the accepting and establishing of universal values – values which we make it our collective responsibility to accept as generally applicable and on the basis of which we can establish authoritative rules which can direct or correct individual and collective action. Shrage's view assumes, in fact, a constitutional democracy and a democratic citizenship, in which people have the freedom and the opportunity to express themselves in public. Unless we adhere to a minimal degree of normative reasoning and well-considered political choice for such a system we quickly reach the limits of radical pluralism. Radical pluralism is only possible if there is a political recognition of basic humanistic values and human rights and a legal order which guarantees these. In this respect democracy is a normative choice: democracy cannot be taken for granted but has to be defended in word and deed. Liberal values such as equality and freedom are crucial in this respect; a pluralist approach forces us, however – and rightly so – to see them as contingent values. They are values, the meaning and effect and validity of which we must continue to specify and argue for, knowing that we will never be able to realize them fully and knowing that there are situations in which we will wish to impose limits on them or in which we will have to conclude that they are not appropriate values for judging this particular issue or situation.[27] In this way, they provide an important 'intellectual horizon' to our normative deliberations (Mouffe 1992).

This implies a conceptualization of both morality and politics in which we can reflect in a situated manner on the value of the virtues of caring. As Lorraine Code has argued, traditionally 'female' values, such as trust, kindness, responsiveness and responsibility, honesty and care can be well fitted into an Aristotelian conception of 'phronesis', or practical wisdom (Code 1991: 108). But, as she says, in some circumstances it would be more appropriate to act 'in accord with efficiency-maximizing and autonomy-promoting values' (ibid.). This depends upon the abilities of moral actors to make an appropriate diagnosis of what is best in specific contexts. According to Code, the Aristotelian orientation of this approach prevents its deterioration into an opportunistic situationism. She concludes that

> modes of deliberation vary qualitatively, according to the character and cognitive capacities of the deliberation. Hence a deliberative morality is at once open-textured, dialogic, and open to criticism, self-criticism and debate. It leaves open scope for trial and error, for showing that some practices are not conducive to the production of social institutions and socio-political environments where people can live well. It requires a finely tuned moral–political awareness to avoid, at once, extreme relativism, conservatism and mere tolerance.
>
> (ibid.: 109)

Such an Aristotelian approach underlines the need to embed the feminist ethics of care in a vision of what good forms of political deliberation and political judgement entail. A politically formulated ethics of care should not make its objective the elimination of power. Rather, it should work with a multi-faceted understanding of power, which can capture both its restraining and enabling, creative and generative dimensions, and which can also differentiate between power and domination. Such an understanding should make one of its goals ensuring that power is recognizable and manageable, and that unfair differences in treatment or arbitrariness cannot take hold of public decision-making. It can also contribute to exposing oppression, repression and systematic forms of dominance and assist in ways of reversing these. It is my contention that we can develop such a vision only by situating the ethics of care in ideas and practices of democratic citizenship. Its ideas about attentiveness, responsiveness and responsibility can have a transformative effect on how we proceed in processes of political judgement and give us a better understanding of the way in which human needs and well-being are treated in politics.

This approach does not, by definition, imply a broad participatory model of politics, in which everybody is always involved in the governance of society, which is what some observers, eager to deconstruct the boundaries between the personal and the political, think that a feminist ethics of care would lead to. The ethics of care fits better into an Aristotelian model of democratic government, where democracy consists of the 'alternation between governing and being governed' (Tronto 1995b). The inclusion of care and an optimal equality in care-giving and care-receiving would indeed enhance the quality of such a model while also enabling individuals to appreciate the different positions which can be adopted in social systems of needs-interpretation and the provision of needs. Because the ethics of care renews our possibilities for responsibility and accountability, it also has the potential to prevent systematic forms of 'privileged irresponsibility', which emerge when there is too little circulation among those who occupy decision-making positions.

This can lead to a political ethics in which, as Joan Tronto has argued, care figures as a political virtue that provides a mean between democracy and justice. Care as a democratic virtue is then a mean between a model of democracy that thinks too much in terms of power and a model of justice that thinks too much in terms of morality. Care is also 'the mean between excessive reliance upon others for our maintenance, and excessive self-reliance. Care stands as a mean, then between excessive dependency and excessive autonomy' (Tronto 1995b: 14). Care demands that we 'constantly assess the position we occupy as we begin to make judgements. We must constantly evaluate whether we are being overly overprotective, too unresponsive, too reliant on our assumed "expertise" and so on' (ibid.). Tronto concludes:

> In a democratic society in which all people are responsible for seeing that the care of all is the premise of justice, we would expect that collective power will be used not to exclude or degrade any groups. Although in democratic societies people will always disagree about the requirements of care and justice, the practice of caring will provide everyone with the concrete basis for making judgments. It is possible, then, to develop our capacity to care beyond the sphere where we give care on a daily basis. Under these conditions, our democratic powers can be directed to serve justice. This vision, then, constitutes the hope of feminist inclusion.
>
> (Tronto 1995b: 18)

Such a vision of politics and democratic citizenship is indeed crucial if we want to find creative modes of combining care and justice in our normative reasoning. The main risk of an overhasty marriage between 'care and justice unmodified' is that it may lead to the construction of an ethical system that excludes politics, or to what Bonnie Honig calls a 'displacement of politics' (Honig 1993).[28] If care and justice are too easily integrated, this can lead to a denial of what politics is all about: strategic action within the context of power relations and the 'art of government', with all its vicissitudes and unpredictabilities. To state this in symbolic terms: if a 'female' symbol of empathy and harmonious care is wedded to a 'male' unity of justice, political action, as unavoidable strategic power-directed action, tends to disappear. This is also the danger of building politics too exclusively on identity while overlooking the crucial importance of (exchange of) opinion. Such a view would lead to a denial of the public sphere as the location where opinions are formulated and reformulated and to a 'reconciliation instead of politicization'. Care would then – paradoxically – be grafted onto an administrative rationality that tends to eradicate the ambivalences and uncertainties that we meet on a daily basis when acting and judging politically. Both the activity of caring and the daily business of politics presume, however, that we face both conflict and complex configurations of power, and the moral and political dilemmas that confront us when developing opinion and judgement. They both imply that we do not avoid 'dirtying our hands' (Tronto 1996). The promise of combining a political ethics of care with renewed conceptions of social justice and citizenship is that it makes us realize, not only that power and conflict as well as ambiguity, contingency and unpredictability are here to stay, but also that we can act 'as well as possible' in order to do what needs to be done.

3

PARADOXES OF GENDER

Ethical and epistemological perspectives
on care in feminist political theory[1]

The problem of the separation of care and politics

For more than fifteen years now, care has been the object of theorizing and research in feminist sociology and political science. Looking back, what strikes me is that the production of knowledge about care and gender has proceeded along different disciplinary tracks. In this chapter I will distinguish two of these 'tracks', each with its own particular structure and goals and its own characteristic discussions.

First, there has been extensive work on caring as an activity, or 'labour of love' (Graham 1983). Sociologists have studied women carers, looking, for example, at the activities, attitudes and problems of mothers, of women who care for relatives, of home-helps, nurses and midwives (Finch and Groves 1983; Reverby 1987; Ungerson 1987; Benner and Wrubel 1989; Simonen 1990; Finch and Mason 1993). Women have also come to the fore as care-receivers: several studies have appeared analysing the power processes by which women's needs for care are interpreted and marginalized by husbands, social services, welfare provisions and legal regulations (Ehrenreich and English 1979; Holtmaat 1992; Addelson 1994). At the same time, studies have also appeared in which care, seen from a feminist perspective, is assigned a meaningful place in the processes of care provision (see, for example, Van Mens-Verhulst and Schilder 1994). Sociologists and political scientists have engaged in research, often of a comparative nature, examining the effects of the modern welfare state's dependence on a social structure in which it is assumed that women will carry out a major part of the caring work. This research has produced all kinds of new insights into the operation and effectiveness of central concepts in the policies of the welfare state, concepts such as equality and individualization (Showstack Sassoon 1987; Ungerson 1990a; Bussemaker 1991b, 1993; Sainsbury 1994, 1996; Knijn and Kremer 1997). Historians and social scientists have carried out innovative research on the part played by women, and by social and political disputes about the meaning of sexual difference, in the founding and construction of welfare states, as well as in the professionalization of care and the organization of social work (Fisher 1990; Gordon 1990; Van Drenth 1991, 1995; De Haan 1995; Waaldijk 1996). In fact, in this line of research, women are clearly present: the idea that gender occupies a central place in modern welfare states has now become widely accepted in feminist thought and is appearing with increasing frequency in the general literature on the welfare state.

Second, at the intersection of psychology, ethics, political theory and feminist jurisprudence, there has been extensive debate among feminist theorists about the ethics of care. For a number of years there was serious and often justified criticism of the concept, albeit accompanied by some confusion and on occasion a tone of ridicule and caricature (Houston 1988; Davis 1992). Gradually, however, the concept seems to be gaining acceptance. Political philosophers are beginning to recognize the value of an ethics of care and it has become a subject which can no longer be overlooked by established writers in the fields of ethics and normative political theory. There is growing recognition of the potential value of an ethics of care, not only for the philosophical aspects of ethics, but also in practical matters, in the private sphere as well as in public issues, such as environmental policy, international relations, family law and criminal law.[2]

The characteristics of an ethics of care have been described in many ways. The most useful definition for the purpose of my discussion is the one put forward by the American political theorist Joan Tronto. In her view, an ethics of care focuses on values such as attentiveness to the need for care, willingness to accept responsibility for others as well as for the results of actions, and responsiveness. In her opinion, this collection of values: attentiveness, responsibility, competence and responsiveness form the core of an ethics of care (Tronto 1993: 127–137). Other authors mention similar characteristics of an ethics of care, such as attention to specific contexts and situations, and the opening up of a moral dialogue in which outcomes are not determined in advance (Walker 1989).

Although there is growing faith in the possibilities of an ethics of care, the role of gender within it remains contested among the feminist thinkers who could, in fact, be regarded as the proponents of this ethic. Some feminist thinkers see women or 'gender' as the epistemological basis of thinking about care (Noddings 1984; Held 1987b, 1990). For others an ethics of care has a future only if the methodological ties between gender and care are broken. Joan Tronto has proposed 'exploring the ethics of care as a moral theory without first associating it with gender' (Tronto 1991: 6). So, while gender is accepted as an important aspect of care in feminist political sociology, it seems that care as a moral concept can be accepted only in feminist political philosophy when its connections with gender are severed. This seems somewhat paradoxical (Davis 1991). Feminists were the first to explore the ethics of care and demonstrate that it could be a fruitful concept, connected to women's moral experiences and their values, as articulated both in personal relationships and the public sphere. At the same time, in feminism the concept has gained only grudging acceptance, and the reasons for its development are often overlooked. And although from empirical sociological research we now know a great deal about women and care, on a political-normative level many feminists prefer to talk about morality and care speaking as non-gendered subjects and employing a gender neutral language.

In this chapter I will argue that the issue of gender cannot be avoided in feminist political theory and social research on an ethics of care. However, in order to develop a fruitful 'gender-methodology' in this field, we need first to reflect on the theoretical unease around gender and sexual difference which emerges in thinking about care. In my opinion, the problem can partly be attributed to the lack of consistency and clarity surrounding the use of the concept of gender in relation to care. The concept of care has been developed and refined in the work of scholars like Hilary Graham, Kari Waerness, Clare Ungerson, Berenice Fisher and Joan Tronto; the concept of gender deserves similarly careful treatment, especially when employed in the context of political theory and epistemological reflection on care. I could now go on to present a definition of what I understand by gender and elaborate on its integration into empirical research and political theory about care. But this would be too simple. Concepts have no meaning in themselves; they only acquire meaning within the context of broader discourses, as part of specific ways of naming, arguing, judging and acting. Hence the sub-title of this chapter: 'ethical and epistemological perspectives on care'. Care and gender are not things 'out there' that can be understood simply by means of a definition. Much depends on how we come to 'know' care and its genderedness, as well as on the normative framework and position from which we conceptualize it.

This assumption poses a serious problem for political theorists who, like myself, were educated in political science in the 1960s and 1970s. In the discipline as I was taught it, care was entirely irrelevant. Empirical political science is about power in the processes of public decision-making, the representation of interests and the distribution of resources, rules and values by the government. Political philosophy concerns itself with such subjects as authority, obedience and resistance; with normative questions around justice and the legitimacy of various forms of government; with tolerance and questions about 'the good life'. In the academic debates on these subjects, care is hardly an issue. It figures only in the margins as something which is there and simply has to be carried out, and which – if one is to arrive at the independent state of mind required for reasoning about justice – needs to be transcended. One could say that modern political theory has defined its object-domain in such a way as to exclude care from its vision: it confines care to the private sphere. In the dominant political–philosophical discourse care has to do with affections, bodies, the 'personal', love and the home, and thus with femininity and women (Jones 1988b, 1993; Pateman 1989). Political theory, according to its own self-image, simply has a different object-domain. In this way gender is inscribed in the borderlines between the academic disciplines; you might as well study sociology or psychology if you want to know more about care. Even large-scale processes such as the political–legal structuring of caring activities in the private sphere and the public regulation of health care belong more to the domain of legal studies and sociology than to that of political science.

Since there are links between political theory and the ways in which issues are conceptualized by social and political movements, this state of affairs has complex consequences for the way in which feminists are able to integrate care into their political arguments. How, for example, can we frame questions about gender and the justice of caring arrangements in our society, if care and family relationships fall outside the scope of arguments about justice? And how can we include considerations of care, concern and attentiveness in notions of justice and injustice? One way of overcoming this discursive handicap is to stretch the conceptual apparatus of the discipline to its limits, in order to be able to frame questions about care within its terms. The most prominent example of this strategy is to be found in the work of the American political scientist Susan Moller Okin, who proposes that gender and care be integrated into the paradigm of distributive justice. I will show that this can lead to contradictory and selective ways of reasoning about gender and care, after which I will develop an interpretation of gender which I consider to be fruitful for feminist social research and feminist political theory on care and ethics.

Gender and care in the paradigm of distributive justice

In *Justice, Gender and the Family*, Susan Okin points out that in spite of the fact that Western political–legal systems uphold the values of equality, justice and democracy, there is still great inequality between men and women (Okin 1989). She argues that this discrepancy can be resolved by including women and gender in the paradigm of distributive justice. Her arguments are based on the view that the family is the main source of gender inequality. Not only are labour and dependency unfairly distributed within the family, but it is also the source of gendered identities, character structures, psychological attributes and moral attitudes. Okin sees gender as the historically produced differentiation of the sexes and thus situates her thinking in the feminist tradition, where sex and gender are distinguished from each other in a manner analogous to the nature–culture divide. In her view there are no natural differences between the sexes. Although she sees the unequal treatment of women in law as a major source of injustice, in her view the main problem is still to be found in the effects of socialization, which reinforce sex roles 'that are commonly regarded as of unequal prestige and worth' (ibid.: 6).

Based on Nancy Chodorow's psychoanalytical object-relations theory, Okin argues that the foundations of gender lie in the unequal assignation of primary parenting (Chodorow 1978; Okin 1989: 6–7). Following Chodorow she finds that boys undergo a stronger individuation process than girls. Because women are responsible for mothering, boys develop a sense of identity by separating themselves from their mother and identifying with their father. Girls, on the other hand, are more likely to develop their gender-identity in close contact with their mother and have weaker ego-boundaries. Thus girls become more oriented towards connection and care. To counteract these inequalities Okin suggests that the principles of distributive justice should be applied to the family. The public–private divide needs to be exposed as a 'false ideology' and eliminated, so that resources like jobs and incomes can be redistributed and personality structures can change.

A major part of Okin's book is aimed at developing the normative principles which can justify this standpoint. Her main strategy consists of showing that her view meets the epistemological criteria of objectivity and impartiality, and complies with arguments on the justification of unequal treatment. In her view, knowledge about gender inequality can be acquired through rational argument and by transcending the particularities of one's own situatedness. She considers the best means for achieving this to be the instrument developed by the philosopher John Rawls in his major work *A Theory of Justice*; this involves taking an 'original position' behind a 'veil of ignorance' (Rawls 1971). Rawls posits that objective principles of justice can be arrived at by imagining a group of free and rational people who have no knowledge of actual human behaviour or of their own position within the group. The principles which they decide on from behind this veil of ignorance can be universalized, because subjects in this situation will always decide that rules must be applied in the same way to others as to themselves. In their own interests they will opt for maximum freedom and compensation of inequality, in order to minimize the differences between those who are less and more fortunate. If this approach is applied to gender and family relationships, it will lead, according to Okin, not only to justice within the family but also to objective and impartial legal rules, which will acquire legitimacy through universal acceptance.

This all sounds quite logical, and to many feminists it is a matter of common sense, a self-evident aim of feminist politics. Indeed, a fairer division of child care and thus of the opportunities and positions available to men and women is one of the most widely accepted aims of feminism. In her book Okin provides the arguments that make these aims acceptable in the dominant paradigm of Western welfare states: the paradigm of distributive justice. From an ethical and epistemological perspective, however, there are a number of highly problematical aspects involved in Okin's approach to gender and care. I will discuss a number of these, not to suggest that Okin is entirely wrong, but to open up discussion on a number of complexities attached to a particular kind of equality discourse, complexities which tend to emerge in the conceptualization of issues concerning gender and care. Okin's approach is representative of what I described in the previous chapter as the 'radical–

liberal version of the distributive paradigm' which determined the policy of many Western welfare states in the 1970s, and which can also be found in the common-sense view held by people who are sympathetic to the 'women's cause'. Her ideas, then, are not simply ideas, but should be analysed as a 'paradigm' or as a discourse in the Foucauldian sense: as an intertwined style of knowledge construction and political intervention, aimed at the construction of a particular type of subject.[3] By analysing Okin's approach in this way, it becomes easier to see more precisely the (often hidden) normative elements in the way care has been conceptualized by many feminists and in influential knowledge practices and research methodologies in women's studies.

First, it should be pointed out that Okin's argument on the overriding importance of object-relations is formalistic, circular and speculative. It is striking that she quotes Chodorow as proof of the 'truth' that men and women in our society represent two genders. Apparently, we can attribute empirical differences between men and women to their 'gendered identities', and thus to the patterns of their socialization. Okin pays little attention, however, to the existence and nature of empirical gender differences in behaviour; in fact she bases the idea that these differences exist to a great extent on the same discourse that she uses to explain them, namely, the object-relations theory. This produces a rather closed or circular method of reasoning. Moreover, her arguments are speculative: she takes an 'obvious' point of different 'treatment' between men and women – the distribution of caring activities and the patterns of socialization supposedly resulting from this – and then goes on to posit the expectation that equality and justice can be realized by following the principle of 'natural' equality.

In this way Okin not only constructs 'women' and 'men' as two homogeneous categories (aspects of each cannot, apparently, be combined in one person), she also makes gender the basic factor of women's identities. Although in one short passage in her book she acknowledges differences of race, class, religion and ethnicity among women, this does not prevent her from concluding that gender – or in her view the gendered nature of the family – affects 'virtually all women' (Okin 1989: 7). She even states that a feminist critique of a homogeneous view of gender diverts 'our' attention from the fundamental importance of gender:

> Some feminists have been criticized for developing theories of gender that do not take account of differences among women, especially race, class, religion and ethnicity. While such critiques should always inform our research and improve our arguments, it would be a mistake to allow them to detract our attention from gender itself, as a factor of significance.
>
> (ibid.: 6)

So in Okin's view the fact that women are primarily responsible for the care of young children not only divides humanity into two clear-cut categories, but also produces homogeneity within each category, because gender, as she sees it, is the basic determining factor of identity.

Not only does Okin thus marginalize the many approaches which differ from hers on this point,[4] she also conceives of identity and subjectivity in ways which are problematical on epistemological and moral grounds. Theoretical knowledge about women's identity, which is based on a manner of thinking which trivializes and excludes subjective experience, and which presupposes a unified and predetermined concept of gender, would seem to be of dubious value. It appears that Okin has adopted a framework of interpretation in which there is no room for considering the fragmented nature of people's identities or the dilemmas and values which individuals and groups formulate for themselves. The phrase 'gender itself' is revealing in this respect: it is as if 'gender itself' can only be incorporated into theory if it is immediately abstracted from the social reality which people actually experience. But how can we speak *as* women and *about* women, if we take this abstraction as an epistemological starting-point?

Seen from this perspective the question of why Okin is so keen to promote the idea of a unified human subject becomes relevant. Why does she embrace this ideal of a universal human subject which only has to be stripped of its gendered character structure in order to reach the right decisions about a just society? The answer lies in her preference for the Rawlsian epistemology of the original position, his 'brilliant idea', as she calls it. According to Okin, feminists should even go so far as to adopt this idea as their most powerful tool of political criticism. But this raises a serious problem: in order to be able to make use of this instrument, it is necessary to presuppose the existence of genderless subjects as both starting-point and aim:

> For if the principles of justice are to be adopted unanimously by representative human beings ignorant of their particularistic characteristics and positions in society, they must be persons whose psychological and moral development is in all essentials identical. This means that the social factors influencing the differences between the sexes – from female parenting to all the manifestations of female subordination and dependence – would have to be replaced by genderless institutions and customs.
>
> (ibid.: 107)

Elsewhere Okin speaks of the 'abolition of gender' or a 'genderless society' as the main goals to be achieved through the redistribution of caring tasks within the family. Equality in parenting is thus seen as an absolute prerequisite for the development of worthy and acceptable forms of moral reasoning:

Only children who are equally mothered and fathered can develop fully the psychological and moral capacities that currently seem to be unevenly distributed between the sexes. *Only* when men participate equally in what have been principally women's realms of meeting the daily psychological and material needs of those close to them, and when women participate equally in what have been principally men's realms of large scale production, government and intellectual and artistic life, will members of both sexes be able to develop a more complete human personality than has hitherto been possible.

(ibid.: 107; emphasis added)

In passages like this we are presented with the ungendered subject as the norm and complete sameness as a necessity, for the sake of consensus and impartiality, the hallmarks of a universalistic approach to justice. Okin encourages feminists to mobilize all their moral reasoning to support this discourse.[5] Elsewhere, however, Okin seems more sensitive to arguments based on an ethics of care, even if in a somewhat ambivalent and contradictory fashion. In the first chapter of her book she brushes aside feminist writers engaged in the ethics of care with the reproach that 'too much energy' has been devoted to an intellectual endeavour, which, because it propagates differences, will automatically lead to naturalism, traditionalism and conservatism (ibid.: 15). However, in a later chapter she takes on certain ideas from these same authors in order to rethink Rawlsian arguments on the justice of laws and procedures. Here she accepts Gilligan's ideas concerning the existence of systematic gender differences in moral reasoning as an empirical given: 'the different voice' of women should be re-evaluated and reassessed in order to arrive at a more completely human approach to moral reasoning.

In accordance with these ideas, Okin reformulates the basic principles of Rawls's theory of justice. In her description of what goes on behind the veil of ignorance, she departs from the Rawlsian language of rational choice and emphasizes empathy and listening as conditions for reaching judgements in which all points of view are represented ('thinking from the perspective of everybody') instead of taking a position which is elevated above any relation to a particular situation ('thinking from a position from nowhere'). So here she invokes care as a moral attitude in order to formulate an even more universalistic perspective than Rawls himself. Yet here again we are caught up in a circular argument. Reasoning about justice inevitably leads to the recognition that there is inequality between gender-roles, but in order for us to be able to see this, gender must be abolished. Only androgynous beings who have been equally cared for by their mother and father can be expected to possess the moral capacities which would enable them to find the correct balance between listening to others and designing fair and impartial rules.

What, then, does this imply for the epistemological dimensions of the debate on the ethics of care? In brief, I would suggest that, in Okin's conceptualization, care receives simultaneously both too much and too little weight. Okin gives care *too much* weight because she overloads it with the expectation that all social problems around gender will be resolved when care is fairly and evenly distributed between men and women.[6] She also places too much weight on care by assuming that those who base their reasoning on care are able to see every political issue from everyone's point of view. Not only is this an impossible task, but even the assumption that it may be possible can lead to unnoticed forms of paternalism (or should I say maternalism in this context?). Even if we suppose that there is a 'somebody' capable of seeing every issue from every perspective, his or her interpretation of 'other' moral voices would inevitably affect the decisions reached on the best and most just laws.[7] On the other hand, Okin gives care *too little* weight because she fails to recognize care as a moral activity, a moral theory or a manner of moral reasoning in its own right. She values thinking about care only to the extent that it meets the dominant epistemological norms of impartiality, objectivity, universality and homogeneity of the subject, or in so far as it contributes to these. This is made apparent by the fact that, in her approach, equality is conflated with sameness.

The contradiction inherent in Okin's interpretation and application of the concept of care becomes even more apparent when we examine her treatment of the issue of how feminists can speak as political subjects about (and in terms of) care. The first point which strikes one is that Okin marginalizes women who practise 'care reasoning' as a means to arriving at moral judgements, by labelling them 'conservative feminists' or 'traditional women', which are categories which few feminists would be eager to associate themselves with. Moreover, she maintains that feminists can only talk about care in public politics by invoking an 'original position' or an imaginary future in which everybody automatically knows what good care is, because everyone has been cared for equally by women and men in their childhood. This implies that feminists should talk in hypothetical terms and adopt a style of reasoning in which they act as if they have become ungendered beings.

The American philosopher Phyllis Rooney has shown how problematic it can be to call on the moral virtues associated with care when making moral judgements about hypothetical situations, because this conflicts with the fundamental nature of these virtues. Compassion and sympathy are generally associated with specific situations:

> The limit imposed on theorizing by means of hypothetical deliberations is not simply a practical one but, more importantly for our purposes, a logical one. Hypothetical reasoning is quite appropriate for consideration of situations which require only the application of

principles of rationality and impartiality. This is because one can hypothetically invoke impartiality and rationality, but *one cannot hypothetically invoke compassion and empathy*. One can certainly articulate consideration of principles of compassion and empathy; one can rationally argue for the need for compassion in a particular type of situation, but that can never be the same as invoking compassion *in the situation itself.*

(Rooney 1991: 351; emphasis in original)

Okin is thus attempting the impossible. The feminist ethics of care and the moral epistemology that goes with it in fact undermine the very feasibility and moral acceptability of constructions such as the 'original position' and 'the veil of ignorance'. The feminist ethics of care also contains a fundamental critique of the related idea of the social contract as the basis for social consensus and the legitimacy of legal regulations (Pateman 1988; Jones 1993). Okin is trying to save something which cannot be saved and which most Anglo-American political philosophers, including Rawls himself, actually left behind quite some time ago. There is now quite broad acceptance for the idea that moral reasoning is always determined by the context and that it reflects the value systems within which people operate and upon which people reflect. From this point of view it would seem more advisable to consider whether and how epistemic qualities associated with the ethics of care, such as empathy and compassion, can improve normative reasoning and can lead to the development of new ideas about partiality and impartiality (Walker 1989; Meyers 1993; Code 1995).

All in all, Okin's approach poses feminist women *and* men with a pretty impossible task when it comes to 'politicizing' care and integrating considerations, experiences and visions about care into their ideal image of citizenship. Feminist women can take part in the normative reasoning about citizenship only if they present themselves as neutral beings, whose only problem is that they have to catch up with men. In fact, care still figures basically as a handicap for women, something which they have to escape from because it stands in the way of their personal development. The marginalization of care in standard political theory is thus reproduced rather than being seriously questioned. This state of affairs not only imposes serious limitations on the positions which feminists can adopt in the public domain, it also limits the epistemological strategies which can be used in research on gender and care.

If research in the field of women's studies regards women who care and who attach a moral and political importance to this as 'traditional' women, it is assigning them to the category of outsiders; they have become 'others', women who under the best of circumstances can only be the object of study. This divide between subject and object limits the further development of feminist knowledge about care in at least two ways. In the first place it restricts the possibilities for employing dilemmas in the social and political practice of feminist theory as a valuable source of reflexive moral reasoning: dilemmas such as the tension between the need for autonomy and for connection, or tensions arising from the social imbalance in the provision of care, whereby women are less often the recipients than the providers of care. It can be quite illuminating when theorists are able to make use of their own dilemmas as 'knowing' subjects instead of looking for problems, whether related to care or not, solely in others (Davis 1995; Shrage 1994). And if we are not able to do this – and this is my second problem – the division between political–sociological and political–normative theory about care, the two 'tracks' mentioned at the beginning of the chapter, will remain. The public debate about the normative dimensions of care still provides no discursive space for the way in which carers frame their moral dilemmas and moral considerations, or the way in which they express their rationality of care. Public discussion about care arrangements in the health service and home-care, for instance, is thus reserved for the academic 'experts', people who generally tend to employ the language of economic, technical and legal rationality, an idiom which is usually far removed from the everyday experience of caring.

Gender and care from the perspective of 'gender in the plural'

These considerations have implications for the development of a 'fruitful' gender methodology in the area of care and ethics. I will now go on to discuss a number of points which I consider useful for the conceptualization of gender in this context, inspired by discussions on concepts and theories of gender in historiography, philosophy, literary theory and feminist psycho-analysis. These sources have provided the starting-point for social science research into gendered processes of care, ethics and moral reasoning. My aim is to explore whether the previously mentioned divisions between the sociological and normative tracks in feminist knowledge about gender and care can be reduced or undermined. This implies, as already mentioned in my introductory chapter, that I am arguing for ethics and moral reasoning to be studied as everyday social and textual practices. I consider moral practices to be forms of communication and interpretation, rather than elevated activities belonging to academics in ivory towers. It is thus not my aim to develop a 'grand' theory about gender, morality and care, nor to reach conclusions on the 'best' ethics or moral theory for feminism. It is rather to reflect upon the different ways in which care can be conceptualized as a practical socio-political activity in moral theorizing and to look for situated ways of reflecting on gender and care which can help to reduce the adverse effects for women brought about by an automatic coupling of these two concepts.

First, I would argue that the concept of gender should be seen as a continuum rather than a binary opposition in which the existence of two 'genders' is assumed.[8] The idea that there are two sexes or sexual identities fits in with the liberal social theory of an original sameness, from which sexual difference

79

is a deviation (Gatens 1991; Chapter 2 of this volume). This approach fails to take account of the fact that there is a wide variety of meanings attached to the concepts of femininity and masculinity, and that these terms are subject to major historical and cultural shifts. It would perhaps be better to think of 'gender' as an element within processes of signification. Seen in this way it refers to the meanings which are attributed to sexual difference in a wide range of social practices, institutions and forms of behaviour, and to the way in which sexual difference is attributed to and accepted by subjects: gender, then, is something that we *do* rather than what we *are* (Kessler and McKenna 1978; West and Zimmerman 1991; Chodorow 1995). If we regard gender as a continuum it then also becomes possible to understand that different aspects of gendered feelings, behaviours and attributes can be combined in one person, and that individuals and groups can experience all kinds of frictions because of this.

The following example will make this clear. Although care is still associated mainly with women and femininity, there are a great many men who are engaged in the practice of care, both in private relationships and in the caring professions. Both women and men have to find a way to deal with the gender symbolism attached to care. Fathers who take care of their children, for example, are confronted with the idea that responsibility for care is not expected from them. They have to deal with a contradictory image: on the one hand the idea that they are 'softies' (i.e., not real men) and on the other that they are doing something extraordinary (Duindam 1996). Just as women have to be able to persevere in their ambitions if they want to combine work and care, so men generally have to scale theirs down. Women more often have to justify their feeling of guilt that they don't care well enough, because this responsibility is more easily ascribed to them and also because it is more often a part of their self-image and their moral identity. However, the ability to display reasoning based on the ethics of care might be much less strictly related to sexual difference than is often assumed; it may also have to do with the position taken by men in caring processes or with the degree to which people are willing to identify with an ethics of care.

Second, feminist research should abandon the concept of gender as a homogeneous category in favour of the idea that different aspects of identity and affinity can be combined within one person or social group. An abstract ideal of sameness often leads to assimilation of the attributes and norms of the dominant groups, as can be seen in political philosophy as well as in everyday political life (Young 1990a). Assimilation goes hand in hand with marginalization, objectification and exclusion of groups which are perceived as different and deviant.[9] This mechanism applies not only to gender, but also to ethnicity and class, and to the complex interaction between these factors.[10] These processes also take place in academic practice, where they are reinforced by the recurrent ways of phrasing problems, methods and concepts, and by all kinds of unspoken assumptions, and cultural and material power processes. Women's studies can counter this by using theories and methodologies that create cognitive and normative space for the situatedness of knowledge and moral reasoning, and thus for agency, interaction, communication and culture, as well as for the symbolic and psychodynamic aspects of gender relations (Haraway 1988; Code 1991; Flax 1993). And it is for this reason that reasoning on justice, care and ethics cannot do without a solid conceptualization of power and oppression as Iris Young has convincingly argued in her book *Justice and the Politics of Difference* (Young 1990a).

Third, gender should be freed from the often false oppositions between nature and culture and between equality and difference. In the first phase of modern feminist theory the conceptualization of gender as a socially constructed identity proved a useful tool for undermining commonly accepted ideas about natural character structures, but in the end the nature–nurture debate and thinking in terms of a dilemma between equality and difference proved a dead end. Ideas about a natural sameness are after all speculative and can thus have widely divergent effects. An approach which sees gender as simply the product of cultural construction can lead to the idea that gender is always something which is wrongfully imposed on women from above, especially if this approach is combined with an exclusively top-down conception of power (Davis 1990, 1995). This easily leads to the body being seen as a *tabula rasa*, or something which only acquires a masculine or feminine form when culture begins to leave its mark (Gatens 1991; Oudshoorn 1991; Orobio de Castro 1993).[11]

I would like to stress that gender, including its embodied aspect, is something which women feel and act upon; they (are able to) employ a whole range of gendered forms of behaviour. Women are not passive victims of their body (Young 1990b; Davis 1995), but use their body in all kinds of ways as a medium of identity, whether this is regarded by themselves or others as something positive or negative, a joy or a burden. This implies that something like 'the abolition of gender' should not be the main aim of feminism, because it is neither feasible nor desirable. Gender constructions will always pervade feelings of identity, and individual and collective forms of moral reasoning, and thus also arguments about care. This means that it is more productive to continue engaging in discussions about where sexual difference *does* matter, and where it does not, rather than to disqualify the voices of women involved in care within the normative frameworks of feminism.

Fourth, gender cannot be located in a single social sphere, nor can it be reduced to patterns of socialization and care within the family. On the contrary, gender plays a role at different levels of social structure and individual and collective behaviour. So it should not only be seen as a continuum, but also as a multi-layered phenomenon. In this book, I distinguish three of these gender layers.[12] Gender works on a *symbolic level*, where images of masculinity and femininity impart meaning to phenomena which would appear to be gender-neutral, such as work, care, citizenship and rationality. Gender works at the level of *individual and collective identity*, because meanings based on sexual difference have an effect on the way in which women and men develop their self-image, are judged by others, and manifest themselves. Gender also works at the level of *social structure* as the availability of (power) resources and the accessibility of social institutions and positions of power are marked by gender norms and gender symbols. The concept of 'layers' allows a more open interpretation than if we start from the premiss that care is characterized by a gender-based dichotomy. It thus becomes easier to address the issue of where and when rifts occur between institutionalized ideologies of gender and care on the one hand, and the way in which people express their self-image, experiences and desire for change on the other. We can also further our understanding of the ways in which meanings of gender and care remain controversial and continue to be the object of interaction, negotiation and interpretation.

This implies, among other things, that feminist research on an ethics of care should not be directed in the first instance towards differences in moral reasoning between men and women. When care is acknowledged as an ethics in its own right, empirical sexual differences are not the most important issue. When sexual differences are taken as a starting-point, the use of 'gender' can easily slip into a 'sophisticated' way of talking about actual men and women, while the symbolic binary constructions of gender and the effect of the discursive power embedded in them are overlooked. The ethics of care, then, tends to be situated too much on the level of experience and (moral) identity, and too little on the level of the conceptual frameworks and the images of sexual difference contained within them. Hence, research into the ethics of care should always be partly concerned with the deconstruction of the gender-load inherent in conceptual schemes and traditions of thought on morality and care. Breaking through the binary logic of gender implies, for example, decoding and overcoming the gender-laden opposition between rationality and emotion, which relegates care to the realm of the emotions.[13] This is why it is useful to realize that concrete and contextual forms of 'care-reasoning' can have their own characteristic structures of rationality and principles of action and interaction (Waerness 1987; Fisher and Tronto 1990; Rooney 1991).

Care as process and practice

Care is a cognitive and moral activity in its own right. This is difficult to understand if we conceive of care solely in terms of the dichotomy between labour and love. Care is not just about changing nappies, cleaning the house and looking after the elderly; it is an activity in which the understanding of needs is central. Unlike individualistically directed care ethicists such as Nel Noddings and Rita Manning, I do not start from the premiss that the ethics of care involves an obligation to care for everyone who elicits a 'caring response' in the moral subject (Noddings 1984; Manning 1992). In my view, the ethics of care then becomes too easily incorporated into the register of the ethics of obligation and its starting-point based too much on the dyadic relationship between carer and cared-for. I think the practice of the ethics of care is marked not so much by a type of obligation different from the ethics of rights, but rather by a different 'moral activity': moral problems are observed and discussed in the first instance from an attitude of caring, that is, with attentiveness, responsibility, responsiveness and the commitment to see issues from differing perspectives. The conclusion of this may not necessarily be a duty to care; it could also mean deciding not to provide care, because one cannot agree with another person's needs-claims, for example, or because one possesses insufficient means to meet or satisfy them, or because these claims conflict too strongly with one's own needs or moral convictions.

The ethics of care is thus related to the activity of caring as a whole; theorizing about care will benefit from a broad conceptualization of what care is and where it takes place. In this broader vision of care as an activity, care is primarily seen as an ability and a willingness to 'see' and to 'hear' needs, and to take responsibility for these needs being met. Berenice Fisher and Joan Tronto have greatly clarified this perception of care as a process by distinguishing four phases, each accompanied by different competences and values (Fisher and Tronto 1990: 35–62). Their description makes it possible to perceive and reflect on the care dimensions of a broad range of activities. It also enables us to develop a socio-political vision of care, which manages to escape from the limitations of the individual–psychological debate.

'Caring about', according to Fisher and Tronto, implies paying attention to the factors which determine survival and well-being, whereby seeing and recognizing care needs is crucial. Knowledge of particular situations is of foremost importance in this. 'Caring about' is not conditional on love or connection in their opinion; it is an orientation rather than a motivation.[14] 'Caring about' has to do with understanding needs, and with selecting means and choosing various strategies of action. 'Caring for', on the other hand, means taking responsibility for initiating caring activities. It demands more sustained effort and detailed knowledge of particular situations than 'caring about'. The main qualities needed here are empathy and judgement: seeing what is necessary in a particular situation and which means can be brought into action. 'Taking care of' is the concrete work of what Fisher and Tronto describe as 'repairing and maintaining the world', carrying out the daily routines and developing a thorough understanding of them. 'Care-receiving' includes the reactions of those towards whom care is directed. Attention to these reactions is important for the quality of the care process and for the motivation of those who care.

In reality these phases may often overlap, or they may be quite separate and fragmented, depending on the power processes involved. The latter may be at the expense of the quality of care provided and the motivation of the carers. Women are overrepresented at the level of 'taking care of', without being able to exert much influence on 'caring about' or 'caring for'. An example of this is the home-help who takes care of elderly clients without a labour contract and without being in a position to influence either the organization of home-care, the way she spends her time or the official diagnosis of the problem. Another example is the volunteer who provides care from a sense of involvement with the people around her, but who has almost no right to the material means which enable her to do this or who cannot reckon on attention for her own care needs. In this sort of situation women carry out work with great responsibility, but little power. They find themselves in countless situations in which the need for care emerges most immediately and in which the appeal for attention is felt most directly; this can lead to feelings of being overburdened and in many cases to severe 'burn-out' (Abel 1990; Miller 1990; Duijnstee 1992).[15]

In principle, all phases of the care process have relational dimensions, although these will be most apparent in the phases of *caring for* and *receiving care*. This is where the direct interaction takes place in which feelings of self and other and connection between people is expressed; this is especially the case when one is caring for close intimates or for oneself. This is why it is so difficult to separate moral problems in the domain of care from the activity of caring or from the people involved. Moral considerations arise in the assessment of needs and in the way in which these must or can be met, if they can be met at all. They arise when the person providing care has to find a balance between his or her own needs and those of the person receiving care, or when the carer and cared-for have conflicting views on what is necessary or possible in a particular situation. Moral considerations become extra complex when care is provided in situations of dependency and where there are major differences in the possession of power resources. A number of these problems can be solved by searching for more opportunities for reciprocity and autonomy in care relations, for the carer as well as for the receiver of care; other problems are inherent to the situation, in particular when those who receive care are dependent on others meeting their needs, as in the bringing up of young children or nursing the ill.

This implies that an ethics of care has to find answers to questions of dependency, vulnerability and the vicissitudes of life. Care as a social and moral activity implies not only dealing with feelings of love, empathy and involvement, but also – and often interwoven with these – dealing with feelings of grief, fear, anger, rejection, guilt, shame and aggression. And this, in turn, implies that it is not sufficient to posit equality and reciprocity as the principle values and normative framework of moral life, and certainly not when these are framed exclusively in the language of rational choice. The moral repertoire in the area of care should allow more discursive space for values associated with trust, respect for differences, and the encouragement of self-respect (Baier 1989, 1991; Jackson 1989). One way to open up space for reflection and moral deliberation on these values is to listen to and interpret the moral deliberations about care expressed by the providers and receivers of care. Research along these lines can be carried out by talking with women about their dilemmas with regard to care, in professional as well as in informal situations, such as in the context of the family, partners and friends (Finch and Mason 1993; Gremmen 1995; Nederland 1995).[16]

This kind of research differs from research into gender differences in the tradition of behaviourist psychology, because women's studies employs concepts of gender in which difference is no longer self-evident and in which it is stripped of its 'natural' and negative connotations. Behavioural differences between men and women in general should not be our main concern. It is often difficult to reach valid and useful conclusions in this area, because differences between men and women have as much to do with social position, cultural background or philosophy of life as with sexual difference as such (Komter 1991). The primary importance of carrying out research among women is that it provides the opportunity for reflecting on different styles of situated moral reasoning, and that only in so doing can justice be done to the moral considerations of women who provide care. And we could also ask *why* it is that we continually seem to feel the need to compare men and women in the first place.[17]

In making this plea, I am not trying to suggest that contextual moral reasoning about care is by definition the source of a 'better' ethic, or that it covers the whole field of feminist ethics. Nor am I trying to suggest that feminism can dispense with deliberation on the issues of equality, justice and rights. In fact, the opposition between care and justice is precisely one of those fruitless oppositions which need a great deal of rethinking. Feminism would benefit from concepts of justice which are not exclusively framed in distributive terms, and which do not automatically lead to taking sameness as the norm where differences would make a better starting-point for political argumentation (Young 1990a; Flax 1993). A fairer distribution of caring activities between men and women does not necessarily have to be framed within the paradigm of rational choice and distributive justice. It can also be argued in terms of social justice for oppressed groups, or from a norm of equal opportunities, although this may well mean that it is more difficult to reach a (hypothetical) consensus on its desirability, since it is impossible to construct a watertight argument for equality being the yardstick in all facets of legal politics and government policy. But the fact that these approaches fail to produce strong universal criteria may be their strength rather than weakness. Politics, after all, has to do with developing arguments in specific situations, directed towards the solution of specific needs and problems. This implies taking account of possible consequences of normative orientations.[18] In other words: open forms of moral reasoning in which the situation and the consequences of possible forms of action are taken into account constitute indispensable elements of a 'good' or responsible politics.[19]

And to take another example: there are many aspects of care processes that need to be reflected on in terms of justice, for instance the question of where, for whom, and for what care is justified, and the question of when it is justified to put limits on the availability of care or to refuse care. Questions such as these cannot be answered in an abstract or general mode. Care is, after all, not simply a matter of distributing 'goods and services'; it has to do primarily with quality of life, and how we experience and interpret this. It also has to do with the way in which power processes are involved in this context. The distribution of goods and services has in a certain sense a merely secondary role in this. Questions with regard to the description, the quality and the distribution of care will always remain controversial issues. It is almost impossible to define care without referring to its qualitative aspects. What counts as good care will be evaluated differently from the perspective of the care-givers and care-receivers. And these positions are not fixed, but circulate among individuals and groups.

The moral and epistemological characteristics of an ethics of care, such as listening, responsiveness, attentiveness and the commitment to see issues from different perspectives offer a sound basis for making situated judgements about the quality of care, which can lead in turn to a 'caring justice'. These characteristics can also be of use in a worthwhile politics of needs-interpretation which, in turn, is essential in shaping public opinion on the issue of which needs should be met, and in which way. There can thus be reasonable discussion about the question of when it is justified to use collective means and about the role of individual responsibility. Only in this way can we come to a more balanced judgement concerning the meaning and applicability of universal values when thinking about the political and legal aspects of care; only in this way can we reach a common decision about the values which can justifiably be applied to everyone.

Conclusion: political theory and ethics

Susan Moller Okin's appeal to the principle of distributive justice (see the second section of this chapter) is inspired by the idea of using political theory as an objective foundation for political critique. Together with this, she employs the most powerful and legitimate political discourse of modern Western states: the liberal principle of equality as enshrined in most constitutions and the related norm of impartiality. Her genre of political theory and the aims of objective criteria and objective knowledge related to it thus offer an attractive perspective for feminists who have decided to focus on gender inequalities in the policies of modern welfare states as their most important target for change. Her approach to political theory ties in with the aims of feminist ethics in the 1990s as formulated at the beginning of the decade by the American philosopher Alison Jaggar, when she stated that feminists' moral critique of social practices and theories should be able to be objectively justified (Jaggar 1991: 94). Like Okin, Jaggar is thus opposed to a feminist ethics of care, which – together with what she terms 'the feminist flirt with postmodernism' – she identifies with 'the spectre of relativism'. Feminist ethics proceeds, in her view, from the recognition that we live in a 'painful pre-feminist world' and she sees her activities as contributing to a transformation of this world into a world in which the fundamental moral principles of feminism are universally accepted.

Seen from Jaggar's perspective, it would hardly be surprising that the two tracks in feminist research about care, that of political sociology and that of the ethics of care, have developed along entirely separate tracks. Moreover, from this perspective it would be better if this situation remained unchanged, because feminism has more to gain from an objective critique than from an ethic which appeals to people's subjective experience. However, Jaggar does not completely discount the idea that a feminist ethic should relate to women's moral experience. In her view, however, feminist ethics should also be able to criticize and transcend these experiences. This explains her appeal to universalism and objectivity, which function for her as a political 'bottom-line' (McLure 1992). It seems to me, though, that there is an unresolvable flaw in her thinking: how is it possible for us to distinguish between those moral experiences which are the products of domination and those which are not, and to decide which experiences can lay a better claim to objective validity?[20] If we really want to validate a diversity of moral experiences we had better ask ourselves which versions of relativism are worthwhile, instead of continuing to regard relativism as a threat (Code 1992; Shrage 1994).

This ties in better with pleas by postmodern feminists to conceive of ethics and moral deliberation as social practices situated in time and space. It seems to me that it is exactly by engaging in an active dialogue with different moral perspectives and moral considerations that we can improve the quality of normative judgements. This would make more acceptable the idea that different gradations and forms of relativism are possible, just as there are stronger and weaker, and well- and badly argued forms of universal norms (Code 1992; Frazer and Lacey 1993). In my view, Jaggar attributes much too ambitious and broad a task to feminist ethics: it must not only be objective, but also prescribe ways of acting. In addition, it must be able to reveal the 'masculine bias' in dominant ethics and develop normative prescriptions for nearly all contexts and areas of life. Through the emphasis on objectivity as the foundation of normative reasoning, this type of theory (and the associated political theory) inevitably reaches a point at which it is no longer able to see the relativity of its own truth claims and comes to regard them as a universally applicable norm. It is striking that Jaggar does not systematically ask who the moral subject of the feminist ethics she supports might actually be, and who, or which institution, should propagate this moral knowledge. In fact Jaggar, like Okin, stays within the parameters of the legalistic ethical codes of modernity and the related view of politics as the domain which should create consensus, and which in turn has the right to prescribe to everybody the norms and lifestyles approved by this consensus. This is a type of ethics which seems more concerned with proving itself right than reflecting on the legitimacy and relativity of its own truth claims. It is an ethics which, in spite of its dutiful salute to moral dialogue, easily leads to moral intolerance rather than tolerance of different moral considerations and viewpoints, or to respect for difference.

It is questionable, then, whether the goal of feminist ethics and political theory should always be to provide a critical perspective on existing practices and to justify existing criticism. The critical standpoint has, of course, been of inestimable importance to modern feminism. However, it can also be taken too far in a boundless urge to politicize every aspect of life, an urge which was launched with the feminist slogan 'the personal is political'. Jaggar's view of ethics and Okin's of political theory are more akin to the broad conception of politics and the malleability of society, more characteristic of the 1970s than the 1990s, the period in relation to which Jaggar framed her normative goal. The latter period is, after all, marked more by a search for the limits of the political in relation to other spheres of life, and by renewed discussion about the boundaries between private and public responsibility. There is also now a more widely shared realization that not all traditions have to be subjected to criticism all the time, and that there is a great deal in existing forms of human society and values which is worth preserving, or which politics cannot simply ignore or overrule. A modest morality would seem, in many ways, to be a more suitable course of action for the 1990s than a morality which makes change its first priority. In this light it is worth noting that both Jaggar and Okin still view the ethics of care, in spite of a few positive qualities, as essentially the negative 'counterpart' to the normative theory which they advocate. It would seem that for many feminists the normative insecurity of the ethics of care is apparently too threatening to be dealt with (Clark 1993). Seen from another perspective this is exactly the strength of the ethics of care, as I argue in this book.

In this respect it is worth noting that Jaggar makes no distinction between ethics and political theory. The task she defines for feminist ethics is actually the same as that which feminists in the 1970s assigned to 'theory' in general. Here, too, we see the influence of the broad conception of politics. A major disadvantage of this inability to recognize the limits of politics is that it means losing useful material for thinking about the particular characteristics of different social practices. The possibility that we might need different moral considerations in different moral contexts is more or less ruled out. In my capacity as a citizen who has to decide whether *in vitro* fertilization should be paid for by public health-care provisions I may well want or need to consider issues beyond my private existence as a mother, or as a friend of a woman with an unfulfilled wish to have a child, or as a feminist who feels critical of the social pressure on women to become mothers and who is worried about the increasing amount of technology involved in human reproduction and the shaping of women's reproductive capacities. The realization that caring relationships with those around me are very valuable will lead me continually to question the primacy of paid labour in concepts of citizenship, however important I find paid work for women's independence. An understanding of social practices is thus indispensable for a feminist ethic, not only because it reminds us of the interrelation of acting and judging, but also because it keeps alive the realization that moral judgements are context-bound.

So, in short, if we want the two tracks of feminist research about care to meet and reinforce each other then we would do well to develop further the situational perspective on knowing and judging (Addelson 1991; Code 1995). A socio-political understanding of social practices in the field of care is indispensable because it can add to our perception of the great diversity in care situations and care policies, and enrich the normative considerations arising in these contexts. The debate about the ethics of care can broaden our insight into the normative dimensions of care and lead to less ambitious and more diverse normative frameworks for socio-political research and political judgement. And both the ethics of care and research on care stand to gain by the normative self-image of the knowing and thinking subject put forward by feminist care ethics: the emphasis on attentiveness, consideration of divergent perspectives, respect, responsibility and practical wisdom. From this perspective, feminist political theory and ethics fit more into an Aristotelian tradition of virtue-ethics and practical wisdom, and a hermeneutical tradition in which language, interpretation and signification are central, than into a conception of political theory and ethics which continues to foster the search for general values and truths (Code 1991; Lugones 1991; McLure 1992; Clark 1993; Warnke 1993; Komter 1995; Tronto 1995b). This is also where the similarity lies with postmodern political theory, at least in so far as this can frame the subjectivity of the knower in terms of positionality, relationships, changes of perspective and embodiment (see, for example, Yeatman 1994). In this case a situated conception of ethics and political theory goes hand in hand with contextual and situated knowledge practices.

4

CARE AND JUSTICE IN THE PUBLIC DEBATE ON CHILD CUSTODY[1]

The transformation of family law

Over the last ten years, readers of Dutch newspapers have been confronted with a number of dramatic stories, in which an appeal is made to their sense of justice in relation to the legal regulation of family ties. Divorced fathers have regularly filled the headlines with fierce accusations of having being denied access to their children. They have organized pressure groups such as the 'Foolish Fathers',[2] who have made frequent appearances on radio and TV, and featured regularly in newspaper articles. Public opinion has also been stirred by the story of an elderly woman, who had been put up for adoption by her (unmarried) mother and was now demanding information about her biological parents from the children's home where she was born (Holtrust 1995). Another well-known case was that of a sperm donor who demanded access to his biological child. While I was finalizing the manuscript of the English edition of this book, the newspapers were reporting on a British surrogate mother who said that she had undergone an abortion because she did not trust the child-raising capacities of the Dutch couple who were to become the parents of her child. After some days she announced that she had made up the story about the abortion, in order to mislead the commissioning couple about her change of mind. The Dutch couple said the English woman had acted 'devilishly' and announced they would go to court, where they have little chance of winning their case since commercial surrogacy is illegal in the Netherlands. This, in turn, was the occasion for British observers to state that the Netherlands has an obsolete legal system. These legal cases are only a few of the many in this area, all related to the question of how biological fatherhood can be legally established and which rights and duties should be linked to non-marital parenthood. And for many years now Dutch parliament has been considering proposed changes to this aspect of family law.

This social, legal and political commotion in the domain of family law is not new. The legal regulation of child custody has been the subject of continual political conflict and legal reform in most Western countries. In the post-war

90

period a fundamental change took place in the legal systems of these countries, which is usually referred to as the modernization or liberalization of family law. A number of changes were introduced in Dutch family law which in one way or another had been on the political agenda since the end of the nineteenth century (Van de Wiel 1985; Sevenhuijsen 1987; Braun 1992). These were the introduction of the capacity for married women to own property and to conclude legal contracts in private law (1957), equality in the exercise of parental power within marriage (1985), the regulation of adoption (1956) and the liberalization of the divorce laws (1971). After 1971 the principles of matrimonial fault and adultery as the principle grounds for divorce were replaced by those of irretrievable breakdown and mutual consent.[3]

The liberalization of family law did not, however, bring an end to the political turmoil, which in many cases had already been going on for more than a century. The 1970s witnessed a fierce political struggle surrounding the legal consequences of divorce: the regulation of alimony, income support for divorced women, maintenance and, associated with this, questions concerning child custody outside marriage and the right to parental access after divorce. This spelt the end of the institution of single custody after divorce, which had been introduced in 1905 and which had given divorced women the chance of an independent existence with their children. The conflicts and discussions on this issue took place not only in the courts but also in parliament, campaigns, lobby groups, the popular media, legal journals, and platforms in the area of social security. From 1975 onwards, divorced men demanded legally enforceable visiting rights, and strengthened their claim by asserting that the institution of single custody withheld men from their 'right to fatherhood' while, on the other hand, they were legally obliged to financial maintenance of their children. In the legal interpretation of these claims, lawyers called on the argument of the 'best interest of the child', which was interpreted as the 'right to have a father', which meant that both children and fathers could claim a mutual right to each other.

Proposals for the further reform of family law have since been directed principally towards designing new regulations for the rights and duties between parents and children in non-marital situations. This reform process began with proposals for the introduction of visiting rights after divorce. Later it was concerned with filiation rules and custody of children born outside wedlock as well as filiation rules in the case of artificial insemination and surrogate motherhood. Parliamentary politics and the courts have each begun to acquire a special role in this field. Around 1980, a bill which aimed to establish a right to access for the non-custodial parent was rejected by parliament. There was clearly a lack of political consensus on the reasoning behind parental access and the precise regulations for its implementation. Women's organizations and welfare organizations cast doubts on the need for an enforceable right to parental access and questioned the one-sided interpretation of 'the interest of the child' (Holtrust, Sevenhuijsen and Verbraken 1989).

Since then the arena of the transformation of family law has shifted. Lawyers have applied themselves to testing Dutch law against the European Convention on Human Rights, which protects people's fundamental freedoms. Article VIII of this treaty states that everyone has the right to respect for their private and family life, their house and correspondence. In 1984, a crucial breakthrough took place in family law when the Supreme Court of the Netherlands decided, in reference to this article, that it should be possible to maintain joint parental power after divorce if this was the wish of both parents. Ending joint parental power would mean that the government was unjustifiably infringing on people's right to family life. Although, at first sight, what seemed to be at stake was the regulation of a private relationship between individuals, the argument took place in terms of the government's obligation to regulate the relationship between its citizens. Later, by invoking the norm of equal treatment of different lifestyles, this ruling was extended to allow the possibility of joint custody between men and women in non-marital situations. The right to parental access in both of these situations was reached by invoking Article VIII, which also provided the grounds for allowing biological fathers, if necessary against the mother's will, to enforce legal recognition and access to or change of custody of children born outside wedlock.[4]

The Civil Code has now been adapted to take account of these developments in case law about child custody and access rights. A law passed in 1995 changed the term 'parental power' into 'parental authority', and sole custody has been abolished in favour of a regulation whereby parental authority continues after divorce. Parents could, under this law, make a request at the moment of divorce that both of them should continue to exercise parental authority over their children. If agreement on this could not be reached, the judge had to decide which parent should exercise parental authority. In 1997 the Second Chamber of the Dutch Parliament accepted a Bill that changed this regulation again. This Bill presumes the continuation of joint parental authority after divorce, unless one or both of the parents submit, in the interests of the child, a request for sole exercise.[5] The 1995 law gave the other parent visiting rights and a right to information about important decisions, while the parent who had been awarded the exercise of parental authority was from then on obliged to consult the other parent on these occasions. This arrangement is also possible in non-marital situations. It is striking that these statutory changes have come into effect with very little political discussion. When the parliamentary decisions were actually taken, there was relatively little controversy in public opinion and the media paid little attention to the changes. To all appearances it thus seemed that there was little normative conflict in this area. In as far as a political–normative debate has taken place in recent years, this has almost exclusively taken the form of a conflict surrounding the legal interpretation of 'the right to family life' and the question of who this right applies to and what it actually means in concrete terms. Conflicts have thus mainly taken place in courtrooms and legal journals. In other words, the statutory changes have found their justification within the internal normativity of the legal system, or, to express this in political–philosophical terms, the 'right' and the 'good' seem to completely coincide here.

As well as the appeal to human rights, principles of equality and the assumption of an abstract equality between the sexes have played an important role in justifying this transformation. This was made possible by the fact that the issue had come to be dominated by legal arguments, in which people are preferably seen as legal entities or 'persons' rather than individuals with social roles and identities, or as people who are living with moral dilemmas and are engaged in conflictual relationships. Through the application of the equality principle, legal discourse constructs parents as de-gendered 'persons' who can appear before the law, in this capacity, according to their genetic ties with specific children (Sevenhuijsen 1992a). Family law treats these 'parents' *as if* they were equal, something which also happens in other parts of the legal system. Equality thus implies the equal treatment of these 'persons' or consistency between the sexes in the application of legal norms, and rights and duties. This then creates the impression that this extension of equal rights is the final culmination of the process of modernization and emancipation which was instigated by the liberalization process. Indeed, policy texts justify this development by referring to the increasing trend towards social equality between men and women, by emphasizing principles such as freedom, equality and consent, and by speaking in terms of sexually neutral 'parents' (see, for example, Partij van de Arbeid 1995).

These changes in the legal system amount to a new 'regime' in family law; the development has led to what is sometimes called a 'patriarchal reconstruction', a revival of fathers' rights (Holtrust 1988; Sevenhuijsen 1988b; Smart and Sevenhuijsen 1989; Deech 1993; Collier 1995) or the introduction of a new (post-divorce) marriage contract (Smart 1997). The public debate, case law and the proposals for statutory change show that there has been a strengthening of the position of fathers as bearers of rights towards women and children without attention being paid to specific living relationships and the issues of care and power relations in this field.[6] Under the old family law regime, fatherhood was linked to legal marriage. The husband of the mother was considered to be the father of the child and the recognition of a child born outside marriage was directed at making the child legitimate, so that the child could grow up under a father's authority (Sevenhuijsen 1987). In nineteenth-century law this was seen as part of a 'natural order', a legal order in which women and children were placed as far as possible under the authority of men and fathers. After 1905, there was some change because paternal power was changed into parental power; however, it was the father who exercised this during the marriage. After divorce this turned into legal custody, which was exercised by the parent who was granted physical custody of the children. So, after divorce, care and control were united and non-custodial parents did not have any right to access.

After the liberalization of family law, marriage no longer fulfilled the 'function' of creating and guaranteeing fatherhood. The number of divorces rose, as did the number of children born outside wedlock. Single custody meant that the parent who was responsible for and took care of the child (mostly the mother) could lead an independent existence; this was also made possible by the 1965 Social Security Act, which gave divorced women the possibility to receive a payment, albeit minimal, from social assistance. Since then a process has started in legal discourse by which biological ties in themselves are gradually coming to be considered sufficient as a foundation for legal family ties. On the basis of this equal biological contribution, an equality of rights and duties has been constructed as the leading normative principle of family law. Behind the facade of legal equality, however, it is clear that what this actually means is a reinstatement of fatherhood as a legal institution (Holtrust and De Hondt 1986). This 'patriarchal logic' is visible in the legal arguments themselves, in their selectivity and in the social science discourses and media representations which are invoked in order to provide them with legitimacy.[7] Fatherhood is predominantly constructed in terms of rights: as an authoritarian and pedagogic principle which can be justified in functionalist terms. Over and over again it is stated that it is the lack of 'legal protection' of the non-custodial parent that justifies the move towards equal rights. Influential psychologists have supported this with the argument that children need a father to acquire the 'correct' sexual identity or the idea that the presence of fathers guarantees 'natural sexual difference' and therewith the maintaining of social cohesion, socio-political order and a stable public morality.

I will not go into the further details of these changes in family law or the ways in which they came about.[8] Instead I am interested in the structure of the argument in the debate on parental rights and particularly in the various feminist conceptual strategies in relation to this issue; in fact, the issue provides a perfect illustration of the limitations and pitfalls of equal rights reasoning for feminism. At the same time it is also shows how difficult it is for feminist political theory to escape from the discourse of equal rights or to accommodate it in a reflexive and meaningful way within its strategies on family law. Feminist lawyers tend to go along with the terminology of legal argumentation and adopt the norms of equality and freedom. They adopt autonomy, freedom and equality as their principal guidelines without recognizing that this line of reasoning also demonstrates a specific style of moral reasoning.

This in turn means that the hidden assumptions, the normative effects and the moral value of (equal) rights arguments have to be subjected to further scrutiny.[9] To make such reflection possible, I propose interpreting equal rights reasoning as an element in discourses where power, knowledge and language are interconnected and grouped around concepts of 'rights'. I see 'rights' not as something which people 'possess', but as a competence granted to them by the state; thus they are elements in a 'mode of governance', a means of regulating the relationship between a state and its subjects. The granting of rights then becomes a way to create a specific type of subject which in turn is set up as the norm. This is why I use the term 'the regime of family law'. In this respect I have been inspired by the approach to discourse analysis introduced by Michel Foucault, and especially by the way in which poststructuralist theories and methods of interpretation have been received and applied in feminist political theory, and in the sociology and the history of law (see, for example, Sevenhuijsen 1987, 1992a; Scott 1988; Smart 1989, 1992, 1995; Fraser 1989; Fairclough 1992; Collier 1995).

In this approach, law is studied as a discursive domain. Thus, I start from the premiss that legal concepts and legal language are subject to their own regime of truth: they have a systematic inclusionary and exclusionary effect on the way in which social problems are interpreted and incorporated into law. Here I follow English discourse theorist Norman Fairclough, who distinguishes three constructive effects of discourse. First, discourse contributes to the construction of social identities and subject positions. Second, it helps construct social relations between people. And third, it contributes to the construction of systems of knowledge and belief (Fairclough 1992: 64). Carol Smart has proposed examining law as a 'gendering machine', or a series of discourses which produce gender (Smart 1992, 1995). Jurisdiction and legislative processes are continuous forms of 'interpretation-work', but this does not take place arbitrarily. In many respects legal discourse functions autonomously as, for example, in its use of specific definitions and its own system of interpretation and rules for evidence and procedure (Mossman 1986; Goldschmidt 1993; Loenen 1994b). This means that it has a selective effect on what can or cannot be counted as legally relevant information. A 'father', in legal idiom, means something quite different from a 'father' in everyday speech. The term 'unmarried mother' derives its meaning from the fact that such a woman falls outside the scope of what is regarded as legally normal. Though not entirely impossible, it remains difficult to open up legal discourse to new concepts and perspectives. It could be polemically argued that feminist legal politics tends to adapt more easily to the discursive process of the law than the other way around. Feminists can make themselves more easily heard if their approach to the law is from liberal feminist legal politics and from an unproblematical concept of 'woman', than if they adopt a critical or deconstructivist attitude and thus problematize the power effects of the law (Smart 1994; Van den Oord 1994).

It is from this perspective that I will analyse, in this chapter, a number of feminist reactions to the juridification of parenthood outside marriage, paying special attention to the effect of this juridification on the way in which the relationship between care and the law or justice can be conceptualized. I start from the assumption that arguments in this domain are not merely arguments but elements in power strategies. They form a justification for social practices and for political decisions about the distribution of rights and duties. This means that discursive strategies in this field influence the manner in which parenthood and care are framed and can be lived, whereby I conceive of care in the double sense of social practice and moral orientation. This approach should make it possible to analyse a number of the central concepts and normative frameworks of feminist attitudes towards family law in terms of ethics, politics and citizenship. The question of how a state regulates, or should regulate, gender, care and kinship is a citizenship issue *par excellence*, although it is not often posed in these terms. Family law is only rarely recognized in modern political science as a citizenship issue; one has to turn to feminist historical–political literature to find food for thought in this direction (Shanley 1982; Okin 1989; Braun 1992; Sevenhuijsen 1992b; Vogel 1994). Although there are many similarities between legal theory and political philosophy, the traditions of thought and argumentational strategies of the latter discipline are much more 'open'. They are not bound to the legal logic and strict argumentational rules of legal discourse. Political philosophy pays more attention to social contexts and historical traditions as well as to the assumptions and normative effects of different lines of arguments. So, a confrontation between these disciplines can also help to further probe the normative aspects of feminist legal politics and to expose the gender-load inherent in the normative dimensions of family law.

In the rest of this chapter I will first go on to analyse formal equal rights arguments on the question of non-marital parental rights and child custody. I will then examine the extent to which theories of justice can provide an approach which avoids the pitfalls of formal equal rights reasoning. And finally I will discuss the question of whether a feminist ethics of care can open up new perspectives on the politics of custody.

Equal rights arguments

At the beginning of the 1980s the introduction of joint custody confronted feminist legal politics and feminist jurisprudence with a complicated doctrinal problem which, paradoxically enough, was prompted by the fact that feminism now found itself in a defensive position. It was, after all, quite clear that the possibility of joint custody outside marriage had been introduced by invoking the equality principle, although this had not generally been at the instigation of the women's movement and was also, quite obviously, a change which was not always in women's favour. Liberal feminists, traditionally the most influential in the field of legal politics, were thus forced either to defend and further substantiate, or to revise their point of view on the relation between formal equal rights and material equality. In the first instance, liberal feminists tended to justify the introduction of joint custody by means of two arguments. The first argument was that it accorded with the natural equality between men and women, and that, if women themselves were willing to go along with it or consented in it, there was nothing wrong with it. The second line of argument was that it could press men to behave more responsibly towards their children and that the government would thus be setting an example.

This made arguments about the place and function of the law ambiguous. Liberal legal theory of law proceeds primarily from the assumption that the law should follow developments in society and adapt itself to these. This was quite clearly not so in this case, and liberal feminism found itself using an argument in which the law was being used to establish a norm. In fact, the second argument reflects a pedagogic approach to the granting of rights: the government should grant rights, not in order to recognize or establish an existing practice, but in the hope of instigating a change in behaviour and identity, thus demonstrating an instrumentalist argument for the granting of rights.[10] The law should be directed towards establishing or compelling a specific sort of moral subjectivity (that is a sense of responsibility towards children) rather than aligning itself with existing practices. In this mode of reasoning, responsibility has the meaning of ascribed responsibility, or obligation, instead of actual or achieved responsibility. Duties are derived from rights. Thinking about duties and responsibilities is then incorporated within a legal logic, because existing rights serve as a starting-point for normative reasoning. The image of human nature of the liberal ethics of rights thus becomes a yardstick for legal politics.

This approach was supported by the arguments underlying liberal feminist assumptions on the relationship between equality, difference and sameness, and the interaction between these concepts, which motivated the first phase of the second wave of feminism (Thornton 1986; Krieger 1987; Chapter 2 of this volume). In the first place, equal rights strategies are based on the expectation that equal treatment and (the granting of) equal rights will lead to an equal outcome. This outcome can be conceived not only in terms of an equal distribution of resources (for instance, jobs, social security benefits and decision-making processes), but also in terms of an equality in traits or identities, as in the idea that the granting of parental rights would lead to a change in attitude, or a 'moral reform'. This line of reasoning did not remain at the level of diffuse 'expectation', but was later incorporated into normative claims about good and just government policy (Okin 1989; Pessers 1994).

In the second place, the formal liberal argument assumes that there are no basic or 'fundamental' differences between men and women. Sexual difference is only recognized in two respects. First, as biological difference in reproductive capacity that can (or must) be compensated for by public provisions. Second, as difference in attitude and psychological make-up. This second type of difference is considered, in liberal feminism, to be principally the result of sex-role socialization or sexual stereotyping. Because this is regarded as something negative it should be ignored; in fact, according to liberal feminism, this type of difference should be eradicated as soon as possible. This is an extension of the general liberal doctrine that, since all people are born equal, they should also receive equal treatment.

The idea that men and women are born equal but, as it were, 'deformed' by culture has always had a strong appeal for feminists, especially for those feminists of the second wave who adhere to a socialization theory about sexual difference. Recognizing or maintaining special rights for women is hard to argue from this point of view. Arguments for special rights have to contend with the idea that they may contribute to keeping gender differences intact by reinforcing outdated images of womanhood. However, on closer inspection, this line of reasoning seems rather speculative: as long as we can find instances of differential treatment we can go on believing that differences in performance are caused by these differential treatments and that somewhere underneath is hidden a natural 'sameness' (Thornton 1986; Chapters 2 and 3 of this volume). When the sex–gender distinction is linked to a nature–culture dichotomy, support for equal rights appears to be an unshakeable element or even the essential dogma of feminist politics.

From this perspective the most important normative criteria to judge the politics of motherhood was the question of whether policy proposals in this area contributed to the 'abolition of gender' and the stimulation of equality in behaviour and self-image. This attitude is evident, for instance, in the arguments put forward by feminists in the 1970s criticizing the traditional principle of family law, the principle of maternal preference, which gave preference to women in custody conflicts. Liberal feminists supported the abolition of this principle with the argument that it maintained a traditional idea of femininity and proceeded from the false assumption that the law should protect women. Instead of this, they felt the law should assume autonomy and encourage women towards independence and individuality. They had obviously failed to realize that this normative attitude could make the political situation with regard to custody conflicts and custody rules much more complicated for women. In a certain sense they were more concerned with granting political authority to a feminist 'truth' than with the problems, needs and dilemmas of women in specific situations.[11] The power of the law had to be exploited for the abstract goal of changing gender relations, rather than improving the actual situation and legal position of divorced women. Or, as Carol Smart has stated in another context, legal discourse is thus granted the cognitive authority and legitimacy to order and organize daily life (Smart 1995).

The liberal feminist dogma could not provide a clear alternative, because within its framework such an alternative could only lie in the argument that women should have special rights as mothers or, derived from this, on the basis of their 'caring identity'. Within the normativity of equal rights, this was generally linked to conservative thinking in terms of sexual difference.[12] Special rights in liberalism are indeed readily associated with the idiom of natural law and a 'natural condition'. Equal rights reasoning generally proceeds from an atomistic image of human nature, whereby arguments about the characteristics and rights of individuals serve as a starting-point (Mendus 1987; Cavarero 1992). When a normative basis has to be found for special rights for women, it is easy to slip into the argument that women are naturally destined for motherhood, thus becoming entangled in the 'equality–difference dilemma'.[13] This dilemma is inherent in contractarian thinking as embedded in Western legal systems (Pateman 1988, 1992). The basic principle of contract theory is that the law treats people *as if* they are equal. In the public space of legal politics and the courts, people meet each other as equal citizens. Unequal characteristics, whether considered to be of social or natural origin, are merely perceived as deviations from this 'fundamental' equality. Modern political theorists have pointed out that this contractarian doctrine is a device for constructing a situation whereby male property-holders can meet each other as equal citizens before the law (Macpherson 1962). The public sphere as conceptualized in contractarian thinking traditionally supposed a private sphere outside politics: a family under the benign reign of the father, where the principles of contractarian thinking do not directly apply, or apply in a different mode.

The standard liberal feminist reaction to this idea of separate spheres has been to emphasize the fictional character of the boundary between the public and the private and to point to the fact that such a demarcation prevents women from fully exercising their rights as citizens. Against this background, liberal feminists have argued that contractarian thinking and the legal dogmas with regard to equality and equal rights should be extended to the private sphere (see, for example, Okin 1979, 1989; O'Donovan 1985). The open or hidden assumption behind this is that other elements of contractarian thinking should be applied in the same way to all aspects of gender relations, particularly concepts of abstract individualism and the rationalist thinking which dominate liberal legal politics and normative political theory. In the later critique of liberal feminism, this normative attitude has been criticized by pointing out that a mode of legal and moral reasoning developed in the sphere of property relations was being transferred to all aspects of the relationship between men and women, without questions being asked about its effects or about whether these assumptions were appropriate for the regulation of intimate relationships.

The American philosopher Janet Farell Smith has argued that dominant ideologies about the rights and duties of parenthood are influenced by a father-related property model (Smith 1984). In this property model, rights are seen in terms of ownership, entitlement, interest and control. They are primarily interpreted as claims or entitlements to do or to have something, while excluding others' claims to these things. Rights are thus enforceable demands, put forward by a detached individual, who creates relationships by laying legal claims (see also Held 1987b, 1989a; Nedelsky 1990). This property model has its roots in property law, but also in the patriarchal family and patriarchal family law, in which the main rights and duties of fatherhood were shaped around concepts such as inheritance, maintenance and the construction of absolute control over women and children (see also Sevenhuijsen 1987). In another context, the philosopher Onora O'Neill has stated that the rights discourse is inherently stamped by a reifying language, which suggests 'that there is some good which the holder of a right is entitled to hold or possess, as though rights were a species of property right'. She says that if (human) rights are taken as a starting point for normative reasoning, the correlation between rights and obligations is ignored and rights discourse becomes the language of people laying claims to something from which they feel they have been excluded (O'Neill, 1986: 117–118). This mode of reasoning can lead to a one-sided 'juridification of daily life' (Sevenhuijsen 1992a; Van den Burg 1993) or an 'externalizing of morality' (Reinders 1994). According to this legalistic ethics, people only have to consider each other when they are compelled to do so by legally established rights and duties. For the rest of the time they can behave as 'self-interested individuals' who can decide for themselves how they will shape the space allowed to them by law. As the Canadian political theorist Jennifer Nedelsky has stated: we can shut ourselves off from the suffering of others, as long as we can tell ourselves that we are acting 'within our rights'. As long as we can continue to believe that 'rights' define our obligations as well as our entitlements, and believe that we have violated no one's rights, we can maintain the illusion that we are doing nothing wrong in our daily non-responsiveness (Nedelsky 1990: 183). An exclusive adherence to an ethics of rights can indeed prevent us from admitting the existence of thorny moral dilemmas, thus also covering up the 'fragility of goodness', to borrow Martha Nussbaum's concept (Nussbaum 1986).

This 'bounded' and property-related style of reasoning can also be seen in recent debates on the reform of child custody, especially in the legal reasoning inspired by fathers' rights movements. Children are perceived as entities to be possessed and the law has the duty to guarantee access to them, even if this is against the interest of others. Along with this, images are often conjured up of malevolent mothers wanting to possess their children and who, by definition, will deny them their right to a father. The fathers' rights movement and the lawyers supporting them have appealed to the 'rights and duties' ethos of the contractarian model: if the government obliges men to pay, then in return they should be granted visiting rights. The popular media have combined this line of reasoning with stories about 'greedy mothers', who are eager to accept money, but shirk all other responsibilities.[14] Divorced fathers and the lobby groups supporting them have always found a willing ear in the media for these kinds of stories, and journalists have been remarkably reluctant to air the other side of the story. The public image thus created acquires political overtones when it is combined with deep-seated fears about radical feminists bent on creating a matriarchal society (Graycar 1989).[15]

Justice and the (re)distribution of care

In reaction to new legal practices and the limitations of equal rights reasoning, feminists have developed a line of reasoning which can be characterized as a revisionist liberal argument. This states that to award rights to men as fathers in situations where women are responsible for children's care is in conflict with the principles of justice. Men and women would then formally be granted equal rights in a situation of material inequality. This line of reasoning can be interpreted as a mixture of conventional justice arguments and Marxist ideas on the relation between labour and control. The conventional Aristotelian justice argument says that it is unjust to treat unequal people in an equal way. Equal rights and equal treatment should only be accorded to people in an equal position. However, when stated in this way, the argument contains all the risks associated with naturalist thinking concerning women as mothers.

To avoid these pitfalls, revisionist liberalism argues that child care is a socially constructed form of labour and that its gender-laden character is the result of social circumstances. Compared to formal equal rights reasoning, this argument contains a number of important advantages. It supports the application of the 'primary caretaker principle' in custody conflicts: the principle that the parent who has provided daily care during marriage is the parent who, after divorce, can lay a greater claim to the right to care for the child and thus to legal custody. It also allows for arguments about the importance of continuity in child care and in children's primary relations. Similarly, it can do justice to situations in which men are the primary carers, or in which women choose, after divorce, not to lay claim to their children and prefer to allow their children to be brought up by their father.

This argument thus accords in many respects with crude measures of social justice: it provides a counterbalance to judgements in which men and women are seen as fixed groups and judged solely according to their sexual difference, while it also gives women a fair amount of protection in what is still predominantly a woman's job (Sandberg 1989). This reasoning can be supported with a further argument about social justice, namely, that decisions about the living conditions of children are closely tied up with the life-plans and lifestyles of those who care for them: decisions about place of residence, choice of school and financial expenditure are difficult to share with someone with whom one is not on good terms or who has very little to do with the daily business of raising the child. Such reasoning in terms of social justice, in contrast to formal equal rights arguments, does not dismiss arguments on the grounds of 'protection' or 'unequal treatment' *a priori* as traditional or old fashioned. Rather, it attempts to weigh up the relevant arguments and see where the social circumstances of child care provide a reason for deviating from an approach in terms of formal equality.

The problem with reasoning in terms of justice lies rather at the normative level: the attempt to find the 'ideal' social situation or a 'just' society. In the social justice discourse this crops up as the question of when 'true' equality will finally be introduced. This question will continue to be posed as long as the principle of equal rights remains the central normative criterion against which all other forms of legal politics must be measured. According to the advocates of revisionist liberalism, the present situation may be maintained but only in expectation of a future time in which the social relations around labour and care have been so equalized between the sexes as to allow the principle of equal rights to be introduced without a problem, a time when 'equal distribution' is the yardstick. The question remains, however, of whether revisionist liberalism has the potential to introduce a more positive and less defensive political vocabulary on the issue of child care into the public debate on the reform of family law, and whether existing theories of justice are able to provide a solution to the issue of just family law. This issue can be approached by examining whether an application of John Rawls's theory of distributive justice can contribute to a just solution of the political controversy surrounding child custody (Rawls 1971). Rawls's theory, although not itself explicitly applied to custody issues, still displays many similarities with revisionist liberal arguments on this issue.

Appeals to nature have no place in the Rawlsian style of reasoning; citizens are addressed as disinterested and impartial persons. This makes the theory attractive to modern feminists trying to escape from and to undermine arguments about innate capacities and provide legitimacy for gender-neutral thinking about justice, especially in the context of parenthood.[16] Rules concerning the distribution of rights, goods, opportunities and other resources have to be argued along rationalist lines, in accordance with the principles of justice. According to Rawls's first and most fundamental principle of justice, everybody has an equal right to certain basic freedoms, such as freedom of conscience and opinion, freedom of association and assembly, and freedom of suffrage. These are liberal freedom rights: political rights enabling everyone to fully participate in the concluding of the social contract. In his second principle of justice, Rawls formulates the rules enabling a choice to be made between equal and unequal treatment. Unequal social and economic treatment is justified on two conditions: first, that it favours those who are less 'well off', and second, that it is connected to functions and positions that are open to everybody by a system of fair and equal opportunities, so that everyone can participate in the competition for social goods.

Any attempt – even just a thought experiment – to apply these principles to the political debate on child custody, as outlined above, immediately shows the limitations of Rawlsian justice reasoning in this field.[17] The extension of the Rawlsian vocabulary into this domain brings with it the same disadvantages which were encountered in the analysis of formal equal rights reasoning. The vocabulary of property rights marks both these ways of thinking. Rawls developed his principles of justice for taking decisions about the distribution of freedom rights, material goods and social services; it is questionable whether these same principles can be applied to issues of culture, power, identity and intimate relations (Young 1990a). Applying this approach to the social–liberal argument about care and custody leads to many problems, which I will summarize point by point below.

In the first place, it has to be decided who are the 'less well off'. The answer to this depends to a large extent on the perspective one takes and the standpoint from which one reasons. It could be argued, for instance, that women, at least until recently, have never had an equal share in parental rights, so they need to catch up arrears in this respect. On the other hand, one could equally well argue that it is men who are the losers in respect to custody, because they are less often awarded physical custody over their children after divorce or because women start from a more advantageous position in the first place, since they are the ones who can actually bear children. Arguing from this point of view, it would then be fair if men were more often awarded child custody in situations of conflict. Indeed, the granting of parental rights outside marriage could also be defended along Rawlsian lines. There are thus no easy solutions to be had in this respect.

To apply the principles of distributive justice to the politics of child custody it must of course be clear, in the second place, what is at stake in custody politics. This is a highly debatable question. If it is simply a matter of the distribution of rights, which rights, exactly, are these? And what is it that is being distributed – children? Can children, or the ability to have a relationship with them, be counted as 'primary goods' in the Rawlsian sense? Rawls himself does not view children in this light. In *A Theory of Justice* (1971) he mentions children on two occasions (English 1977; Kearns 1983). First when he asks himself whether we can assume that minors are bound by the social contract. His answer is that, in this respect, children are represented by the head of the family. Apart from this, he also mentions children, following the classical tradition of thought in liberal political theory, in the context of transference of goods and morality between the generations. Here, having and maintaining children is constructed as an important motive for people to acquire income and possessions. Rawls also sees the family as the place where children develop a 'feeling of love', a feeling which is important for the reciprocal relationships within which decisions about the principles of justice and the content of the social contract are taken.[18] Now it may well be possible to stretch the Rawlsian perspective to include the bond with children as a 'primary good', but such a statement overlooks the question of whether it is morally justified to see children as entities to which people can claim rights, which is what an approach in terms of primary goods would quickly lead to.

In the third place, the level at which the justice arguments apply needs to be specified: are we concerned here with individual conflicts about guardianship and custody, or political decisions about the content of family law? Individual and collective dimensions of rights are often confused in discussions about

103

custody. In this context it should be remembered that Rawlsian arguments are meant as a guideline for reaching collective decisions on broad rules of distribution, in order to determine whether social systems are just or not. In the political debate about custody, feminists, it is true, use Rawlsian arguments primarily at a collective level, in the sense that the law should not be changed as long as mothers are the main carers. The weakness of this argument, however, is that it then becomes difficult to specify when the moment has arrived when change *is* acceptable. Should that be quantitatively determined: for example when a certain percentage of men are responsible for the daily care of children? Even then there will undoubtedly still be individual conflicts which demand just decision-making. The Rawlsian principles leave us empty-handed when it comes to deciding what is just in specific situations. In my opinion, the argument of the primary caretaker will always continue to serve a purpose in conflict situations. It would thus be better to continue 'making do' with an approach in terms of social justice without going on to take the further, logical step of assuming an ideal image in terms of distributive justice.

Fourth, an (imaginary) application of Rawlsian thinking makes it clear that a political theory which completely distances itself from an embodied subjectivity is inadequate when it comes to the politics of child custody. Such a vocabulary excludes the possibility of speaking in terms of the reproductive differences between women and men. Here we can see the drawbacks of the nature–culture dichotomy at their sharpest. Applying Rawlsian concepts in this area, it immediately becomes clear that the 'functions and positions' in regard to childbirth are bodily differentiated. On the one hand, it is quite easy – and in many respects valuable – to design a Rawlsian scheme of compensatory inequalities in order to attain more equality with respect to child care: public child-care provisions, shorter working days, maternity or paternity leave for both parents. However, on the other hand, it is important that feminist theory does not concentrate *too* much on a moral language of equality. In any case, equality should be differentiated from 'sameness', or becoming identical, as has been argued in earlier chapters of this book. If this distinction is overlooked, it can easily be forgotten that motherhood is a lived identity and in many respects a specifically feminine experience. Issues concerning pregnancy and childbirth clearly affect men and women differently and will continue to do so unless a future is envisaged in which men can become pregnant, give birth and breastfeed thanks to genetic engineering. Indeed, there are people who feel that this vision of the future is close at hand, making a 'true' equality between the sexes possible (Badinter 1988). The ease with which this idea is welcomed is striking. Obviously the medical and political risks of genetic engineering seem worth enduring for the fulfilment of a contested ideal, which could just as well be described as an inability to deal with sexual difference and embodied subjectivity in a woman-friendly and meaningful way (Cavarero 1992; Schott 1993; Sevenhuijsen 1995; Gatens

1996). Proposals like this in fact come down to an endeavour at 'engineering' the subject in a homogeneous way, in accordance with the universalist ethical codes of modernity.

And last, but certainly not least, the application of a Rawlsian vocabulary gives little indication of what is *un*just in the present politics of custody. The issue remains framed as a problem of distribution, which can be solved by universal, abstract reasoning. The Rawlsian discourse offers little space for deliberating on the claims of specific groups who experience injustice in specific contexts (Shklar 1990). Nor does it provide space for deliberating on the moral worth or political background of the concept of a 'right to family life'. The universalist pretensions of Rawls's theory of justice and the epistemological device that supports this (the veil of ignorance) exclude claims from specific groups by labelling them as 'particularistic'. Or, as the philosopher Seyla Benhabib has stated: the form of moral deliberation of Kantian justice reasoning excludes thinking in terms of difference because it presupposes a 'generalized other' who is identical to the moral actor (Benhabib 1987). Not only differences are excluded from this moral deliberation; the ideal of abstract reasoning also excludes power and subordination as relevant concepts (Sevenhuijsen 1986; Young 1990a; Cavarero 1992). The application of contractarian thinking gives the illusion that issues of parenting can be decided in a power-free space. Thus, we are deprived of the conceptual means of perceiving and analysing family law itself as a strategic field of power relations and discursive apparatus; nor are we enabled to review the historical context and political tensions within which arguments are mobilized, applied and awarded significance.[19] Arguments about fatherhood as a legal institution, about the limited power of women in the legal system or about the institutionalized mistrust of women and the symbolically feminine embodied in law are thus placed 'outside the order of discourse'.

In short, it makes little sense to extend the application of the Rawlsian principles of justice to the politics of custody. Fitting this issue into the paradigm of distributive justice would create more problems than it solves. Indeed, the simpler approaches of social justice seem more appropriate here. In addition, the paradigm of distributive justice allows no satisfactory discursive space for thinking about the relation between care and justice; this is a problem which is connected to the moral epistemology, social ontology and image of human nature in Rawlsian contractarian thinking, in which care is continually subordinated to justice and the law. This is clear, for example, in the argument that a good family is necessary for a good political contract. Contractarian thinking is also marked by methodological individualism: abstract individuals are the entities in its imaginary social world. These individuals are, in the first instance, constructed as owners of rights, as persons carrying rights: a person is someone who has rights, and possession of rights is what makes someone a 'person'. This can then serve as the starting-point for deriving duties. Or, conversely: if the state demands duties, then it should also grant rights. Legal discourse thus remains trapped in circular arguments of an ethics in terms of duties and rights.

Because the image of human nature inherent to contractarian thinking is based on a 'bounded self' (a detached individual guided by enlightened self-interest), care and its accompanying relational perspective tend to be left out of the contractual discourse; at best, they form a subsidiary argument. Legal discourse, which rests on contractarian thinking, closes itself off from arguments to do with care; it creates almost no discursive space for the 'voice' of care or groups who speak with that voice (Conley and O'Barr 1990; Reinders 1994; Verkerk 1994, 1995, 1996; Loenen 1995b). This atomistic view of human nature assumes that the identities of contract-bound individuals are separate from the relationships which have formed them and that affectivity and relationships are not relevant in the normative model of moral reasoning. Because the freedom of individuals to realize their goals is the overriding moral value in the liberal rights discourse, there is no moral space for thinking in terms of what it means to lead a meaningful life or for notions of connectedness to others. By taking the image of the free, choosing individual as its normative image of the human subject, the discourse of rights, in fact, upholds an attitude of moral indifference, or carelessness, to issues such as these. Because the moral agent is assumed to be detached from his or her situatedness and connections, he or she is *unable* to reflect on moral dilemmas in relation to concrete others. The discourse of equal rights lacks the potential to recognize as fully moral the considerations of those who 'deviate' from its standard subjectivity and instead tends to disqualify their moral considerations. This applies for example to women who are struggling with the moral dilemma of whether to stay in or leave an abusive marriage or a marriage that simply fails to satisfy their need for a loving and caring relationship. Often these women tend to stay because they experience complicated dilemmas between their own need to leave and their children's need to remain with their father. Carol Smart and Bren Neale have shown that women who finally decide on divorce, and thus have to break the daily relationship with the father, are easily disqualified as 'acting immorally' (Smart and Neale 1997b). Their analysis shows that legal discourse neglects or undermines 'ordinary people's' confidence in making moral decisions. According to Smart and Neale, most of the divorced parents they interviewed were 'competent moral philosophers, who did not need lessons in how to approach moral dilemmas'. Rather than abandoning moral values they were going through a process of 'balancing' different needs and obligations and were negotiating a route through competing value judgements.

A contractarian way of thinking prevents us from posing questions about how to proceed in specific situations involving the care of children, both at the individual as well as the collective level. Contractarian thinking also forms a barrier to developing, within the public debate, a moral sensibility to the diversity of social problems and moral perspectives which can occur in relation to care and responsibility for children, just as it leaves little space for moral reflection about dependency (Tronto 1993; Kittay 1995). It provides insufficient points of departure for deliberating and arguing on the question of which are good and just forms of behaviour in relation to caring for and forming relationships with children, and how we can reach a responsible set of rules in this area which can apply to specific social practices of care.

The ethics of care and responsibility

Against this background, the feminist ethics of care might be able to provide new perspectives on the politics of custody, provided that it is carefully inter-preted and that we take care not to become entangled in the controversies surrounding sexual difference in moral reasoning (see also Clement 1996). The ethics of care, as argued in previous chapters, is a specific form of ethics which can also imply new types of normativity. This interpretation offers a better approach for mobilizing various ideas from the care ethics debate in public deliberations about child care and custody than thinking in terms of female or male forms of morality, or maintaining that women are better at caring than men. Following Joan Tronto, I start from the premiss that the ethics of care differs in three respects from what Carol Gilligan has described as an ethics of rights (Tronto 1987: 648). First of all, the ethics of care involves different moral concepts: responsibilities and relationships rather than rules and rights. Second, it is bound to concrete situations rather than being formal and abstract. And third, the ethics of care can be described as a moral activity, the 'activity of caring', rather than as a set of principles which can simply be followed. The central question in the ethics of care – how to deal with dependency and responsibility – differs radically from that of rights ethics: what are the highest normative principles and rights in situations of moral conflict? Various authors have compared the ethics of care and its accompanying moral epistemology with the moral theory of authors in the tradition of the eighteenth-century Scottish enlightenment, such as David Hume and Adam Smith. A number of feminist philosophers have reread Hume's work and compared it to that of other moral traditions, in order to assess its value for a feminist moral theory (Baier 1987, 1993; Merill 1994; see also Werkman 1993; Reinders 1994). I will summarize a number of points which could be relevant for political decision-making on care and custody.

According to Hume, and here he differs from Kant, ethics is not a matter of obeying universal laws or developing a general argument which can identify such laws; rather, it involves cultivating specific character traits, and in par-ticular a 'corrected sympathy'. Hume finds the source of moral reasoning to lie, not in universal rules, but in a combination of instrumental reason, self-interest, custom and historical chance. The best moral stance is to participate in a community and to communicate opinions and feelings. Morality depends more on context-bound opinions than on universal reason. Hume does not exclude desires and emotional needs from moral reasoning, provided they are corrected by reflection, self-control and social discipline. His work thus belongs to the tradition of virtue-ethics. An important point to note in relation to this is that moral respect is not derived from legal personhood. Morality is not based on respecting other people's rights, but on the ability to recognize their individuality. People do not exist as individuals, but in their ability to be recognized by others, for example by being able express their feelings to each other. Morality is thus bound to social practices and customs, and to people's feelings and motives. Through knowing others one can deliberate on feelings and opinions, and thus 'corrected sympathy', the hallmark of good judgement, can be realized.

Hume's moral philosophy and Kantian theory are diametrically opposed when it comes to the question of which problem morality is supposed to solve. For Kantians and other contractarians the main problem is that of the relation between freedom and autonomy on the one hand and obedience to political and legal authority on the other. The principal problems of Kantian thinking are thus those of legitimacy: contract has to mediate and solve the paradox between individual freedom and collective duties. In Hume's moral theory, on the other hand, the moral tensions and ambivalences to be solved are both intrapersonal as well as interpersonal: the contradiction, conflict and instability which can present themselves within any one person's individual desires over time as well as conflicts between people. Morality points to the issue of how to minimize oppositions of interests, how to arrange life so that sympathy and not hostile comparison will be the principle relating our desires to those of our fellow human beings. Whereas in the contractarian model morality regulates and arbitrates opposing interests, in a Humean view morality's main task is to rearrange situations so that interests are no longer by definition opposed.

Implications of the ethics of care

Without embracing a Humean approach to morality altogether, I would like to say that these ideas can provide various openings to the public debate on child custody. I will again describe its implications in a number of steps. My starting-point is that moral problems can be expressed in different ways, according to the moral vocabulary used; the definition of the problem thus forms part of the moral deliberation. Thinking in terms of virtue-ethics would urge us to frame moral problems of parenthood and custody in such a way that the interests of men and women are no longer seen as fundamentally opposed. Or, in political terms: which forms of collective responsibility and institutional virtue are necessary to make the relationship with and authority over children into a less contested and 'gender-antagonized' issue?[20] The key to this lies in the main proposition of the ethics of care: what is the best way to deal with dependency, vulnerability and responsibility in specific situations? In the context of parenthood, this question refers directly to the moral meaning of reproductive sexual difference. In an individualistic rights ethics this difference is usually described in the seemingly objective statement that women become pregnant and bear children while men 'donate the sperm'. The next question is then which rights and duties men and women can derive from this biological 'truth'.

A relational ethics of care formulates the problem differently. Because dependency and responsibility are of primary importance, a care ethics perspective proceeds from the question of how the fundamental dependency between the sexes in the area of reproduction and relationships with children should be approached and which social ordering would meet the criteria of the 'good life', responsibility and justice. Just as women are not anxious to be reduced to 'walking wombs', so also it is difficult to morally justify describing men as 'sperm donors'. Biological 'facts' have no meaning in themselves, but acquire meaning within discourses and social practices. In the ethics of care the asymmetry in the sexual and existential dependency between the sexes is exactly what constitutes the essential moral problem. Women need men to become pregnant, but men need a relationship with a woman in order to form a relationship with a child. For both 'parties' this dependency also involves vulnerability, although the nature of this is different in each case. Feminine vulnerability consists, for example, in easily becoming pregnant through sexual intercourse and being primarily responsible for the consequences of this: pregnancy, childbirth and primary child care. Women can only share this care and responsibility if others are willing to do so and if promises and commitments in this respect are fulfilled. Women and men land up in all kinds of forms of mutual dependence when they have children together and want to care for these children in a relational context, whatever form that may take. The exact situation a woman finds herself in will depend on whether she is married or not and whether or not she has chosen to become a mother. Marriage in itself, however, is no guarantee against vulnerability, among other things because of its imbalance of power between men and women implied in current marriage practices and family law. Because of the uncertainties of life, the relations surrounding child care can often take a different form than expected. Responsibility for children thus creates a mutual dependency between women and men, and of course children themselves are also dependent on a satisfactory regulation of care and responsibility.

Feminist arguments often overlook these complex existential problems, for example, through their unwillingness to discuss the reproductive difference between the sexes in normative terms or to interpret motherhood as a relationship, rather than an identity. Feminist discourse still tends to display traces of the radical-feminist image of society, in which it is argued that, historically, men have transformed their fear of dependency and the potential power of women into an urge to control women's reproductive capacity through marriage rights (Rich 1976; O'Brian 1981; Corea 1985). The only solution is then for women to become independent of men. When feminist political judgement starts from an image of men driven by fear and aggression it can soon end up with a Hobbesian view of society, but then in a feminist version. According to Hobbes, social contract and strong political hierarchical authority are needed in order to keep fear and the aggression which accompanies it under control. In the Hobbesian view the 'state of nature' preceding this contract consists not of families, but of individuals, which is the reason why feminists have often called on his idea of an 'original equality'. Indeed, it is not difficult to imagine the Hobbesian person as a male driven by fear and aggression, as someone who is unwilling to grant moral accountability to the fact that people are 'of woman born'. According to the political philosopher Carol Pateman, the liberal contract can best be seen as a contract between brothers, preceded by sexual aggression and rape (Pateman 1988).

If this line of thought is followed to its logical conclusion, one would soon arrive at a legal system in which the primary objective is the protection of women against male oppression. This would in fact amount to a form of 'feminist foundationalism'. This would imply that women always have the 'first right' to children. The problem with such reasoning is that it is informed by a fixed image of masculinity and femininity, with – as a reflection of this – women being seen as a special interest group. Although this approach is linked to a critique of contractarian thinking, it still remains within its parameters: feminist legal politics should aim at a 'woman-friendly' contract, in which women are fully accepted as independent individuals. Contractarian thinking continually leads to the dilemma of whether women and men should be viewed as individuals or as a social group. In the Hobbesian image of human nature, 'rights' function as a guarantee of autonomous personhood, as a safeguard against dependency. The government then has the obligation to conceive of people as 'legal individuals' and to give them the possibility of asserting rights against others while, at the same time, protecting them against the claims of others; or it may play an intermediary role. This is why the feminist versions of contractarian thinking so easily slip into thinking in terms of conflicting interests between men and women as social groups, thus resulting in claims for a strong constitutional state, where the power of the law is extended to nearly every aspect of human life (see, for example, West 1988; MacKinnon 1989).[21]

The feminist ethics of care, as argued for in this book, provides a different moral perspective on this issue, because it starts from the premiss of an existential situation of mutual dependency, without attaching a negative value to this, and without thinking in terms of an opposition between dependency and autonomy (see also Manschot 1994; Verkerk 1996). If we start from the idea that the potential to maintain intimate relations and care for others is an important formative human value, a different sort of collective responsibility can be expected from public provisions and political regulations. In a care ethics perspective, instead of guaranteeing men authority rights to protect them from a (potential) dependency on women, the government should see its primary task as enabling men to build intimate and caring relationships with women and children, by making this possible in terms of time, space and material resources. This would imply that a more satisfactory distribution of labour and care between men and women would be a political priority. When care is re-evaluated and freed from its gender-load and its associations with sexual difference, it also becomes a less daunting and more attractive proposition for men to identify with care and to adopt a caring identity.[22]

This is not a plea for 'compulsory love', as contained in proposals for a 'care duty', which, according to some observers, governments should enforce in the interests of emancipation. The concept of a 'care duty' remains, in fact, within the tradition of contractarian thinking. Or, as Marian Verkerk has argued, friendship, connectedness, intimacy, dignity and respect are not needs which can be claimed, but needs which are necessary to allow a truly human existence (Verkerk 1994: 69). The feminist ethics of care can lead to a rethinking of obligations in the direction of responsibility as well as reflection on how responsibilities and obligations can be realized in conditions of uncertainty and instability (Hirschmann 1992). In the ethics of care, the central moral issue is not 'what am I obliged to do, in general terms?' but 'how should I deal with dependency and responsibility?' The political corollary of this is government policy which creates necessary conditions rather than imposing obligations. In this sense, the feminist ethics of care leads us continually to reconsider and redraw the boundaries between justice, morality and politics. An appeal for strong authority does not fit in with this, whether it be the authority of fathers, governments or a combination of these.

A parallel government obligation should be to support women in their responsibility for children and to make satisfactory forms of shared care possible, both within the context of intimate relationships as well as through collective provisions. This can also be argued in terms of the vulnerability which goes together with pregnancy and child care, and the need to protect women from the disadvantages arising from this in the organization of labour in instrumentalist, achievement-oriented cultures and its strict patterns of time allocation. Certainly, in the postmodern condition, in which professional labour, the means of sustaining life and interpersonal relations are organized in new ways, and in which priority is given to flexibility and plurality, the objectives of the ethics of care should contribute to leading a 'good life'. However, because of the vulnerability and fragility of intimate relations, this moral claim is less easy to justify in legal terms than an abstract norm of equality. It is also more difficult to implement, even if only because of the problems arising from the inflexibility of power relations in the labour market. It is difficult to develop a caring masculine identity because, among other things, the collective cultural images of 'masculine' self-fulfilment are so tied to career, self-sufficiency, invulnerability and an existence in the public sphere. However, the fragility and uncertainty of the ethics of care also demonstrates its importance and points to the necessity of 'judging with care' when we pose the question of where and how legal rules should take account of care as a social practice and human need.

A collective attitude on this basis would not only improve intimate relations and the distribution of care between women and men, but would also cast new light on the issue of post-divorce child custody. If it becomes possible for children to maintain caring relationships with both parents during marriage, decisions surrounding separation and divorce will acquire different dimensions. A mutual bond developed through daily care may help to guarantee the continuation of a relationship in a new situation, or to make it easier to find new ways of shaping relationships which are mutually acceptable. The question of who has legal authority is then of less importance, because the exercising of authority is no longer a means of enforcing something on others. This allows another dimension of parental authority to come to the fore: the question of which parent is primarily regarded as responsible by external bodies in relation to the child's upbringing and education. Regulations concerning parental authority can then indeed be seen as ways of regulating the relations between the state and its subjects.

Where there is mutual agreement on upbringing and living conditions, parental authority can just as easily be single or shared. In this respect, the granting of shared authority by legislators can be interpreted as a symbolic gesture, a means of restoring 'rights' to parents who are first constructed as 'being deprived of rights', and a way to set up a norm of abstract equality and good consultation between parents. The critical perspective of the ethics of care makes clear that the public debate about access rights and child custody is still influenced by the patriarchal view that, for men, connections can only be achieved by enforceable rights. A collective mistrust of the legal independence of women and their moral agency overshadows moral trust in people's ability to solve problems for themselves within a relational context.

When fathers take care of children it also makes it easier for them to develop an orientation towards an ethics of care and to empathize with others and their needs. This makes them better equipped to take account of children's experience in their moral deliberations about the way they run their lives and in the way they describe and deal with the moral dilemmas which they encounter. By this I do not wish to suggest that developing a caring moral orientation is dependent on a 'fifty-fifty' sharing of child care. An empathetic moral attitude can be fostered in many different ways: there is no linear connection between the number of hours that people take care of others and their ability to develop a caring orientation. One can think and argue about the ethics of care without necessarily fully participating in the practice of care. This is one of the reasons why simply arguing for an equal sharing of care and paid labour is not enough. A minimal assumption is that there is a willingness to listen to the moral deliberations of those who care or to pay adequate attention to one's own 'caring voice'; it also means creating the discursive space for this in the different forms of judgement on issues of care. Another important condition is that academic moral and political philosophy allows room for the care perspective and the plea which it makes for a new understanding of issues such as dependency, individuality and autonomy (Nedelsky 1988; Tronto 1993; Young 1995). This in turn implies that a revision of the conceptual framework of authority, as expressed in family law, is long overdue.

Compassionate authority

Traditions in political theory about authority can be of help in analysing legal concepts of authority. In the patriarchal tradition in political theory, authority is conceived in terms of sovereignty, as the capacity to generate the obedience of others, and as the condition for being a 'self-governing subject'. Judging with authority assumes that one stands above a situation, free of relationships and intimate ties. In this sense, thinking in terms of authority certainly rules out care as a relevant factor. Feminist thinkers have argued that this concept of authority is based on the construction of an autonomous will and a detached self. This means that representations of the autonomous subject are symbolically linked to a masculine self and the symbolism of the father. Fatherhood and authority are thus linked at the symbolic–metaphoric level, an image in which the father rights play an important role (De Kanter 1987; Dimen 1987; Mulder 1987, 1988). Care and dependency are not absent in this subject ideal, but emerge in the form of a repressed fear of both dependency and fusion as well as in the fear of rejection by the mother. Symbols of gender are thus actually contained within dominant conceptions of authority such as 'self-control', and in the combination of fear and desire which these embody.

From this perspective, femininity is certainly not absent in the law and citizenship. In fact, at a symbolic level, it is present in many ways, though often in a secondary and repressed manner, and as something which needs to be kept under control (Coltheart 1986; Keller 1986; Eisenstein 1988; Pateman 1989; Nedelsky 1990; Cavarero 1992; Scheman 1993; Van den Oord 1994). Authority and care presuppose each other, but in the dualistic patriarchal conception of authority this is undermined by an internal barrier, through mechanisms which Val Plumwood has termed 'hyper-separation, backgrounding and denial' (Plumwood 1993; see also Chapter 5, note 11 of this volume). According to Kathleen Jones, this authoritarian image is linked to an instrumentalist vision of political life and collective agency and to a model of appropriation of otherness (Jones 1993; Chapter 4; see also Cavarero 1992; Plumwood 1993). In public life, social integration and stable social interaction are pursued through the attribution of authoritarian rights. Authority thus serves as a shield against the threats of social contact and social interaction.[23] Situations governed by the rule of authority are necessary as protection against intimate contact. The seemingly disembodied, autonomous subject who exercises authority thus does this in order to close himself off from the vulnerable aspects of human life: natality, nurture, finiteness, insecurity, ambiguity and fragility. Conceptions of authority which repress and exclude the capacity for caring and compassion with others thus contain a dimension of destruction, dominance or domination (Sennet 1981; Benjamin 1988).

In contrast to this, Jones posits the concept of 'compassionate authority', a caring or 'empathic' authority, inspired by the work of the political theorist Hannah Arendt. According to Jones, compassionate authority reveals that which remains hidden in authoritarian conceptions of authority: the accident of being born and being dependent for one's existence on a woman's body and a woman's dedication. Through its recognition of dependency, compassionate authority has a creative and positive connotation associated with the ability to act and be creative. It is linked to the capacity and willingness to recognize the other *as other*, as different from the self, as possessing individual desires and needs. Because this implies a recognition of ambiguity, compassionate authority accepts instability as inherent to human social practices. Instead of trying to control this instability through the false security of contract, it takes – in the spirit of Arendt and the neo-republican version of virtue-ethics – communicative values as its starting-point in the regulation of human interactions and, in particular, moral attitudes such as representative thinking, promising, forgiveness, attentive love and beginning anew (natality) (see also Elshtain 1992).[24] This means that care too can then be liberated from thinking in terms of binding authority, legal power and legal obligation, and – above all – from its association with oppositional logic. Thinking about relationships, dependency, intimacy, eroticism and sexuality could then gain a more positive place in ethics and in conceptions of democratic citizenship (see also Young 1983, 1990a, 1990b, 1995; Hirschmann 1992; James 1992; Vegetti Finzi 1992; Frazer and Lacey 1993; Tronto 1993).[25] This diminishes the contractarian dilemma of whether to obey a central authority or one's own conscience, because compassionate authority is based on interaction and dialogue, and on the ability to reach judgements through consideration of different perspectives. This is why it is so important that political ethics moves away from the symbolic power of fatherhood, instead of retreating into the safety and security of outdated symbols of patriarchal authority.[26]

On both an individual and collective level, this perspective of compassionate authority can instigate new ways of describing and dealing with the moral dilemmas arising from broken relationships and different solutions for maintaining relationships with children than merely the claiming of rights to access or authority, or the legal honouring of such claims. The acceptance of a care ethics perspective also implies assuming a responsibility not to hurt others unnecessarily and not to saddle them with impossible problems and dilemmas. This moral orientation is apparent, for instance, in the stories of mothers who voluntarily entrust the care of their children to the father after divorce. From these stories it is apparent that, although emotionally torn, these women often become convinced after some time that this solution is best for their own lives and need not entail losing a bond with their children; living arrangements in such cases may take a variety of different, and perhaps untraditional, forms (Franks 1990; Thooft 1992; Van Hennik 1996). Acting according to the ethics of care can mean waiving one's claims to rights over children, because they are incompatible with the children's needs.

It is indeed the difference between 'caring about' and 'taking care of' that can clarify moral dilemmas in situations like this. 'Caring about' may lead one to refrain from enforcing 'rights' to 'taking care of' and allow space for moral trust that spontaneous forms of contact may be restored after some time. This implies, however, an ability to live with uncertainty. This observation also underlines the idea that moral agency does not necessarily imply that one should always 'do something': it can also imply refraining from action. It can also mean making concessions in one's career or mobility after divorce, in order to remain near children and maintain a relationship with them. Values such as continuity, clarity and providing the conditions for trust, which are crucial in relationships with children, are indeed inherent to the thinking of the first proponents of the ethics of care such as Sarah Ruddick (1989). Reasoning in the terms proposed in this book underlines the idea that it is not contact and access themselves which are the problem. In fact, an ethics of care would support the idea that a continuation of the relationship between divorced parents and children is, in principle, desirable. It is, however, the legal enforcement of contact in situations where this may be considered harmful and the legal presumptions, as well as the concomitant suppositions about 'good' and 'bad' moral behaviour, that should be critically considered from the perspective of the feminist ethics of care. Indeed, the ethics of care reminds us that 'right and wrong' do not necessarily coincide with 'good and bad'. On the contrary, there can be a huge gap between established legal codes about 'the right thing to do' and everyday moral considerations about the 'best thing to do'; moreover legalistic ethical codes often lack the capacity to do justice in an appropriate way to the ambiguities and nuances of 'lived' social moralities. The voice of care may indeed be too marked by fragility and multiplicity to be able to be registered by legal discourse, directed as this is at establishing robust and fixed systems of meaning. In this respect too, care remains in a position of defence against the normalizing effects of the Law.

From a law-oriented harmony model to an ethics of care

My reasoning until now has been based on a situation in which care and attention are more evenly divided between the sexes than is usually the case at present. In this situation, I assume that authority will acquire a different meaning: that, rather than using legal authority to enforce contact, legal agreements will take care and dependency into account. In a situation such as this, it would probably be easier to take a model of mutual agreement as the normative principle for the legal regulation of parental authority; the practice of a 'caring authority' can then emerge as a form of responsible behaviour. This approach draws, in a political respect, however, on strong forms of social policies that enable women and men to share care and responsibility for children. In other words, it is directed at issues of social citizenship more than at the rules of family law, although there should be an intertwining and attuning between these two legal domains once we adopt the perspective of care. The problem, however, is that in its recent institution of shared parental authority, the government has taken a generalized harmony model as a guideline for reforming family law, on the assumption of a fictive rather than an existing equality between the sexes. In spite of the fact that we live in social relationships in which both care and authority as well as the relationship between these two are variously marked by gender, men and women are constructed as equal individuals before the law and in principle granted equal parental rights under all conditions, whereby authority is still primarily regarded as the legal right to control, to enforced entry to others' lives and to 'self-governance'.

The law also has the task, however, of mediating in conflicts, just as it has the responsibility to protect weaker and more vulnerable parties where necessary. Both functions assume a clear set of rules and the competence to create clarity by means of quick and just procedures. Harmony is a difficult starting-point for thinking about divorce, because in most cases divorce is accompanied precisely by conflict and opposed interests.[27] The harmony model is based on the ideology of a 'clean break' or a smooth continuation of relations after divorce, on the illusion, that is, that both marriage and divorce are based on equality (of power) (Mossman 1993). In fact, what is more often found in divorce is inequality in power and a lack of agreement and compromise. When we approach the issue from the perspective of the ethics of care and interpret divorce as a moral situation or as a moral transition, we can acknowledge, however, that it is not merely power that is at stake in situations of divorce, but also the experiencing of complex moral dilemmas and often 'moral collisions' between the mothers and fathers involved. Interpreting divorce solely in terms of power does not enable us to undermine the stereotypical image of the power-prone mother, who uses her legal prerogatives in order to withhold men from their rights; thus women's moral dilemmas and moral competence to live with these dilemmas or find ways of solving conflicting responsibilities remain invisible. Proposals for the reform of family law should take this into account and the law should provide the necessary space and moral sensitivity to allow for this.

The present Dutch regulation is also rather 'careless' in the way it formulates the duty to share information and to engage in consultation. It provides these rights in cases where there is no shared authority or access right, in order to give the parents concerned a minimum amount of involvement. According to the Minister who defended the Bill, relationships should be maintained as far as possible and a parent wishing to remain involved in the upbringing of his or her child should be given every opportunity to do this by the other parent. However, precisely in those situations in which shared authority and access have broken down, a legal duty to share information is a rather illusory and far-fetched concept or, as Elsbeth Boor argues: every 'foolish father', having exhausted the possibilities of the law, can disturb the peace of mother and children, aided by the new right to consultation, without this solving anything (Boor 1995: 107). Here, too, it seems that the law is more ready to assume the (political) task of enforcing relationships – or at least to maintain the illusion that it is doing so – than to guarantee peace and stability in situations of conflict or to protect women from coercive or neglectful behaviour on the part of men.[28] This demonstrates that the process of separating care and authority, and the separation of different aspects of parental authority, which has been going on for the past fifteen years and which is now enshrined in the new regulation of parental authority, in fact often amounts to nothing more than a legal supervision of women's day-to-day care, based on a deep-seated mistrust of their moral capabilities.

All in all, there are insufficient guarantees in the new legal regulations to protect women against legal imperatives, or against men who are not afraid to resume their use of force on a legal basis after divorce. This can be especially harmful in marriages which have already involved domestic violence and sexual or child abuse. It is striking that this problem has entered so little into the political consciousness regarding divorce and that there is so little awareness of the legal protection which women and children may need in such situations.[29] Similarly, in a care ethics model, claims made by biological parents solely on the grounds of genetic ties would not be recognized; instead, different criteria would be developed for determining additional demands in regard to care and relationships (Boor 1995; Loenen 1995b; Shanley 1995). This would be possible, for example, by deciding on a broader definition of the 'child's interest' and the 'right to protection of family life' as grounds for refusal of joint parental authority and by granting judges more discretionary power to judge each case on its own merits. Moreover – also on this point – it should not be forgotten that women's opinions and lifestyles deserve respect and protection in this area.

If political judgment was guided by an ethics of care it would be possible, and justified, to involve considerations of power differences and the quality of care in the way in which family and kinship relations are regulated; an ethics of rights is unable to deal with these aspects because it takes equality as its starting-point (O'Neill 1988; Van den Burg 1993). However, it is also true that an ethics of care does not exclude normative reasoning in terms of justice and rights. Arguments about vulnerability and dependency can, for example, lead to an appeal to the liberal principles of autonomy, conceived as negative freedom: the right to be safeguarded from force and abuse of power by others. In this respect it would be desirable to guarantee women's rights to privacy in the family sphere too (Holtrust and De Hondt 1991) and to reflect from a feminist perspective on the legal use of terms such as 'harm' and 'injury' (Howe 1987; Smart 1995: 182).[30] This attitude can draw on an approach in terms of social justice that argues against institutionalized patterns of violence and normalization (Young 1990a).

Reasoning in terms of dependency and moral virtues makes it possible to arouse public discussion on the issue of what good care entails and how a responsible society should act towards children and those who care for them. It opens the way to looking at the moral problems in this area from different perspectives and to involving arguments and images of femininity and masculinity, motherhood and fatherhood, in the deliberations on issues of care (Young 1995). It also makes it possible to fit considerations of care into a politics of needs-interpretation by, for example, posing the question of what women need to care well for their children without this conflicting with their wish (and nowadays also the legal obligation) to lead an independent economic existence. The feminist ethics of care also offers a critical perspective on the idea that it is possible to achieve entirely just and harmonious laws in this area. The emotional bond between parents and children is, after all, often so complex that there is no single satisfactory solution. The law should pay attention precisely to the fragility of the relationships between people and to the different situations in which people need the law because they are unable to sort things out for themselves. The law and the intermediary institutions of government, such as child protection agencies and welfare organizations, should protect children, as the most vulnerable party, in situations in which parents' care is inadequate. There thus needs to be a 'pluriform' law which takes account of different situations (Goldschmidt 1993) and which abstains as far as possible from positing an abstract ideal of 'good family life'.

Concluding remarks

These are only a few of the many examples which could be given to demonstrate the possibilities which are opened up through reasoning from the perspective of a feminist ethics of care. There now exists an extensive body of literature on moral issues arising in the domain of family law, issues such as people's demand for access to information about their biological origins, the conflicting claims and obligations arising in cases of adoption and surrogacy, and the question of whether sperm donors can claim the right to contact with their biological children. Although it is certainly the case that family law should become attuned to these issues, it is also striking – and in a sense discouraging – how little change has occurred in the established manner in which legal discourse speaks about these issues, in spite of twenty years of feminist involvement and feminist arguments about alternative moral approaches. It is as if the belief in a combination of what Zygmunt Bauman has called 'reason-dictated rules and rule-dictated reason' is too deeply entrenched in the ethical codes of modern family law systems and their legal discourse (Bauman 1992: 67). There is still a solid congruence here between law and Law, or legal rules and the symbolic Law of the Father, that is supposed to bring universality, harmony and moral order. This ideology has the status of a 'logic', a subterranean set of assumptions underlying legal reasoning and the predominant expectations attached to legal regulation in this field. But it is not difficult to perceive this logic once we note the persistence with which the principle of biological descent is cherished as the leading normative principle in family law. We might even speculate that family law is one of the discursive domains that is supposed to bring socio-political certainty to a postmodern age, in which pleas for plurality and ambiguity are becoming louder and in which those who want to believe in the certainties of rule-bound ethics can project their fears of a 'loosening' of morality onto modernity's 'others', i.e., 'Hostile Mothers' who are accused of withholding what is due to men: their rights of access to children. There is a powerful political rhetoric, which wants us to believe that The Family is the one social institution that should not change, and that 'natural' responsibilities can easily be restored by Law when they temporarily fail (see also Young 1995, Smart 1997).[31]

But we can also see developments and strategies that undermine this logic, as well as reflected arguments about alternative moral approaches. There have been several attempts to engage in discussions about the social nature of care and the desirability and justification of rights claims in the light of care and an ethics of care (see, for example, Zipper and Sevenhuijsen 1987; Deech 1993; Holtrust 1993; Loenen 1995b; Shanley 1995). In the Netherlands the norm of heterosexuality contained in family law has been criticized by appealing to the ethics of care, combined with the liberal injunction of non-discrimination. Feminist lawyers have argued in this way in order to enable lesbian couples to share custody rights (Loenen 1994a) and since the latest Bill this has now almost been accomplished.[32] These alternative approaches will certainly not always provide us with simple solutions for moral dilemmas or legal conflicts. Intimate relations and kinship ties will continue to be marked by tragic dilemmas, often amounting to fierce conflicts between the individuals involved. It is this experience of being morally torn which marks moral existence as part of our everyday life, as well as the ways in which we choose to identify ourselves as part of a kinship network. An ethics of care, however, can counterbalance potentially fatalistic feelings about the insolubility of each and every moral conflict, not just by posing the question 'who has done the caring work?' in order to establish who may have prior rights, but also, and especially, because the values and virtues of responsiveness, forgiveness, acceptance and starting anew can prevent us from remaining entangled in the illusion that Just Law can free us from our moral dilemmas. The quality of care can be publicly disputed, but this is less easy for the law, as I hope to have shown here.

The principle of biological descent is in fact seriously distorted and long overdue for replacement. We live in social relationships in which biological descent is no longer appropriate as the central basis for regulating kinship ties and caring relationships. A diversity of possible fatherhoods have come into existence and this is now also true of motherhood: the possibility of egg donation makes it possible to differentiate between the genetic mother, the pregnancy mother and the caring mother or mothers. Transsexual operations allow fathers to change into mothers and mothers into fathers. Gender roles and identities, and the gendered division of labour, are more open to change and transformation than ever. Children grow up in the most diverse situations and there is no real reason to doubt the child-rearing qualities of the 'new' family relations any more than those of the traditional family. Actually existing human relationships and care practices and the connections, ambivalences and conflict situations arising within them form a better starting-point for reflecting on legal rules than an abstract legal norm such as the 'right to family life' or 'equality-as-sameness'. This should be the stimulus for open forms of public consideration on the importance of care and such issues as vulnerability, dependency and social justice. The public debate would be served more by this than by the positing of abstract legal equality or the enforcing of a 'right to family life' with no consideration of the underlying human, social and moral problems this entails.

When the practice of care, together with the feminist ethics of care's formulation of social problems and moral questions, as well as its idea of moral agency, forms the starting-point for political reasoning this can lead to new conceptions of social justice, whereas the reverse process is much more difficult to achieve. This would mean that instead of the abstract individual forming the starting-point for normative reasoning about rights and responsibilities, concepts such as autonomy and rights could be embedded in a relational vocabulary (Nedelsky 1988; Minow 1990). Family law and its regulation of kinship and caring relationships should be an integral part of our conceptions of citizenship, because the way we can shape our mutual relations as parents and children is firmly influenced by its discourse. These identities shape the way in which we can act in the public sphere and deliberate about good ways of caring and accounting for relations of (inter)dependence. The ethics of care is indispensable in this respect, because it provides meaningful modes of moral reasoning at the interstices between public and private, where the legal regulation of family life is situated.

As I have argued elsewhere, an acceptance of the care ethics implies a double move with regard to citizenship (Sevenhuijsen 1997b). On the one hand, integrating the ethics of care into conceptions of citizenship broadens the idea of what citizenship entails, because its values can then be included in public deliberation and political judgement. On the other hand, it narrows the scope of citizenship because the ethics of care makes us acknowledge that acting morally cannot be derived from legalistic ethical codes, but instead presumes forms of autonomous judgement based on interaction with and attentiveness to others. This may remind us about the boundaries of the political and the 'hubris' embodied in conceptions of coercive normative regulation. The ethics of care provides us with more balanced styles of moral reasoning, and thus of political judgement, compared to the liberal tradition, which takes the detached, disinterested individual as its starting-point, but which at the same time needs the fiction of biological ties and the logic of rights to create connections and unity. It has the capacity to provide a fuller and richer moral idiom that is better attuned to the manifold and often complicated moral dilemmas that people experience in their intimate relations. Such an approach is a condition for a viable and creative politics in which the interests of women and children are not submerged under a universalist ethics of equal rights and in which the masculine legal subject does not, implicitly or explicitly, continue to serve as the privileged point of reference.

5

FEMINIST ETHICS AND PUBLIC HEALTH-CARE POLICIES

A case-study on the Netherlands

Introduction

In recent years the reform of public health-care policies has been high on the political agenda. Several governments have installed special committees to produce proposals on such issues as new systems of insurance, the criteria for access to medical technology or the provision of care for the elderly. There is also a search for new institutional settings and decision-making procedures that can change the deeply entrenched power relations in the medical sector. The context of these new policy designs is that of the restructuring of modern welfare states. There are of course many relevant differences between countries in this respect. While in the United States the Clinton administration has tried to introduce a scheme of mandatory health-care insurance, successive Dutch governments have tried to save public funds by distinguishing a 'basic package' of necessary health services from less necessary services to be paid for privately.[1] A common denominator in both these policies, however, is the fact that new relations and balances between public and private health-care provisions are being discussed. There seems to be a widely shared view that while, on the one hand, nation-states cannot make available all the health-care services technologically possible, on the other hand, market forces cannot provide these services in accordance with the basic principles of social justice and political solidarity.

In 1991 the Dutch government published an important policy document entitled *Choices in Health Care*.[2] This report presents a framework for public decision-making about the availability of and access to health-care services, as well as proposals for a public debate on these issues. After its publication a wide variety of medical, political and cultural organizations as well as the media were invited to participate in this debate; among those invited were women's health organizations and the National Women's Council. Positive as this might seem from a feminist perspective, it also confronted the leadership of women's organizations with a complex situation. It was by no means clear with which voice, on which issues or from which position they should speak in the public domain when discussing health-care policies. And in spite of the open invitation to participate, it was striking that the main text of the report that was to serve as the basis for the public discussion referred neither to feminist approaches to health care nor to women's complex position in the care system. This in turn made it clear that there was a need for a critical analysis of the terms of the political discourse which would shape public discussion as well as reflection on the way in which these terms would inform political judgement.

In a sense this approach was suggested by *Choices in Health Care* itself, because a considerable part of the report is devoted to an evaluation of the normative frameworks which can guide public decision-making on health care. This facilitated the idea of launching the feminist involvement in the debate with an analysis and evaluation of the normative frameworks of the report itself from the perspective of feminist ethics and political theory. This chapter is the result of various insights arising from these discussions.[3] My approach can be seen as an exercise in the gender-reading of a public policy document such as *Choices in Health Care*. Policy documents can be analysed as vehicles of normative paradigms. A paradigm can be defined as a configuration of knowledge which orders the description of social problems, in order to pave the way for regulation. In this sense, a policy paradigm constitutes an element of a 'mode of governance', a way of giving form to the relationship between the public authorities and their subjects or, in more democratic terms, a way in which citizens can perceive themselves as part of a political community.

Iris Young's definition of a paradigm is a useful tool of analysis here: 'a configuration of elements and practices which define an inquiry: metaphysical suppositions, unquestioned terminology, characteristic questions, lines of reasoning, specific theories and their typical scope and mode of application' (Young 1990a: 16). Policy texts are sites of power, because their modes of speaking structure the way individuals and social groups (in this case women and their political representatives) can formulate legitimate speaking positions and acceptable considerations, thus creating a distinct profile for themselves in the public sphere. By establishing narrative conventions, authoritative repertoires of interpretation and frameworks of argumentation and communication, they confer power upon preferred modes of speaking and judging, and upon certain ways of expressing moral and political subjectivity. Through examining official documents in this way it becomes possible to trace both the overt and hidden gender-load contained in their vocabulary. And it can help us to analyse the inclusionary and exclusionary effects of texts with regard to gender by examining the degree to which they are able to speak about women and issues of gender. Starting from an analysis of the way in which 'women', women's issues and women's speaking positions are conceptualized in the terminology of *Choices in Health Care*, I will work my way through the text and analyse the gender-load of its most important normative concepts and frameworks. In doing so, I will use gender as an analytic category (Harding 1986; Scott 1986), in order to show how gender assigns meaning to seemingly gender-neutral concepts, such as 'necessary care' or 'normal social participation', which are presented in the report as guidelines for political judgements about public health care. Through analysing the gender-load implied in these concepts and their surrounding normative frameworks, I will assess the effects of these frameworks on feminist concerns. I will then argue that a feminist ethics of care, conceptualized in a communicative and relational political paradigm, can provide the basis for reformulating established normative concepts which are used as guidelines for thinking about health-care policies.

In doing this I have two goals. First, to reflect on the question of which policy framework provides the best opportunity for including feminist concerns about women as receivers and providers of care. My second interest is even broader and more ambitious. By reflecting upon the gender dimensions of public speech on health-care policies, I hope to contribute to a more general discussion of policy frameworks in the field of care in modern societies.[4] In my opinion, bringing the hidden dimensions of 'care talk' out into the daylight of public speech can help to enrich normative thinking about the availability and quality of care in modern societies. In order to do this I will situate discussions about care within conceptions of citizenship. Public discourse constructs 'citizenship positions', images of how a good citizen should think and act, in this case when engaging in political action concerning care or when making use of the health-care system. By analysing the vocabularies of citizenship that have implicitly informed *Choices in Health Care*, I will try to develop discursive space for integrating feminist political theories of care into the public debate; in my view, these theories offer the potential for a more solid and inclusive way of talking about care than the frameworks proposed in *Choices in Health Care*. First, however, I will sketch the outlines of the report.

The normative framework of *Choices in Health Care*

In 1990 the Dutch Minister for Welfare, Health and Cultural Affairs, Hans Simons, formulated the guiding question for the committee on choices in health care as follows: what limits should be imposed on the use of new medical technologies and how can public support be found for solutions to the problems caused by insufficient resources and rationing of care which would entail the selection of patients? The committee was supposed not only to formulate normative considerations and criteria with regard to these questions but also to instigate a public debate of the following question: *should everything possible be done?*[5]

The report argues for the necessity of making choices by referring to the growing proportion of the national income spent on health care, the waiting lists for operations and the growing shortage of provisions for the mentally handicapped and psycho-geriatric patients. According to the committee, the lack of sufficient resources is not simply a financial issue; it also raises the moral problem of distribution in accordance with the principles of justice. The issue of distribution is brought in by asking how we can protect weaker groups in society (the elderly and the chronically ill) in a situation where the possibilities for prolonging life are steadily growing. Making the health-care system more efficient or providing more money would not solve the problem because, as the report puts it, 'we are caught in an upward spiral of expectations': 'in an understandable desire to banish all illness and defect, we often expect the impossible from our health-care system, particularly when the system itself contributes to this expectation'. To counter this development the report recommends that political choices are made as to which forms of care are deemed 'necessary' and which should be regarded as the responsibility of the individual.

The report goes on to discuss the issue of how criteria can be developed for deciding what constitutes 'necessary care'. It distinguishes three approaches to questions of health and health care. The first is labelled the *individual approach*. Here, health is linked to self-determination, autonomy and the fulfilment of individual life-plans. Health care is thus dependent upon individual goals, needs and preferences. The committee condemns this approach, because it would deny the possibility of collective choices; the range of individual preferences would be too broad and it would be impossible to distinguish between individual health preferences and social problems. Definitions of basic needs differ from one person to another, so it would be impossible to decide what constitutes necessary care.

The second approach is labelled the *medical–professional approach*. Here health is defined as normal biological functioning or the absence of illness and handicaps. Biomedical knowledge about the internal construction and the biological functioning of the body would then lead to decisions on what constitutes necessary health care. The committee criticizes this approach on two grounds. First, it does not allow for psychological and social determinants of health; arguments in favour of the necessity of contraceptives in an over-populated society, for example, would find no room in this approach. Second, the complaints of patients could only be interpreted in medical terms. Medical and economic norms would then continue to dominate in the process of choosing.

The committee sees the solution in a third approach, which they call the *community-oriented approach*. Here health is perceived as the 'means for every member of a community to function normally according to the prevailing norms in (Dutch) society'. The committee argues for this approach in the following terms:

> The choices here are made at the level of the society because individual health is seen to be linked to the possibility of participating in

social life. According to the community-oriented approach, care is necessary when it enables an individual to share, maintain and if possible to improve his/her life together with other members of the community. Individual preferences and needs are not given priority here; the central question is which care is necessary care from the point of view of the community.

(Choices in Health Care 1992: 53–54)

The committee acknowledges that there is a problem residing in this approach: not all societies will define 'normal social functioning' in the same way, because there are great differences between their norms and values. This problem is solved by arguing that the most important norms and values in the Dutch democratic social–constitutional state have been laid down in international treaties and the constitution. This leads to three fundamental norms which should be applied to the process of choosing: first, the equality of all human beings, as laid down in the constitution; second, the fundamental protection of human life, as laid down in international conventions; and third, the principle of solidarity, as laid down in the construction of the public health-care system (Choices in Health Care 1991: 17).

The community-oriented approach would allow for a description of necessary care, independent of individual needs. It would enable limits to be imposed on both individual choices and patients' autonomy, as well as on the professional autonomy of medical professionals.[6] The report argues for a system of distributive justice in which principles of equal access are combined with a just distribution of resources. In this way care could be guaranteed for those members of society who cannot take care of themselves, such as the elderly and the mentally handicapped. According to the committee the principle of 'necessary care' would then be the principle criterion for guiding decision-making procedures.[7] Three additional criteria are mentioned: is the provision effective, is it efficient, and could it be left to individual responsibility? Taken together these four criteria are then hierarchically arranged in a 'funnel', with, as it were, four filters. Every medical provision has to pass through these filters in order to qualify for inclusion in mandatory basic insurance schemes. If a provision passes the test of 'necessary care', it then has to be examined for effectiveness and efficiency, and whether it can be left to individual responsibility. The report follows with a discussion of examples such as in vitro fertilization, homes for the elderly, homeopathic medicines, sports injuries and adult dental care, and reaches the conclusion that even with these four criteria it is hard to reach just decisions in accordance with the principles of solidarity. In view of this, the committee argues that agreement on what constitutes 'appropriate use' should be a crucial goal of public discussion in order to arrive at the appropriate criteria for government policy.[8]

The report ends with a proposal for a public campaign, entitled 'a communication plan', in which a wide range of organizations will be invited to participate in a two-year, government-funded project. The main goal of this project is to convince the general public that choice is necessary and desirable, and that individuals and organizations are capable of making choices at all levels of society. The aim is to work towards a new awareness about 'appropriate use' of care provisions and to create new kinds of social consensus in order to pave the way for public decision-making. At this point, women's health organizations were asked to participate in the campaign, because they had developed critiques of unnecessary medicalization processes and thus have 'experience in dealing with choice' (ibid.: 80). Here, women's groups are addressed as the vanguards of autonomy and free choice, as opposed to medicalization. But prior to this women are mentioned in the first paragraph of the communication plan in a more general mode. There they are addressed as people who can influence the care consumption of others and thus fulfil the role of potential intermediaries in the furthering of appropriate use:

> Women generally have great influence on the care-consumption of many others. Mothers decide the care choices for their children, women usually advise their partners on care choices and adult women are often involved in the care choices of their parents.
>
> (*Choices in Health Care* 1992: 149)

So, while women's health organizations are addressed as the political vanguards of free choice, women as a category are addressed in a rather traditional role, as the central actors in families, where they can influence the 'care consumption' of their near and dear.

Legal equality and necessary care

Choices in Health Care has been both praised and criticized for its introduction of a community-oriented approach into public discussion on health care. A closer look at the report reveals, however, that its considerations are framed in a peculiar mixture of normative vocabularies, combining communitarian arguments with those of a liberal-rights discourse and distributive justice. To this mixture are then added notions from communicative ethics, through the proposal for a public discussion on the question of whether everything possible should always be done. This idea of communicative ethics tends to turn into a top-down moral–pedagogical discourse, however, when it comes to a furthering of 'appropriate use', particularly when women are addressed as the social guardians of the responsible use of health-care services. The normative approach in *Choices in Health Care* thus represents a mixture of elements from conflicting, and sometimes incompatible, normative frameworks, rather than a clear-cut paradigm. In what follows I will take the leading concept of the report, 'necessary care' as a starting-point for reflection on these normative contradictions. By analysing these frictions in terms of gender and citizenship, I will also try to open up discursive space for bringing feminist theories of care into the public debate on health care.

I would like to start by taking a closer look at the supposed aim of the concept of 'necessary care'. The committee uses this concept in its attempt to develop objective criteria for deciding which medical provisions should be covered by a legally guaranteed basic insurance scheme. By invoking a community-oriented approach, the committee hopes to curtail, on the one hand, the discursive power of individual consumers with their supposedly infinite needs and, on the other, the medical professionals who can argue only in bio-medical terms. 'Normal social participation' should thus become the norm for access to public health-care provisions. Herein resides, of course, a familiar problem for political philosophy: is it possible to establish reasonable or generalizable norms for social participation? After all, societies contain a great variety of moral convictions about what 'normal' social behaviour should entail. The crucial question for philosophers from different viewpoints is whether it is possible to find a 'minimal consensus' on these points which can lead to policy decisions while maximally conforming to standards of justice and solidarity.

Questions such as these belong in the domain of discourse ethics or procedural justice. The committee has, however, evaded the philosophical and political complexities of these questions by resorting to a more familiar vocabulary, the constitutional language of equal rights and solidarity. The value of these abstract legal norms lies, according to the committee, in their general acceptability, universality and enforceability. Although the concepts of necessary care and social participation are derived from a communitarian approach,[9] the committee has selected normative concepts from a liberal ethics of rights and of distributive justice in order to operationalize the demands of community life. This leads to the question of how the relationship between 'social participation' on the one hand, and 'equality, solidarity and the protection of human life' on the other, could be worked out in more detail. Do these norms offer the potential for reaching a responsible and well thought out selection of health-care services which are guaranteed for all? I will discuss the way the report deals with two examples of women's health-care provisions in order to show the selective workings of the normative framework of *Choices in Health Care*.

The first example concerns the way the report uses the criteria of 'normal social participation' to argue that *in vitro* fertilization (IVF) and cosmetic surgery should not be counted as necessary care. IVF is not considered necessary because, according to the majority of the committee, involuntary childlessness does not hinder women's 'normal participation'. The same would hold for cosmetic surgery, which could be considered a 'luxury' and thus unnecessary for women's social participation. There is a striking absence of any explicit reflection on the meaning of 'normal social participation' here. The implicit norms for normal social participation are, however, clearly visible between the lines: they entail participation in the public sphere of paid labour and political participation. Until recently these were also the most important aims of the Dutch government's policies on women's emancipation (Outshoorn 1991). The IVF example shows that having children is apparently not considered to be 'social participation' (Van Berkel 1994). And the example of cosmetic surgery shows that subjective feelings of identity, which are inherent to 'bodily images', are labelled as 'extra-social' phenomena (Davis 1995). Issues of women's reproductive capacities and women's identities are relegated to a private sphere of individual preference and thus to individual responsibility. Women's health issues are thus brought under the normative regime of 'independence' and 'equality', norms which govern the public sphere, and which are conceptualized from the perspective of participation in the labour market.

The second example concerns the way in which the report calls on equality norms in order to argue the case for 'necessary care' for the 'weaker' groups in society. The report invokes the constitutional rule of equality in order to find normative foundations for solidarity with the elderly and the mentally handicapped, and to guarantee them access to the health-care system. These groups are then constructed as 'people who cannot take care of themselves' (ibid.: 35). In the first instance this proposition evokes moral and political sympathy: solidarity with and care for the weak and vulnerable should indeed, as many people feel, be regarded as a fundamental moral obligation. But it is also possible to interpret the committee's standpoint from different perspectives: first, as a generalizing and potentially stigmatizing way of talking about the elderly, because they are presented as weak and needy; and second, as a statement which proceeds from a questionable counter-norm, the idea that 'normal' citizens can take care of themselves.

Gender, citizenship and care

This view of citizenship and care is not spelled out in further detail in the report. It can be traced, however, through the previously proposed paradigm study, by looking at 'metaphysical suppositions and unquestioned terminology' and by tracing implicit meanings and subject positions, and institutionalized patterns of interpretation: suppositions which are regarded as self-evident or which belong to the parameters of hegemonic discourse (Fraser 1989: 146). Thinking in terms of citizenship and care can be helpful for several reasons when developing this approach, at least if we are prepared to stretch the language of citizenship beyond the liberal vocabulary of individuals, rights and duties and include in it normative questions about the adequacy of public discussion and political debate, and questions about the 'good life'. An approach which employs a broad concept of citizenship makes it possible to place considerations regarding care firmly in the public domain, the sphere where deliberations about the best social arrangements for care (should) take place. And it can provide the springboard for discussions on identity and human nature, which inform public policies on health care. A condition for this is that we recognize and consciously employ the normative dimensions of the concepts of both citizenship and care.

The contours of the views on citizenship and care in *Choices in Health Care* become clearer when we relate the committee's normative ideas about the self-sufficient individual to its assumptions about 'normal' social participation. The idea of the independent individual fits into a neo-liberal conception of citizenship, where it figures as the central normative ideal for human personhood. In the neo-liberal view, normality is constructed as self-sufficiency or the ability to lead an independent life in economic, social and political respects. The self-sufficient individual is someone who has no need of care during his or her 'normal social participation'. I describe this view of citizenship as neo-liberal because it corresponds to the mode of regulation which guides the restructuring of many Western welfare states at this historical juncture. The idea of the self-sufficient individual fits into the current programme of privatization of public services and the growth of market-oriented forms of regulation. 'Normal' citizens are constructed then, first and foremost, as individual participants in the exchange of labour and provisions. These individuals are supposed to translate their care needs into market-oriented behaviour, thus conceiving of themselves as care consumers, participating in a system of care provisions which works according to the principles of supply and demand.

This view of citizenship and care has its origins in the history of Western political thought. It was Aristotle who first laid the foundation for this mode of conceptualizing citizenship and politics in his demarcation of the 'polis' and the household (Tronto 1995c; Spelman 1989). While the household was seen as the place where life-sustaining activities take place in the form of labour carried out by wives and slaves, the polis was seen as the place where free men come together to engage in socially important affairs and to deliberate on and live the 'good life'. According to Aristotle, it was this gathering in the polis which was the constitutive act of human freedom. Political participation and freedom are thus closely connected, and their connection is dependent on the distinction between freedom and necessity. The public sphere is thus considered as the domain where free men can transcend not only their embodiedness but also the finite and mortal aspects of the human condition. Some people (women and slaves), in accordance with a 'natural' or 'functional' order, had to make sacrifices to enable the independence of others (the free citizens). Free men gathered in the polis in order to carry out deeds and make works of art which would leave their traces in history and thus provide them, as citizens, with immortality. As a result, the Western tradition has since been left with a mode of theorizing politics in which care is associated with immanence, necessity and the private sphere, while politics is constructed as a social activity that enhances the freedom of the human subject, by freeing *him* from the burdens of necessity and the fear of mortality and death.

These short genealogical remarks can enable us to identify some of the hidden traces of gender in the normative idiom of *Choices in Health Care*. The report not only exhibits a gendered mode of thinking about politics, it also leaves us with a paradoxical mode of speaking when deliberating about care and public responsibility. While citizens are invited to participate in a public discussion about necessary care, care is at the same time situated *outside* the realm of 'normal social participation'. Care is supposed to have a primarily supportive function: the 'repairing' of citizens so that they can once more take part in their normal social participation. This exemplifies a thoroughly instrumental vision of health, a vision in which health is a condition for the achievement of other ends and thus something that should be evaluated against the background of individual 'life-plans'. As Joan Tronto has pointed out, it is a model that overemphasizes the autonomous, rational, life-project, choosing vision of the (male) individual, who perceives illness as a 'foreign invasion' (Tronto 1995c: 6). Doctors are imagined as heroes, who can transform patients back into independent agents by means of the 'rescue principle' (Tronto 1995c: 7). Illness is thus perceived as a deviation from normal social functioning, rather than as an inherent, even if often disturbing, part of human life. Some philosophers do indeed regard illness as a threat, as the object of a fundamental human fear, from which the state should protect its citizens (see, for example, Callahan 1994). The construction of a stable and healthy body is thus the starting-point for collective bargaining. This accords with the construction of care as a 'necessary evil', as something which is needed, but which also has to be contained; this is an image which returns in the central proposition of *Choices in Health Care*, which suggests that individuals, unless corrected by collective decisions about boundaries, will have 'endless' needs.

The general feminist response to the constructions of normality in *Choices in Health Care* must be that they are permeated with gender-laden images. When care is situated outside the sphere of social participation, it is consigned to the 'black box' of the private realm, where so-called informal arrangements guarantee that care is provided spontaneously. While the report argues on the one hand for priority to be given to care for the elderly, it does not even touch upon the question of how this care should be provided, nor does it refer to the complex socio-political problems surrounding informal care. It simply draws on the silent logic of a 'natural' provision of care within the family and kinship networks, where it seems just as self-evident that it will be women who care spontaneously for others whenever the need arises (Sevenhuijsen 1993b; Knijn 1994).[10] The effects of this 'gender-logic' extend not only to the social arrangements of care, the question of who cares for whom, but also to the institutionalized, symbolic meanings of care. In this respect gender is a

powerful factor giving meaning to care. Images of care still have strong connotations of femininity, privacy and dependency, while their opposites –
labour, independence and a public identity – are more readily associated
with masculinity. One could indeed speculate that care is constantly 'banished'
from the public sphere and thus from full political consideration *because* it is
marked by hidden meanings of femininity.[11] An approach that takes public
'male' norms as the normal perspective can easily adopt the viewpoint of the
privileged and the powerful, who can speak from a position where receiving
care is taken for granted without having to realize fully what providing care
actually entails; this is a position which Joan Tronto has described as one of
'privileged irresponsibility' (Tronto 1993: 174).

We can conclude, then, that the endeavour to find principles of 'necessary
care' in a combination of ideas about 'normal social participation' and constitutional norms of equality is bound to lead to a contradictory and selective
mode of moral reasoning about care. It leads to a discursive track where
judgements about medical provisions are brought under the normative
regime of labour market participation. This normative regime tends to marginalize care, by considering it as a precondition for social participation,
rather than as a social phenomenon and a meaningful social activity in itself.
This framework can include feminist issues only if they are phrased in the language of individualism, independency and 'equality-as-sameness'. Women
are then fitted into the regulatory parameters of late modernity by being
asked to enter the world of paid labour and independent citizenship, and see
the world of care as a 'traditional' barrier to freedom and equality.[12] Seen
from this perspective it is not surprising that the main text of *Choices in Health
Care* does not talk explicitly about women. In its normative framework of
distributive justice and legal equality, women are addressed as gender-
neutral citizens, for whom sexual difference is supposed to be irrelevant or
marginal. Differences between the sexes are considered relevant only when
they can be phrased in terms of differences in health conditions.

The opposition between individual and community: how to talk about needs

It could be said, then, that the normative framework of *Choices in Health Care* is
informed by the perspective of the independent citizen, who needs as little
care as possible and does not reflect upon the nature of his or her needs and
the moral dilemmas to which they can give rise (Tronto 1995c). A basic
problem in this respect lies in the report's strict distinction between an individual and a community-oriented approach. Needs are unequivocally relegated to the domain of the so-called 'individual approach' to health and
health care. Needs are depicted as 'preferences' belonging to 'individuals', as
entities springing from individuals' psychic dispositions. This confirms the
liberal approach to the relationship between the individual and society, and

the individual and politics. Liberalism in its most 'pure' form sees individuals as prior to society. In liberal contract theory society is seen as a compact between individuals who bring their needs and preferences into the public sphere. Since Thomas Hobbes and John Locke, liberal politics has explicitly or implicitly involved the construction of a social–political contract, which is necessary to 'curb' these individuals in their drive to satisfy their needs, because otherwise they would harm each other through unmitigated self-interest, violence, theft or the usurpation of power (Pateman 1988; DiStefano 1991; Jones 1993).

Choices in Health Care tries to depart from the liberal framework by invoking communitarian solutions or by selectively stating that needs might be socially constructed. Communitarians, however, would go much further: they would deny the image of the 'unencumbered individual', and would regard individuals, together with their needs, preferences, values and moral considerations, as part of communities, and thus as the basis for moral and political life. In *Choices in Health Care*, however, the liberal individual remains the prototypical human subject. This individual is held responsible for recognizing needs and translating them into claims on the health-care system. Needs are overwhelmingly constructed as 'unlimited', as entities that must be curbed in order to facilitate an orderly discussion about responsible choices. This individual irresponsibility is then contrasted with the positive image of a responsible community as the socio-political norm.

This leads to a mode of reasoning in which the individual and the community are seen as opposites and played out against each other.[13] Instead of viewing individuals with their needs, feelings of identity, hopes and fears about illness, and moral considerations as an inherent part of political life, 'the' individual should be seen as a threat to community values. And instead of constructing human communities as entities that ought to respond to the needs of their members, we are asked to imagine a political community that argues about care with abstract, legal norms as its main point of reference. Citizens in the public debate are thus confronted with the paradoxical task of being asked to air their views about *Choices in Health Care*, while at the same time being forbidden to bring forward their needs as a legitimate topic of collective deliberation. The only discursive space for 'needs-talk' is that reserved for considering (negatively marked) individual preferences, such as the discussion of such 'luxury' treatments as cosmetic surgery and expensive fertility treatments. This discursive strategy leads to paradoxical modes of public speech; it is, moreover, ineffective. People *do* consider their own needs and desires, and those of others, when they talk about health and illness and about complex moral questions in the domain of care. One could even say that it is rather immoral *not* to reserve discursive space for talking about needs in a discussion about care. For how can a community ever care properly about and for its members, if there is no space to communicate and deliberate about the way in which people experience needs? Judgements about the necessity of care are, then, by implication, evaluations of needs.

In spite of these critical remarks I do not wish to suggest that the concept of 'necessary care' should be dropped from our political vocabulary. On the contrary, considerations about the necessity of care and social participation might provide fruitful points of departure for public discussion about health care, provided that we do not start our normative deliberations by invoking objective norms and images of human nature derived from a liberal ethics of rights; and also provided that we overcome the manifold ways in which gender-laden binary thinking has invaded the frameworks of public discourse as, for instance, in the dichotomy between the individual and the community, and that between needs and social participation. 'Necessary care' might be a fruitful concept if we can acknowledge the contextual and narrative character of people's need for care. It is exactly the search for objectivity, universalizability and economic rationality that obscures many of the moral discourses about care and needs. It is, for example, often presumed that if we want to take needs into account, we have to reach consensus over a list of 'basic needs', that would be inherent to human nature. Lists like this are usually limited to a very general overview, i.e., the need for shelter, food and adequate health care; they fail to tackle the more complex question of which provisions are necessary under which specific circumstances. A more important problem, however, is that this approach is again linked to an individualistic perspective on human nature and to implicitly or explicitly gendered images.

An alternative approach, as I have argued in previous chapters, could draw upon social constructivism and narrativity, which have recently begun to inform social and normative theory, and which have led to creative research and theorizing within women's studies (Walker 1989; Addelson 1994; Shrage 1994; Davis 1995). These approaches open up space for reflection about the way needs are constructed by social practices and interactions. By regarding needs as narrative events we can also see how they become the object of negotiation and contestation. Gender analysis should be an integral part of such an approach, since it enables us to see how, for example, the ascription and experience of gendered identities influence the way women and men experience their bodies and state of health, and the way in which they care for and about themselves and others. This approach can also counter the effects of power and privilege in discourses about needs. It can, for example, sensitize us to the ease with which professionals lay claim to cognitive authority when interpreting the needs of the 'needy'. It also helps us to see how professionals can use their discursive power to construct entire (often gendered) social groups as *needy*, thus making them objects for social regulation and intervention. This enables professionals not only to justify their position as protectors of the 'needy', but also to use this position to speak on behalf of the 'needy' in the public domain (Fraser 1989; Addelson 1994). There are indeed many historical traditions in which needs are discussed in patronizing and paternalistic – or maternalistic – modes of objectifying and 'othering' the needy (Tronto 1993). By constructing 'situated knowledges' about needs and care, it becomes possible to empower the subjects who are the bearers of needs, and to make *their* considerations on their condition an integral part of public deliberations. This would enable us to engage in public discussion about the relevance of gender in specific situations rather than ignoring it, as is customary in the liberal discourse of equality-as-sameness which informs countless public policy documents.

This is especially relevant when arguments from a feminist perspective are to be validated in political discussions on health care. Until recently, women have predominantly been the *object* of medical science and medical discourse. The medical profession and related experts have extensive powers to define and structure what count as women's needs, and even to decide what counts as femininity and 'true' feminine behaviour, so that 'women' are somehow reduced to a sexually defined body (Martin 1987; Schiebinger 1989; Jacobus, Fox Keller and Shuttleworth 1990; Schoon 1995). A recent example of this is the way in which the menopause and osteoporosis have been constructed as cases of hormonal failure, and thus as a possible threat to the 'feminine' aspects of women's lives (Van Hall 1994; Van Wingerden 1994). The feminist health movement has, since the 1970s, in its critiques of medicalization processes proffered a broad spectrum of alternative views on women's needs in which needs are seen in context and care is placed in a relational paradigm (Van Mens-Verhulst and Schilder 1994). This has brought to light a number of controversies surrounding needs which, rather than being excluded, clearly merit a place in public debate. This calls for what Nancy Fraser has termed a 'politics of needs-interpretation' (Fraser 1989). According to this model, public discussions should take the form of open debates about the origins of needs and the issues of why and how needs should be met, and where the boundaries between private and public responsibilities should be drawn.

Approaching health-care policies from the ethics of care

Choices in Health Care is, all in all, rather ambivalent about the nature of the public deliberations that could lead to responsible political choices in the health-care system. Although the report opens important doors by taking solidarity and social participation as the starting-point for decision-making, it proceeds to close them again by resorting to the language of rights and individualism in its search for objective criteria for 'necessary care'. Because needs are excluded from the debate about necessary care, and because the report hardly reflects on the conditions under which care is provided, we are left with a fragmented view of care and health, in which care is primarily seen as and moulded into a commodity. This market-oriented approach is echoed in the communication plan. Citizens are supposed to talk about 'appropriate use' and to channel their choices in that direction, rather than reflecting on their needs. The general public and the decision-makers are asked to reach normative judgements about care in terms of the distribution of goods and services, rather than in terms of needs, social relations, social processes, systems of knowledge, cultural images and value systems. Health-care policies are principally constructed as a strengthening of the market system, though corrected and regulated by a neo-corporatist political system of negotiations and bargaining. Thus, the tendency towards the creation of new 'care bureaucracies' is strengthened. Because the logic in such a system confines policy issues to choices about insurance schedules and designing uniform standards of behaviour, *Choices in Health Care* has missed the chance of optimally contributing to the implementation of one of its central goals, that of countering the culture of medicine.[14]

In the end, the report remains caught in the parameters of the distributive paradigm, a framework which, to use Iris Young's words, is marked by a 'tendency to conceive social justice and distribution as coextensive concepts' (Young 1990a: 16). Because this framework can deal with issues of gender only in marginal and distorted ways, it cannot satisfactorily incorporate many of the considerations brought forward by feminists in the last decade. The assignment of women to a 'gatekeeper' function in the health-care system accords with the market-oriented individualism of the report. The report can best be understood as an endeavour to regulate the demand side of the 'health-care market'. This conclusion is supported by the report's assertion that the power structure on the supply side is too resistant to political regulation. Apparently, women, as housewives and gatekeepers, are 'easier to regulate'. This observation gains in relevance once we realize that women are addressed here in a social role with many responsibilities, but (in most cases) little access to power resources; they thus have little opportunity to stand up for their own needs.

Feminist scholars have questioned in many ways the feasibility of moral theories which start from the assumption of a self-interested, calculating and exchange-oriented human being. If, instead of this, moral and political deliberations, in accordance with the feminist ethics of care, started by confirming the importance of interaction, interdependence and relationships, a considerable number of the assumptions about the self and about needs and interests now circulating in our political system and its hegemonic normative frameworks would have to be modified. A feminist ethics of care certainly offers the potential for such innovation, because it leads to a reformulation of the moral domain and moral subjectivity, and thus to a redefinition both of which issues need to be judged as well as how these judgements could or should proceed. And since judgement is such an intrinsic part of citizenship, the ethics of care has the potential to shift the boundaries between ethics and politics (Tronto 1993, 1995a; Chapter 1 of this volume). Joan Tronto and Berenice Fisher have defined care as 'a species activity that includes everything that we do to maintain, continue and repair "our" world so that we can live in it as well as possible. That world includes our bodies, our selves and our environment, all of which we seek to interweave in a complex, life-sustaining web' (Fisher and Tronto 1990: 40; Tronto 1993: 103). Care, thus conceived, is not a marginal activity of life but one of the central procedures of human existence. Care is not confined to the family or personal relationships but is also situated in formalized social and political institutions in our society.

Tronto and Fisher's definition of care is quite broad: it could refer to nearly all the activities that humans engage in. This makes it difficult and perhaps undesirable to distinguish caring from non-caring practices. For the purpose of discussing the politics of health care, however, I would prefer a narrower definition in which needs are conceptualized as the quintessential object of care and in which the ethics of care is seen as a moral orientation.[15] According to Fisher and Tronto, care can be viewed as a process taking place in four phases, each of which is linked to different moral attitudes, values and activities. These phases can help to clarify how individuals and institutions deal with care. Fisher and Tronto distinguish between caring about (recognizing that there is a need that should be met), caring for (the assuming of responsibility for the meeting of the need), taking care of (the actual practice and work of caring), and care-receiving. Each of these phases is linked to moral dimensions of care or specific moral values. Tronto calls these in turn 'attentiveness', 'responsibility', 'competence' and 'responsiveness' (Tronto 1993; see also Chapter 3 this volume, esp. p. 83). In order to understand the political dimensions of these values, it should be emphasized that they are not abstract norms that can be invoked when considering a particular situation; rather, they should be seen as moral and cognitive attitudes, or 'epistemological virtues' (Code 1991; Rooney 1991).

This implies that there is no such thing as an 'objective' situation of need for which politicians can then seek a solution. How we come to know people's needs and the situations in which they occur depends on our willingness to see things from a 'care' perspective and to bring into practice the epistemological virtues of care when talking and deliberating about needs (Parlevliet and Sevenhuijsen 1993). The question of how a social situation can best 'be known' thus forms an indispensable part of moral and normative deliberation (Code 1991). If care is defined as an activity or practice, we can look in an integrated manner at such phenomena as acting, thinking and judging in relation to care. Defining care in this way counters tendencies to narrow it down to an emotional disposition, for example, or a moral intuition, or to conceptualize it primarily in an economic vocabulary of labour. Instead, we are invited to think about the way social practices give rise to certain attitudes and moral frameworks, and vice versa. Seeing care as a practice also enables us to draw upon women's experiences and moral considerations as carers, without linking these to useless speculations that these considerations are about a special 'feminine' or 'female disposition' towards caring (Gremmen 1995).[16]

Such a political approach to care also makes it possible to perceive and address issues of power, and to adapt our judgements about care politics to the fact that power and conflict are involved in every phase of the caring process, as well as in our collective discussions about the way social institutions should care about and for human beings. Deliberations about what constitutes necessary care are structured by power and depend upon the position from which one speaks. Needs are often perceived differently, depending on whether they are seen from the perspective of the providers or receivers of care, whose 'negotiations' about needs may well be informed by a wide range of motives and considerations. Providers of care, through their lack of access to power resources and limited control over their work situation for instance, are often not in a position to provide care in a way that meets their own standards of quality; this is the case, for example, when home-carers are expected to do only cleaning work for the elderly or the washing of their clients, without engaging in social interaction (Morée and Oldersma 1991; Gremmen 1995). As mentioned earlier, needs are the object of both negotiation and contestation, and thus of power struggles about who gets what. Power and privilege are important factors shaping the social relations of 'giving and receiving', and of 'speaking and listening'. And these social relations are marked by structural factors of gender, race and class, and by the ways in which these factors coincide in individual lives.

If we take it as a goal of moral and political judgement to counter these power mechanisms in care processes, several of the central concepts in the political discussion on health care need to be redefined. A well-considered ethics of care enables us to do this. I will now go on to consider six such concepts: social participation, autonomy, choice, equality, justice and solidarity. Again I will discuss them as concepts of citizenship: my aim is to rethink them from the perspective of a collective discussion about the availability of and access to good health care in modern societies, and thus in a sense to 'prepare' them as leading normative concepts for public decision-making.

Social participation

In order to arrive at responsible forms of political judgement about the availability of health-care services, it is important to pose the question of how caring arrangements contribute to meaningful social participation. Rather than answering this question in abstract or general terms, it would be better to talk about meaningful forms of social participation in a variety of social groups and social practices, and to do this from the perspective of the individuals concerned. Arguing from the perspective of care can help us to avoid confining social participation to paid labour, without forgetting of course that a considerable proportion of caring is carried out in professional situations. Proceeding from this view of care is precisely what opens up space for normative deliberation about where to draw boundaries between public and private forms of providing care, and allows consideration of how the further professionalization of care can be achieved in a responsible way. It enables us to take into account the fact that individuals will alternate between the roles of care-providers and care-receivers at different points in their lives and in different contexts.

If we want to do justice to care as a crucial element in the life of a community, the opportunity to provide care should be included in the economic arrangements and social policies which structure people's life-plans.[17] Similarly, attention should be paid to the fact that dealing with health and illness is an integral part of human life. Social participation may well turn out to be a just standard for judging the availability of health-care services, if we start from the assumption that diversity, vicissitude, fragility, vulnerability and dependency are basic aspects of the human condition, rather than proceeding from a standard life-script or a standard healthy human body. This would, for example, imply that working conditions, the design of public space, access to cultural events and to modes of expressing sexual pleasure should take into account the fact that a considerable part of the population live lives that are marked by disability or chronic disease.

Autonomy and choice

'Choice' is actually the central normative concept in *Choices in Health Care*. In this sense the report is permeated by a view of human nature drawn from liberal political theory: the autonomous, choosing individual. Because choice is presented as a guiding principle in almost every situation, it is used in a rather one-dimensional and unreflective mode, as if there were a direct connection between the choices we make as patients or individuals and the choices which politicians should make when discussing modes of regulation (Mol 1991). This hides the fact that different situations demand different criteria and different forms of judgement. The concept of choice is not invoked in an 'innocent' mode in the report. Citizens are expected to make choices in such a way that the collective need for care services can be kept within reasonable limits. In other words, choice is conceptualized as a shield against an inordinate need for care. Until recently, the Dutch welfare state held itself responsible for providing an adequate system of care for its citizens, but now these same citizens are viewed as a problem, at least when they translate their needs into claims. Choice and autonomy are thus placed in opposition to care.

An approach based on feminist moral philosophy, on the other hand, would start by questioning the ways in which care and autonomy are positioned as binary, hierarchically ordered opposites. Indeed, autonomy is often assigned the task of freeing individuals (or *the* prototypical human subject) from dependency, contingency, vulnerability and the disorders of embodiment. An ethics of care would replace the idea that dependency forms an obstacle to

139

autonomy with the concept of interdependency and recognition of the ways in which good care can contribute to behaviours and choices which enhance people's feelings of self-respect. Care should not be reserved for interaction with 'needy' persons but seen instead as a phenomenon that structures and enables human interaction in a great diversity of modes. Or, as Marian Verkerk puts it, following the French philosopher Paul Ricoeur: 'essential to the self-esteem of autonomous individuals in the fulfilment of their life-plan is bearing the responsibility for care, because through this they experience the imperfections of human existence' (Verkerk 1994: 64).

There are also all kinds of situations in which the norm of autonomy provides little help in deciding what care is necessary. It would seem pointless to ask an elderly woman suffering from an advanced case of Alzheimer's disease what she needs, and to shower her – in accordance with the principals of individual choice – with information enabling her to make her choice (Widdershoven 1995). Weak and dependent people simply need care, and it demands a proportionate quantity of commitment, time and patience to find out what they need to live with dignity. If we disregard this we run the risk of ending up in a position of 'moral arrogance', of weighing up the need for provisions for psycho-geriatrics in terms of business economics or programming care in time units, without seeing what is actually needed.

In short, it is important to recognize the moral value of relationships: to recognize that good relationships and time for human interaction are a prerequisite for adequate care, just as good care should affirm the receivers of care in their individual uniqueness. The way we give form to our relationships with others is an important moral event in itself, since the ability to maintain human relationships is decisive for the way we enable ourselves and others to experience and handle the moral dilemmas we face in our individual and collective lives. Intimacy and the ability to maintain relationships should be counted as fundamental human values (Young 1983; Nussbaum 1995). If such a relational approach were combined with diverse and balanced forms of responsibility and accountability on the part of the different actors involved in the care process, in both formal and informal contexts, the care–autonomy opposition would cease to exist, and in its place would come a whole range of moral practices and public discussions about care and about the ways in which care and autonomy can support each other.

These ideas could also contribute towards one of the quintessential goals of *Choices in Health Care*, that of a more thorough reflection on the sources of the culture of medicine. When autonomy is one-sidedly conceptualized as self-sufficiency, self-governance and freedom from contingency, it can indeed fuel the promise of medical technology to free the human subject from a wide variety of physical inconveniences.[18] This discourse, for example, plays quite a powerful role in the bio-ethical texts which dominate the public discussion on reproductive technology and genetic engineering (Sevenhuijsen 1995), just as it contributes to the ease with which medical–technical solutions are sought for human problems. Dethroning 'autonomous man' from his privileged status in moral reasoning and indeed as the central goal of moral politics (in the sense of engineering the human subject) could lead to more humane, contextualized forms of deliberation about the desirability and thus the social necessity of specific forms of medical knowledge and technology. The fiction of an autonomous moral actor is still too often linked to an instrumental view of the body: the idea that the body is a means to an end and that it is in the service of the mind, or that it should be kept under control by the mind. People with specific problems are thus turned into patients (a mechanism that could be termed 'patientizing') rather than being seen as ordinary moral subjects, who are trying to find their way through the trials and tribulations of daily life and deal with the ever-present threat of over-medicalization which constantly confronts them (Martin 1987).

Taking the ethics of care as a point of reference also cuts through the ease with which women are prescribed tranquillizers and sleeping-pills, without attention being paid to underlying social problems. A more adequate form of care can break through the 'addiction spiral' (Van der Waals 1994). In more general terms, an ethics of care can open the way to constant reflection on the question of whether the medical domain and the medical–ethical idiom are suited to the task of dealing with issues surrounding human fragility and finiteness. This ties in with the women's movement's attempt to promote different forms of communication, treatment and understanding between medical professionals and patients. In this sense medical science should have a much stronger social dimension and social involvement.

Equality

Equality figures in *Choices in Health Care* on two levels: that of constitutional equal rights and that of 'equivalence' or the injunction to regard fellow citizens as equals. These norms, together with the norm of solidarity, are invoked with the aim of protecting weaker parties in society (the elderly and the mentally handicapped), and arguing that care for these groups should be given priority over the development of expensive life-saving medical technology (a plea which is captured in the Dutch policy maxim 'care before cure'). This implies that equality is invoked in terms of the paradigm of distributive justice, in order to protect those who would suffer if goods and services were equally distributed with equal claims for all. In accordance with the argumentational rules of the paradigm of distributive justice, the report identifies relevant differences between individuals and determines these as differences in the seriousness of the illness and in the degree to which individuals are capable of taking care of themselves.

As I argued before, this approach has an inherent tendency towards blindness to social differences and social relations, because it starts from a norm of equality-as-sameness. This approach tends to see difference as deviance from the dominant norms or to naturalize difference; if differences cannot be corrected by just patterns of distribution, they are in the end attributed to 'natural' differences between individuals (Thornton 1986; Young 1990a). When feminist politics is phrased in the terminology of the distributive paradigm, it remains caught in a dilemma between equality and difference. When invoking equality the adaptation to 'male' norms seems inescapable (as is clear, for instance, in the dominance of paid labour as the norm for social participation), but talking in terms of difference can seem daunting as well, because it often leads to fruitless speculations about 'natural' sexual differences. This is particularly risky in a medical context, because thinking in terms of sexual difference in this context is usually derived from gender-laden images of the body in which, for example, a 'reproductive body' or a 'hormonal body' are taken as characteristic of femininity (Schiebinger 1989; Oudshoorn 1994; Schoon 1995). Thinking in terms of the distributive justice paradigm then, has adverse effects on the way social groups can profile themselves in the public sphere, just as it restricts modes of normative theorizing. When the norm of equality is interpreted as sameness, we lose sight of the fact that it is necessary to reflect upon patterns of 'othering' and the value attached to difference.

My negative appraisal of equality-as-sameness and of the argumentational rules of the paradigm of distributive justice should not be read, however, as an argument that we could dispense with equality norms and (re)distributive politics completely, when trying to reach responsible judgements about health-care policies. On the contrary, we need to reframe norms of equality and access to public provisions in such a way that they meet basic standards of social justice. This is also important in order to counter the deeply entrenched tendency towards thinking in terms of an opposition between an ethics of care and an ethics of justice, and to mark these as 'female' and 'male' forms of moral reasoning, thus reifying them into gender-divided ethical systems. At least three concepts of equality are crucial in this respect.

First, the norm of *equality in access and voice* in the public domain is important, because this is where the social groups concerned can discuss their experiences and develop their views about health and necessary care (Young 1992). This is not just a question of interest representation, but rather of the opportunity to participate in public deliberations in which concepts of the self as well as needs and interests are shaped. Participation in the public sphere is also important because this is the domain where ways of thinking and acting are open to discussion, and where cultural symbols relating to the body, health and the relationship between mind and body are formed and transformed. Equality in access and voice are important guarantees against traditional images and paternalism in the medical professions and against tendencies towards the 'othering' of social groups by marking them as different and thus deviant. This approach is relevant, for example, to the current discussion in the Netherlands about the issue of whether medical operations to reconstruct the hymen should be made available to Islamic girls by the Dutch health-care system. If there is no place in such a discussion for the views of the women concerned, the debate can easily slip into institutionalized patterns of aversion against 'strange habits' or 'traditional customs', thus blaming the women concerned instead of trying to understand their dilemmas and motives.

Another example concerns the availability of health-care services for HIV-positive women, who are often heroin addicts, ex-addicts or prostitutes. They need special health-care services, specialized forms of medical research and guaranteed access to the health-care system, not only in view of their own health condition but also when they are pregnant and bringing up children. An approach which proceeds from the principle of equality in access and voice ensures that their need for adequate care is taken into account. This counters the tendency towards punishing them for their 'irresponsible' behaviour, thus labelling them as 'deviants' compared to 'normal' persons (Young 1994). The ethics of care is of help here, because such values as attentiveness and responsiveness have the potential to orchestrate various moral considerations in an open-ended way and to question the way in which patterns of normality are constructed.

The principle of equality of access and voice paves the way for the second important equality norm, that of *equal opportunities*. By giving different social groups the opportunity to make themselves heard we get a richer view of the domains that need to be discussed when talking about equal opportunities and a broader range of arguments with which to justify claims to equal opportunities. This is relevant in the context of *Choices in Health Care*, because policy strategies are at present directed towards replacing formal care with informal care, often without due attention being paid to the considerable gender-effects of these strategic interventions. Public policies relating to the structuring of paid labour should be evaluated against the criteria that men and women should have equal chances of providing and receiving care when needed, not least because the possibility of having intimate relationships is one of the basic values of human life and a crucial condition for human development. Equality in the tradition of contract theory posits that people have equal rights, in this case to care provisions. Compensation for inequality then becomes an issue for normative theory. Equality from the perspective of an ethics of care means recognizing the fact that everyone needs care, but also that equality can only be achieved by paying sufficient attention to the diversity of needs. The issue of normativity is then to be found in questions such as 'how should we deal with plurality in care needs?'; 'how can we guarantee that groups of people are not unnecessarily privileged in their ability to acquire care?'; and 'how can dependency be given a place in thinking about necessary care?'

The principle of equal opportunities should also provide a counterweight to the logic of thinking in terms of heterosexual couples when designing just care provisions. A 'heterosexual logic' has unfair repercussions for the position and opportunities of lesbians and gay men, effectively removing their care needs from view. Similarly, the model of the heterosexual couple and the standard family can easily lead to the stigmatization of women who raise children alone (Young 1995). Moreover, it overlooks the fact that the majority of the elderly are women, often widowed, who have no partner to take care of them (Nelissen 1994; Nederland 1995). Policy proposals in which the kernel of the care system for the elderly depends on informal care mean, in effect, that daughters (and daughters-in-law) and women friends are made responsible for primary care, so that care remains principally in the hands of women.

The third important equality principle is that of *equal rights*, if we can at least shape these in such a way that they can account for differences in needs and values among individuals and social groups. This means, for example, guaranteeing women the right to health-care services that adequately support them in problems resulting from sexual assault as well as in pregnancy and childbirth. The possibility of a home delivery, for example, should be guaranteed, not only because it is preferred by many women, but also because the furthering of home deliveries can counter tendencies towards the medicalization and 'technologization' of human reproduction (Treichler 1990; Van der Hulst 1993; Cuppen 1995). Equal entitlements to social services can provide a safeguard against processes of marginalization and exclusion, and thus guarantee equal opportunities for full development to all. This is, again, of crucial importance against the background of immigration and the need to create fair and just multicultural societies. Neo-liberal regimes have a tendency to exclude immigrants from social services, and thus from public health care, on the grounds that newcomers should first attain full legal citizenship of the receiving country. By implication a large number of women – and their children – could be excluded from maternity and health care. Care is then literally reduced to charity; worse still, caring behaviour on the part of people who are willing to provide care to those who need it can even mean that these people are engaging in illegal activities. Even settled immigrants can suffer from exclusionary processes. Lack of understanding for the lifestyle and needs of immigrant women is increased by adherence to ethnocentric interpretation-repertoires (Van der Zwaard 1993; Özçelik 1994). So, in designing new social care practices, it is important to take immigration and the intercultural society into account; this underlines the need to take diversity as a guiding principle in social and health-care provisions.

Justice and solidarity: reformulating the political

By thus revising the arguments surrounding social participation, autonomy and equality from the perspective of a communicative and relational paradigm which provides space for diversity and situated forms of subjectivity the dichotomy between care and justice starts to lose ground in our deliberations about justice.[19] Again, it remains important to remember that the care–justice dichotomy is at its sharpest when justice is framed in the epistemological parameters of the paradigm of distributive justice, in which abstract rationality, impartiality and sameness are paramount. If we base our moral arguments, instead, on social practices and an explicit awareness of the way these are affected by power and domination, we may be able to arrive at enriched notions of justice. The moral and epistemological orientation of the ethics of care can contribute to this awareness, which is also the goal of social justice; this is a consideration which remains of crucial importance for public decision-making. A combination of these normative orientations should make it possible to counter arbitrary and authoritarian practices, ensuring that norms of social justice can encompass measures of what constitutes fair and reasonable treatment of individuals in law and the just provision of public services. Considerations of social justice should enable people to participate in the *res publica*, the public domain where we meet in order to establish common norms for living and acting together.

Seen from this perspective, justice cannot be formulated as a standard set of norms and rules, be they procedural or substantive. Justice cannot be separated, any more than care, from the way in which we give shape to our social and political participation. Justice is a *process* in which content and form are interwoven in specific ways, or a common commitment to structure our collective lives in accordance with situational considerations on just rules and public provisions. Justice should be based on values such as reconciliation, reciprocity, diversity and responsibility, and on the willingness and ability of citizens to accept responsibility for each other's well-being (Flax 1993; Frazer and Lacey 1993: 206). Justice, thus conceived, explicitly opens discursive space for deliberating about what constitutes *injustice* or, in other words, for continuous reflection on which 'social evils' we need to address (Shklar 1990). This can serve to strengthen the collective will to do something about the cruelties suffered by women on account of male violence, whether it be violence within intimate relationships or in contexts such as mass rape or war atrocities. These collective feelings of responsibility can be given shape by regarding provisions such as shelters, counselling and psychotherapy for the victims of rape and sexual abuse as part of the collective health-care system.

This concept of justice also opens avenues for dealing with difference and diversity, and for countering the tendency of the paradigm of distributive justice to turn difference into deviance and 'otherness', accompanied by the urge to control or eliminate the 'other'. This is important when assessing political issues in the area of health care, because respect for difference provides a counterweight to prevailing tendencies towards governing 'the' human subject by standardizing bodies with the help of medical technology, for example through the further development of pre-implantation diagnosis and early interventions in fertilization processes. The moral impulse towards respect for diversity can thus strengthen democratic citizenship, at least if we accept, in the spirit of Hannah Arendt (Arendt 1958), that the most fundamental task of democratic societies is to find just ways of dealing with plurality. However, this would by no means imply that every posited difference should be accepted at face value, nor indeed that every claim to health care made by individuals and social groups should always be met with public means.

Nor does it imply that everyone should always participate in a direct form of public decision-making or that we should adopt a political model which allows for the group representation of oppressed groups, with or without the right of veto, on issues which determine their lives, as has been proposed by Iris Young (Young 1990a). Group representation assumes that members of the group have a clearly defined identity which makes it necessary for them to have a separate political voice. This has become a thriving model in health care, as witnessed by the large number of patients' organizations, aimed at protecting patients' interests. The risk attached to this model is that people become tied to a citizenship identity as 'patient', which in turn can dominate their whole life. This can encourage thinking in terms of 'them' and 'us', as well as an inability to see the public sphere as a place in which we can give shape to commonality on the basis of diversity. As an alternative to group representation, it is quite possible to frame the politics of health care within models of representative democracy, provided that positions of power and decision-making are open to representatives of all social groups, and provided that there is room for different voices to be heard in the public sphere and for different forms of accountability to be developed (Mouffe 1992; Voet 1995).

If care assumes a more important place in public morality and if the recognition of vulnerability is incorporated into the concept of a 'normal' subject in politics, then it will depend less on the presence of specific groups whether political decision-making is carried out 'with care'. In this sense, we need to be able to put our trust in politics without always having to be involved. If care is seen as a normal human activity and a normal need, then it will be possible to combat the various forms of privileged irresponsibility which are still too often to be found in administrative logic and the public debate. Clearer ideas about what constitutes necessary care can be gained by granting those who are the 'object' of care cognitive authority over their needs, and giving them the opportunity to express these in a heterogeneous public sphere which allows open and honest debate. Politicians in decision-making positions can, in turn, decide whether they find it justifiable to meet these needs with public funds. It is then up to the public debate to decide whether they have done this with care and responsibility.

Such an approach to politics and justice would also imply revised notions of solidarity. The distributive justice paradigm is attractive for many social groups and political theorists because at first sight it seems to offer a suitable measure of solidarity with those who are most in need. I would argue, however, that these forms of solidarity, as laid down in *Choices in Health Care*, are overwhelmingly based on rationalistic arguments which can easily take on the form of 'calculating', monologic and even self-centred forms of solidarity: because I now have the right to something from you, you will then have the right to demand something similar from me, should you find yourself in a similar situation. This mode of reasoning, which belongs to a subject-centred form of ethics, presumes a norm of sameness and, accompanying this, different constructions of a uniform normality. It encourages a solidarity of giving and taking, and points to an ethics dominated by mutual exchange. We provide care, not because it is needed, but because one day we can expect to get something in return when we are in the same situation. The feminist ethics of care points to forms of solidarity in which there is room for difference, and in which we find out what people in particular situations need in order for them to live with dignity. People must be able to count on solidarity, because vulnerability and dependency, as we know, are a part of human existence; we need each other's disinterested support at expected and unexpected moments.

Therefore we need to conceive of the ethics of care as a form of political ethics. It may be that care structures human relationships and makes them possible, but these relationships take place for an important part within political contexts, in situations of communal interaction and collective deliberation and decision-making. How we can care depends to a great extent on how we give shape to our society. If we fail to give due consideration to these sorts of issues in our thinking about care, then care will rapidly be reduced to private charity. The notion of solidarity gives a political meaning to care and to mutual commitment. Solidarity without care leads to an impoverished sense of morality and collective responsibility, because it can only recognize others if they are exactly 'like us' or needy, pathetic, pitiful and worthy of 'our' commiseration because of their comparative deprivation in relation to 'ourselves'. Solidarity thus depends on an 'us-and-them' distinction, which is exactly what forms an obstacle to thinking about care in a 'human' way. On the other hand, care without collective solidarity strengthens the privatization and moralization of care. We need caring solidarity not because the 'needy' are dependent on the solidarity of the 'strong', or because the 'strong' need to defend themselves against the looming threat of society's corruption by the 'needy' – an idea which has been fast gaining in popularity in recent years – but because everyone in different ways and to different degrees needs care at some point in their lives.

Dependence on care should not be seen as something which can suddenly overtake us; rather it should be seen as an integral part of human existence. This does not exclude the existence of different gradations of dependence; there are all sorts of situations in which care is needed suddenly and in which we cannot survive without it. Through speaking in terms of caring solidarity we can do justice to the idea that people are differently situated and that this is exactly what makes public dialogue and collective support so necessary. This 'caring solidarity' offers more potential for understanding the diversity of needs and lifestyles than a solidarity which takes for granted the norms of homogeneity and a 'standard' human subject. In this respect, care marks the difference between policy as control and policy as an enabling activity.

Seen from this perspective, the contradictions in *Choices in Health Care* can be made productive. Through combining a policy document with a public campaign, the Dutch government has opened the door to an ongoing public debate about the availability and quality of health care. This discussion would be improved, however, by a revision of the proposed normative model. The feminist ethics of care, a politics of needs-interpretation and caring solidarity could be integrated into dialogic open-ended forms of discourse ethics. This shows how important it is that citizenship is not conceptualized exclusively in terms of a liberal rights model but first and foremost as an activity and a normative approach which can lead to a search for the best course of action in public contexts. This does not preclude thinking in terms of rights; indeed, it can lead to a recognition of situated rights to (health) care, and thus to public provisions which meet the standards of social justice. It can, in other words, lead to judging with care.

NOTES

1 'HAS HEAD, HANDS, FEET AND HEART'

1 'Judging with care' was indeed the title of the Dutch version of this book.
2 For an illuminating overview of the different dimensions of feminist theorizing about care, see Gremmen 1995: 21–48.
3 I have outlined the historical background to this problem in a number of articles not included in this collection (Sevenhuijsen 1988b, 1992b).
4 The following passages dealing with Held's work are taken from Sevenhuijsen 1993c. The articles by Held which I have drawn on the most have been reprinted in Held 1993.
5 The feminist view of neo-republican citizenship has been inspired by the work of the political theoretician Hannah Arendt. See, for example, Voet 1988, 1995; Mouffe 1992; Hermsen 1994. See also Passerin D'Entrèves 1994; Honig 1995, Benhabib 1996, Bickford 1996.
6 A number of feminist authors are critical about the possibilities of the ethics of care in relation to ethnocentrism and the undermining of a (post-)colonial mentality. See for example Lugones 1991; Spelman 1991; Schrage 1994; Narayan 1995. However I am inclined to give the ethics of care at least the benefit of the doubt, on the condition that its epistemological bases and moral and political implications are formulated as carefully as possible, and on condition that it is made sufficiently explicit in which contexts the ethics of care can or cannot lead to appropriate political judgement.
7 A more sympathetic and inspiring argument about the congruence between postmodernism and a feminist ethics of care is made by the American political theorist Stephen White in his *Political Theory and Postmodernism* (1991). More than I would do, he situates the ethics of care in a barely substantiated concept of 'difference feminism', whereby his thoughts could get pigeon-holed in the 'equality–difference' debate in feminist theory. Moreover, he tends, more than I would argue for, to situate the need for an ethics of care in a Heideggerian philosophical ontology, defining care as an attitude, i.e., one of humility towards 'the world beyond one's control', and of the acceptance of otherness and finitude. Although similar arguments recur in my plea for a postmodern form of care ethics, my version of the ethics of care is more firmly linked with caring as an activity, in the sense of a fully human praxis, and would thus expose a split between being, thinking and doing. Only by decoding the gender-load of thinking in terms of 'otherness' and by thoroughly accepting human plurality, can we arrive at forms of moral subjectivity that can break with harmful patterns of 'othering'. It is indeed this idea of human plurality,

that marks a crucial difference between Hannah Arendt's political theory and the philosophy of her teacher, Heidegger (see, for example, Passerin D'Entrèves 1994). Her definition of plurality ('the fact that men, not Man, live on earth and inhabit the world') makes her thought a much more attractive partner for feminist theory than a Heideggerian ontology. This is, again, an argument for conceptualizing the political dimensions of an ethics of care in a renewed concept of citizenship. In my view, White positions the need for an ethics of care too exclusively in the need for cultivating a 'mood', albeit a crucial one; namely, a mood of listening to otherness. But this moral–epistemological strategy only has a chance of success if we radically and explicitly alter real-life patterns of backgrounding and the lived everyday gender dynamics in speaking and listening, and thus in attentiveness and responsiveness, both in public and private life. At the same time White's argument about ontology is a solid reminder of the fact that 'caring' has many existential dimensions, and that human intimacy should stay aloof as much as possible from regulative administrative rationality.

8 In her 1950s study of the upbringing and supervision of the so-called 'Philips girls' Annemieke van Drenth developed the concept of 'caring power' (Van Drenth 1991, 1994), that is inspired by Foucault's concept of pastoral power, but without Foucault's forgetfulness about the symbolic roles of gender and the role of women's agency in this discursive domain.

9 The historical roots of this lie for a major part in nineteenth-century Christian feminism, in particular in the different forms of social work which were set up in this circle, for example help for women prisoners, prostitutes and unmarried mothers. See for this Sevenhuijsen 1987; De Haan 1995; Van Drenth 1995; De Vries 1997.

10 Frazer and Lacey use the term 'dialogic communitarianism' in this respect (Frazer and Lacey 1993: 193). This notion accepts the social ontology of communitarianism, whereby people are considered as living in interpretative communities which attribute meaning and which are important for the formation of moral subjectivity. However, it is critical of the normative dimensions of the images of a homogeneous subject which are linked to most versions of communitarianism, and which often amount to a nostalgic longing for 'old certainties' and fixed boundaries between 'them' and 'us' in constructions of group membership. Dialogic communitarianism, on the other hand, is dynamic in nature. It assumes that people participate in different social practices and have layered identities, and moreover that this has a positive value for morality and politics. While the conservative versions of communitarianism view fragmentation as a threat, in dialogic communitarianism it is seen as positive, both on the level of the individual subject and of social communication. Though I share this commitment to dialogue and communicative ethics, I would be hesitant to qualify this approach as 'communitarian', overloaded as this term is with traditional notions of community and harmony. I would argue that the moral epistemology proposed by Frazer and Lacey better fits an openended model of communicative ethics than some form of communitarianism.

11 In spite of this remark I do not want to suggest that care and the perception of needs are by definition linguistic events or that care needs are always transparent for cognitive acts. Many forms of care indeed suppose that the care-giver can silently perceive the needs of the cared for, and has the capacity for attentive love and displacement of the self into the other. If we limit care to linguistic communications this would preclude caring for those who cannot speak and for physical objects from our moral considerations and our moral being.

12 This means that I have difficulty with the definition of care introduced by Berenice Fisher and Joan Tronto. They argue that we can distinguish care practices by

their aims and that we can recognize care as a practice which is directed 'towards the maintaining, continuing or repairing of "our" world so that we can live in it as well as possible'. Playing, fulfilling desires, marketing a new product or creating a work of art do not constitute care in this respect (Tronto 1993: 104). Such attempts at delineation, however, continually capsize because it is not clear which criteria can be used to judge practices other than an evaluation of the motives of the caring agents and the well-being of the cared-for. In short, if we want to see care as a practice and a virtue, we cannot escape giving first priority to the aspects of agency, orientation and motivation: a hermeneutical, interpretative approach to care and ethics is thus most appropriate.

13 The metaphor of the 'stranger within' has recently been used, principally in black women's studies, to refer to the productive, creative and critical position which can be chosen for cultural and political action. See, for example, hooks 1990; Collins 1991. The metaphor goes back to the work of Virginia Woolf (1938), who pointed out that by adopting a 'bridge position' intellectual women could avoid surrendering uncritically to patriarchal society and its intellectual culture.

14 With thanks to Annelies van Heijst who pointed this out to me when discussing the Dutch version of this book with me in an interview for the Dutch Journal of Women's Studies.

15 Since 1991 there has been a considerable change in this situation. The redistribution of paid and unpaid labour has become one of the spearheads of Dutch emancipation policy. Informal and voluntary care are now evaluated from an emancipatory perspective. Even so, the importance of care is still most derived from paid labour and from 'independence' as the overarching normative goal for government policies. In addition the dominant paradigm is still the distributive paradigm, which means that several aspects of care and the ethics of care are difficult to thematize. Chapter 3 of this book will go further into this. I discuss these issues further in Sevenhuijsen 1997b.

16 The English neo-Kantian political philosopher Susan Mendus has argued for an ethics of vulnerability, which she contrasts with the ethics of care (Mendus 1993). In her opinion, the ethics of care is based too much on a controversial concept of a 'motherly' identity of women and linked too closely to an apolitical communitarianism à la MacIntyre. She argues that an ethics of vulnerability could certainly draw on the moral experiences of mothers, because mothers have more contact with the vulnerable and fragile sides of existence and because the duties of motherhood are not freely chosen, but often have more to do with destiny. Even though I can sympathize with this observation I fail to see why this should lead us to dispense with the concept of an ethics of care. At most it warns against founding the ethics of care in a motherly identity. Mendus's suggestion, however, is not free from foundationalism either, because why should the ethics of care necessarily find its foundations in a vulnerable subject? And how can we make vulnerability a moral theme without posing the question (arising from an ethics of care) of how to deal with vulnerability? This problem can only be overcome in my opinion by grounding the ethics of care not in a concept of identity, but by finding its sources of inspiration in social practices and virtue-ethics.

17 For a convincing philosophical argument about the possibility and necessity of such an approach, see Fraser 1989, in particular Chapters 2 and 3. See also Haber 1994; White 1991.

18 I have used this concept in Sevenhuijsen 1993b, where I borrow it from the philosopher Marli Huyer, who introduced it into the Dutch care debate.

19 For this, see further Chapter 3.

20 For this, see Chapters 4 and 5. In women's studies in the Netherlands there are now many examples of applications of such an approach, for example: Holtmaat 1992; Keuzenkamp and Teunissen 1990; Mossink and Nederland 1993; Bussemaker 1993; Verloo and Roggeband 1994; Halsema 1994; Parlevliet 1995; Nederland 1995; Römkens 1995; Ten Dam and Volman 1995. See for the methodology of this approach, for example: Smith 1990; Fairclough 1992.

21 For this idea I would like to thank Jeanine Suurmond, who is writing her Ph.D. about care and justice reasoning in Dutch media debates about female circumcision and immigration policies (see, for example, Suurmond 1992).

22 With this remark I certainly do not want to say that the actions of the nurse can be in any way justified by appealing to motives of care and compassion with suffering, as she indeed tried to when explaining her actions in the courtroom. This would amount to a view in which care and justice are indeed on a 'strange footing' with each other. What I do want to say is that a perspective of care may give us a better moral understanding of the moral complexity and the (potential) burden of caring for the frail elderly, but also of the difficulties of living with finitude and death as 'moral experiences'. Justice within a perspective of care may imply that we have to protect the weak and vulnerable from too much compassion and thus from tragic combinations of desperation and hubris in matters of life and death.

23 A creative way of both distinguishing and combining care and justice arguments that bears many similarities to my approach can be found in Clement 1996, which I received only when finalizing the English version of this book.

2 THE MORALITY OF FEMINISM

1 This chapter is a thorough reworking of the speech which I gave on 16 May 1990 on the occasion of my appointment as Professor of Women's Studies at the Faculty of Social Sciences at the University of Utrecht. Several passages in the original text have been further thought through, developed and brought up to date. I have also extended the argument on the question of why a feminist ethics of care should be considered a political ethic. I would like to thank the following people for their constructive criticism of the provisional text of the inaugural lecture in 1990: Christien Binkgreve, Kathy Davis, Aafke Komter, Wibo Koole, Joyce Outshoorn, Henk van Nieuwenhuijzen and Renée Römkens. In addition I have benefited from reviews and other reactions which I received after the delivery and publication of the text. An English translation of the original text appeared in the American philosophical journal *Hypatia* (Sevenhuijsen 1991a).

2 In this sense I agree with the feminist theologian Annelies van Heijst, who argues:

> I consider 'moralistic' to mean the absolute presentation of morality, a presentation which forces acceptance or rejection on the basis of authoritarian arguments or rhetorical overkill. A text has a moralistic effect if the ethical judgement of the reader is extinguished by the force of its moral appeal. A text interpretation is moralistic if the reader reduces the plurality of meanings in a text to one absolute value-laden meaning; or simply imposes her one meaning on the text.
>
> (Van Heijst 1992: 51)

3 Here too I agree with Annelies van Heijst's description, with the difference that she is concerned with sexually differentiated reflection. That seems to me to be too great a limitation for a first definition, because it closes the path to ethical reflection on the issue of when 'sexual difference' plays a role in thinking and behaving, and when sexual difference may or may not be a relevant moral category for the practice of ethics.

4 For an overview and analysis of the debate see, among others, Kittay and Meyers 1987; Benhabib and Cornell 1987; Prins 1988, 1989; Sevenhuijsen 1988a; Komter 1989b; Benhabib 1992; Davis 1992; Larrabee 1993. An overview of the literature with a keyword index can be found in Krol and Sevenhuijsen 1992.

5 In Dutch women's studies this link has been made by Saskia Poldervaart, among others. She interpreted my oration as a plea for an equation of the ethics of care with motherhood and femininity, and in so doing accused me of a universal and unhistorical view of femininity (Poldervaart 1991: 151).

6 In this chapter I discuss liberalism in general terms, which fails to do justice to the great variation within liberalisms in the history of ideas and in the political reality. The modern feminist criticism of liberalism is mostly directed towards contractual and deontological varieties, as found in John Rawls's influential work *A Theory of Justice* (Rawls 1971). From a feminist perspective the most important philosophical themes in the debate about liberalism are its use of the concept of 'person', the idea of impartiality, of abstract and instrumental rationality and abstract individualism. These are also the themes which I deal with in this book. For a clear and nuanced treatment of the feminist criticism of liberalism see, Naffine 1990; Porter 1991; Frazer and Lacey 1993; and also the literature mentioned in the footnotes to this book.

7 Like the concept of 'liberalism', the concept of 'universalism' needs further detailed explanation. In my argument the concept refers to abstract universalism, which takes a general and homogeneous human image as its starting-point and as the norm for moral reasoning. This does not mean that I want to exclude the possibility of reasoning in terms of universal values or of using them as a standard of political action and judgement. Chantal Mouffe has, for example, argued that norms such as equality and freedom can form an important 'political intellectual horizon' in order to judge existing practices critically from a feminist perspective (Mouffe 1992; see also Frazer and Lacey 1993: 191 ff.). The ethics of care can also provide the opportunity to take a number of general human values as the starting-point for moral deliberations (see the examples mentioned in Chapters 4 and 5 of this book).

8 This distinction goes back to one of the founders of liberal feminism in political philosophy, the nineteenth-century English philosopher John Stuart Mill, and in particular to his standard work, which appeared in 1869, *The Subjection of Women*.

9 In this way the concept of distributive justice is applied consistently to gender issues. This approach has been most explicitly expressed by the American political philosopher Susan Moller Okin (Okin 1987, 1989). In Chapter 3 this point will be dealt with in more detail.

10 This is certainly so, if 'difference' and 'equality' are seen as mutually exclusive norms or even political positions, as was the case for a long time in the equality–difference debate. The opposition between equality and difference was first criticized in the Netherlands by the psychologist Aafke Komter (Komter 1990) and in Anglo-Saxon women's studies literature by the American historian Joan Wallack Scott (Scott 1988). The Australian historian Carol Bacchi has analysed in detail how much the equality–difference dilemma is generated by legal discourses and

by the way in which Western welfare states have dealt with a number of women's issues and incorporated them into the law (Bacchi 1990, 1991).

11 For this, see further Chapter 3.

12 The Australian political scientist Merle Thornton has described this mode of arguing as 'the dogmatic argument for equality' (Thornton 1986; see also Plumwood 1993).

13 This can lead at best to a 'high-handed' and at worst to something approximating to a totalitarian form of political life, in which the government is by definition justified in determining what the desirable forms of its subjects' existence are. This tension between freedom and coercion is still paid too little attention by radical–liberal feminists.

14 The criticism of dualism and the logic of identity can now be found in many women's studies publications. The most important contributions are: Lloyd 1984, 1993; Benhabib 1987; Arnault 1989; Van der Haegen 1989; Spelman 1989; Young 1990a; Braidotti 1991, 1994; Jay 1991; Plumwood 1993; Braidotti and Haakma 1994. The Australian philosopher Elizabeth Porter has described the effect of dualism in moral philosophy in a way which is similar to my own work (Porter 1991, in particular Chapter 2).

15 For this, see among others the authors mentioned in note 12, as well as Bordo 1986; Coltheart 1986; Diprose 1994; Hermsen 1994; Schott 1994; Waters 1994; Gatens 1996.

16 Many authors have introduced concepts such as gender-load and gender-symbolism as an instrument for research into gender. See, for example, Harding 1986; Scott 1986 and Hagemann-White 1989.

17 Barbara Houston has made an intriguing analysis of the marginalizing terms which authors who work within a universalist discourse have unleashed on Gilligan's research. As well as methodological carelessness, she has also been accused among other things of particularism, conservatism, traditionalism, (crypto)separatism, anti-feminism and moral essentialism (Houston 1988). Kathy Davis shows in her rhetorical analysis of the debate about Gilligan's work that academic and political arguments were continually cutting across each other in their evaluation of it (Davis 1992).

18 The moral philosopher Anette Baier is the most explicit representative of the idea that Gilligan's work should be placed in an anti-Kantian tradition in moral philosophy, which goes back to the work of David Hume (Baier 1987). From a more critical angle this is argued by the political theorist Joan Tronto (Tronto 1987).

19 The idea of a paradigm change has been developed in steps over the years in a number of publications about the ethics of care. See, for example, Calhoun 1988; Maihofer 1988; Addelson 1991; Rooney 1991; Sevenhuijsen 1991a; Tronto 1993, 1995c; Verkerk 1994; and most explicitly by Hekman 1995.

20 In Chapter 3 I develop this argument for moral issues in the area of parental authority: on pornography see Cohen 1986; Assiter 1988 and MacGregor Davies 1988; on abortion Whitbeck 1984; Hursthouse 1987; Himmelweit 1988; Addelson 1993; on reproductive technology Sevenhuijsen 1995.

21 It might be evident that the word 'duty' cannot rely on a great deal of popularity when rights, freedom and autonomy are considered as exclusive values for feminism. Reflection on ethics should thus in fact lead to a feminist re-evaluation and reformulation of the concepts of 'obligation' and 'duty'. See, for example, Hirschmann 1992. For many philosophers categories such as obligation and responsibility are even the characteristic concepts of ethics, because the tensions between the striving to be an autonomous self and accepting responsibility for others who are different from the self, is basic to moral dilemmas. Without the willingness to set

aside a definite idea of the self and the desires and objectives of the self, ethics is hardly imaginable.

22 I work this theme out further in Chapter 5.

23 In nursing and home-care ethics this has led for example to different pleas for a restoration of the unity between 'hand, head and heart', as a counterbalance to the instrumental ethics which is becoming more and more dominant in the care sector. See among others Benner and Wrubel 1989; Simonen 1990; Gremmen 1995. For a similar appeal from a hermeneutical viewpoint see Widdershoven 1995.

24 Even though the feminist ethics of care has given an important impetus to this mode of thinking, it is of course by no means the property of this ethic. The existence of links between reason, emotion and thinking has meanwhile become commonplace in feminism (see, for example, Lloyd 1984; Jaggar 1989; Code 1991). The idea of the rationality and moral relevance of emotions has been elaborated in different philosophical traditions, among which that of the Aristotelian virtues tradition has attracted most attention, for example, Nussbaum 1990, 1995. There are thus, as mentioned in the introductory chapter to this book, all kinds of connections between different moral vocabularies.

25 The French philosopher Luce Irigaray has formulated the principle of moral respect for sexual and bodily inviolability as the basis for a visionary design for a women's law (Irigaray 1989).

26 For this, see further Chapter 3 of this book.

27 In Chapter 5 I further develop the relevance of this approach for the way in which justice can be conceptualized in the public debate about the health-care system.

28 With thanks to Mary Dietz, who has, starting from a Machiavellian idea about politics, formulated an astute critique of communicative ethics in the tradition of Jürgen Habermas and Seyla Benhabib (Dietz 1996).

3 PARADOXES OF GENDER

1 An earlier version of this chapter was presented as a paper at the BSA/PSA congress 'The Politics of Care' at the London School of Economics in February 1992 and published in *Acta Politica* (Sevenhuijsen 1993a). I would like to thank Diemuth Bubeck, Diana Coole and Ann Showstack Sassoon for their stimulating and detailed comments on the original version of the paper. Participants in the Dutch interuniversity project 'Gender and Care' have also contributed useful suggestions for the further development of a number of lines of thought in this article. I would like to thank Annemieke van Drenth in particular for her helpfully critical remarks.

2 For relevant discussions on this point see, for example, various issues of journals such as *Hypatia: A Journal for Feminist Philosophy and Ethics*. For a bibliography on this area see Krol and Sevenhuijsen 1992.

3 See for example the chapter in Young (1990a) about the paradigm of distributive justice and my ideas about the influence of this paradigm in the areas of family law and health care as set out in Chapters 4 and 5 of this volume.

4 For a thorough critique of homogeneous conceptions of gender see, for example, hooks 1981; Spelman 1989; Butler 1990; Gatens 1991; Haraway 1991; Lugones 1991.

5 The dilemmas arising from this recommendation by Okin are further worked out in Chapter 2 of this book.

6 In adopting this reasoning, Okin not only expects an inordinate amount from the

redistribution of child care, but also discredits the quality of the moral arguments of those who do not live or have not been brought up in the modern egalitarian heterosexual family. This works through into her concept of democracy, which depends on citizens having been brought up in modern egalitarian families. The concept of democracy as the ability to live with plurality and difference is thus quite far removed.

7 There is a great risk of paternalism or maternalism connected to the assumption that a single (hypothetical or actual) person could reach the 'true' moral judgements. Moral judgements of course are dependent on interpretation. 'Empathy' in itself forms no guarantee that someone's moral considerations are free of projection or misconception. The promotion of empathy is in itself insufficient to break the dominance of cognitive processes, in which 'others' are objectified, and along with this the sexism, classism, and ethnocentrism in dominant currents in Western philosophy. For this to happen it is necessary that the so-called 'others' speak for themselves. 'Listening', 'communicating', 'interacting' and 'understanding' are more important cognitive elements of an ethics of care, seen in this way, than 'empathy', just as the encouragement of pluriformity and compromise, in my opinion, is a better aim of moral debate than the creation of consensus. See also Code (1992) and Meyers (1993) on the relationship between empathy and impartiality as elements of moral reasoning. See Bickford (1996) for the importance of listening.

8 The idea that gender can be represented as a continuum was introduced into women's studies in the Netherlands by Carol Hageman-White (1989) and Kathy Davis (1989). See also Gremmen (1991). In using this metaphor I am not suggesting that people take up a fixed position on a line. On the contrary, they may display a great deal of flexibility and change during the course of their lives. Moreover 'gender' as an aspect of a person's character is always interrelated with other aspects in a complex way.

9 For further discussion of this point see Chapter 2.

10 I thus do not agree with the argument that a uniform or unambiguous concept of 'Women' is necessary as a political basis of feminism. This need for unambiguity means that oppressed groups are marginalized or silenced, and keeps alive the cultural myth of the homogeneous subject as the centre of political activity. Moreover, in this way it can all too easily be forgotten that the subject who *is* speaking *does* have a gender, a body, a class identity and an ethnic identity. The spread of feminism is thus served more by emphasizing rather than denying differences, ambiguity, plurality and discord.

11 Moira Gatens (1991) has criticized the distinction between sexual difference and gender by pointing to the fact that it rests on a desire to see the psyche as a *tabula rasa*, on which gender is inscribed via the body which is then seen as a passive medium. She makes a connection between this wish and the liberal tradition of the 're-education' of subjects:

> The effect of the use of the sex/gender distinction . . . has been to encourage or engender a neutralization of sexual differences and sexual politics. This neutralizing process is not novel, it can be traced to nineteenth-century liberal environmentalism where 're-education' is the catchcry of radical social transformation. Much of contemporary radical politics is, perhaps unwittingly, enmeshed in this liberal tradition. A feminism based on difference rather than on *a priori* equality is representative of a decisive break with this tradition.
>
> (Gatens 1991: 140; see also Gatens 1996)

12 The layered concept of gender was introduced by Sandra Harding (1986), Joan Scott (1986) and Carol Hagemann-White (1989), for example. Ine Gremmen has elaborated this approach more fully in her dissertation about the ethics of home-helpers (Gremmen 1995). Myra Keizer has drawn on this approach in the research for her dissertation on gender and professionalism in medical specialisms (Keizer 1997). The layered gender concept is also laid down in the programme for the Dutch Research Council project 'Gender and Care: Identity, Labour and Morality' (Gender en Zorg 1991), and in the research programme of the Netherlands Research School of Women's Studies (NOV [Netherlands Research School of Women's Studies] 1994).

13 For this see further Chapters 1 and 2 of this book. Rooney writes the following on this point:

> In other words, the gender dimensions of principles must be examined from both directions, in terms of the tendency to automatically hear male voicings as essentially involving principles deliberations, and the corresponding tendency not to hear principles operating in female deliberations. In the end, of course, this should help propel a reconceptualization of the role of principles and 'rational' deliberation in moral theorizing itself.
>
> (Rooney 1991: 341)

14 When love and empathy are seen as the chief characteristics of care, traditional definitions of femininity play a determining role. This problem will always arise when the motivation of those who care is the only starting-point for an understanding of care (Fisher and Tronto 1990; Tronto 1993).

15 Informal care for the elderly and relatives is a typical area in which the shift in the feminist viewpoint on care is clearly apparent. In the 1980s informal care was turned into a political issue through the care = work paradigm. In this, informal care figured as unpaid work, a burden, from which women could not derive any rights. Informal carers were seen as a specific group, which could be fitted into a trade union model of political interest promotion. Payment for care was presented as an important demand, while organization of informal care was seen as an obstacle to emancipation: emancipation would have to be accompanied by professionalization of care. If care, on the other hand, is seen as a normal human need and a social process, this leads to a different view on informal care: it is just a part of life and in principle is no worse or better than paid work or making use of professional care. A great deal depends on the conditions under which informal care is carried out and the amount of support which the carer receives. This leads to a differentiated policy on care, in which for example care leave, integrated care and support for carers are compatible with emanicipatory aims (Duijnstee *et al.* 1994). I have supported this 'different view' on voluntary work and women's liberation in Sevenhuijsen 1993d. See also Emancipatieraad 1993.

16 When only intimate situations are described as situations in which care can be involved, the danger exists that the ethics of care is considered as something which is only relevant in close relationships. As Sarah Hoagland has argued, however, an ethics of care should be able to account not only for responsibility for the 'proximate intimate', but also for the 'distant stranger'. When the accent lies on care for proximate intimates, fear of proximate and distant strangers can even be increased. Or, in Hoagland's words:

> If an ethics of caring is going to be morally successful in replacing an ethics located in principles and duty, particularly within the context of oppression, then it must provide for the possibility of ethical behaviour in relation to what is foreign, it must consider analyses of oppression, it must acknowledge a self that is both related and separate, and it must have a vision of, if not a program for, change. In my opinion, care stripped of these elements isn't a caring that benefits us.
>
> (Hoagland 1991: 261)

17 This does not mean that I would deny that comparisons between the moral reasoning of women and men can provide useful knowledge. I am more in favour of this sort of research being carried out in relation to a context; that is, in relation to specific issues in specific situations. For an example of this see the previously mentioned dissertation by Myra Keizer on gender and professionalism in medical specialisms, in particular the section in which she analyses men and women specialists' reasoning on the dilemma between making a career and responsibility for children (Keizer 1997).

18 Such an approach which is based on the shift in the paradigm of care is slowly beginning to be heard in the Dutch political debate. See, for example, Van Lieshout 1995.

19 This approach is set out in a well-considered way in the report 'Onbetaalde zorg gelijk verdeeld' (Unpaid work equally shared) published in 1995 by the Dutch Commission for Future Scenarios for the Redistribution of Unpaid Work. This report comes out in favour of an even division between paid and unpaid care and the gradual introduction of more equality between men and women in this respect. A choice is also made for a strong encouragement policy rather than a normative policy. It is still striking, however, that the commission is reluctant to support the value of intimate relationships and a relational perspective in itself. In the introduction to the report the need for a better division of unpaid care is primarily argued by referring to factors derived from paid work, such as the increasing stress suffered by working women and higher absence due to illness, which arise from their 'compromise strategies' now that they 'are expected' to carry out paid work. In this sense the report can be read as an expression of the belated realization that the implementation of an obligation for women to participate in the labour market, without measures directed at the redistribution of care, could well turn out to be counterproductive. The policy perspective adopted is still mainly based on the rational choice-theory view of human nature or, in other words, the idea that the government can change human behaviour through material stimuli. Factors such as representation, identity and culture receive short shrift in this view, while the moral worth of care is only mentioned marginally, in connection to the idea of 'the quality of care' or 'cultural habits'. I have elaborated the viewpoint of the ethics of care on this policy conception in Sevenhuijsen 1997b.

20 In this respect it is striking that Jaggar concentrates her criticism of the ethics of care on interpretations of it which are based on the specifically female experiences of menstruation, sexuality, childbirth and breastfeeding, and which propose that women derive from these a morality of connection. Jaggar associates this with biological determinism, and reproaches this type of thinking for making feminist ethics thus only accessible to women. A 'good ethics' should, in her view, be accessible to everyone (Jaggar 1991: 94). I find this a problematic line of reasoning, because it rules out the possibility that there could be moral experiences (such as pregnancy) which cannot be shared with others, and which could still be worthwhile for others or which could even serve as an example for moral reasoning

about other issues. Iris Young, for example, has argued that the experience of pregnancy is accompanied by an image of human subjectivity in which the relation between self and other and between inside and outside is directly opposed to the homogeneous ideal of human subjectivity. Pregnancy can also be seen as a specific creative experience, which implies a non-linear image of time and space (Young 1990b: 160 ff.; see also Schott 1993; Diprose 1994; Sevenhuijsen 1995). Jaggar's reasoning in fact removes the possibility for thinking about the moral relevance of an embodied subjectivity and physical sexual differences, and makes it impossible to see that the question of how to deal with difference could be a crucial task for ethics.

4 CARE AND JUSTICE IN THE PUBLIC DEBATE ON CHILD CUSTODY

1 This chapter is a thoroughly reworked and updated version of an earlier article (Sevenhuijsen 1991b). I would like to thank the participants of workshops in Paris, Leeds, Warwick, Manchester, Enschede, Madison and Utrecht for fruitful discussions on earlier versions of the text of that article and Ian Forbes and Aafke Komter for their stimulating and carefully considered comments. In rewriting the 1991 article I have included ideas from other publications, particularly Sevenhuijsen 1988b and 1992b. Titia Loenen supplied thoughtful comments on earlier versions, which I was able to incorporate in the reworked chapter. Nora Holtrust and Ineke de Hondt kindly went through the last version once more, checking all legal details.
2 The 'Foolish Fathers' ('Dwaze vaders') is the name of a recent Dutch fathers' rights group, which has sought extensive media attention and has set up exemplary case law. They shamelessly appropriated the Dutch term 'dwaze moeders' (foolish mothers), the name of the mothers of the Plaza de Mayo – 'Las Locas'. As the American political philosopher Jean Eshtain argues, Las Locas, by their public presence and courageous action shattered the systematic deceit that had shrouded the disappearance of their children: they transgressed official orders by marching in the plaza and thus went ouside the boundaries of legitimate politics (Elshtain 1992: 120). Elshtain indeed uses the example of Las Locas to speculate on how a perspective of care might become a wider social imperative and argues that their persistent demonstrations and their language, in which they combined their grief about a mother's loss and human rights, was an important element in the re-emergence of democracy in Argentina. The 'foolish fathers', on the contrary, appealed to a seemingly legitimate political principle: the legal rights of fathers. But they did not refrain from 'illegitimate' action either, by, for example, supporting men in kidnapping children from the homes and the custody of their former wives. Apart from this, the implied analogy between a military regime that abducted and killed many thousands of people and divorced mothers who want to protect themselves against forceful behaviour of former husbands, is quite misplaced, to say the least.
3 Until 1995 the official Dutch legal term for parental rights was 'parental power'. Though this term may sound strange in English, I use the literal translation of this term here, in order to sensitize my international readers to the connotations of different terms and concepts, as well as to the ideologies that underlie changes in legal concepts.

4 According to Dutch civil law, an unmarried mother must give permission for a man to recognize her child. Although, under nineteenth-century law, her declaration was viewed as a form of evidence of the 'truth' of the man's paternity, it was also interpreted as a freedom right of the woman concerned and a protection against would-be fathers who wanted to impose themselves. It is striking that with the liberalization of family law in the 1960s, it was precisely this women's freedom right which came under attack. Lawyers for the fathers' rights movement transformed it, in their writings, from a liberal freedom right into a 'right of veto'. Since 1984, judges have been allowed to scrutinize women's motives for refusing permission, whereby once again the right to family life laid down in Article VIII acts as the highest norm. See further on this Holtrust, Sevenhuijsen and Verbraken 1989; Sevenhuijsen 1991b; Holtrust 1993.

5 At the time of finalizing this manuscript this Bill has not passed the First Chamber of Parliament, so it does not have legal status (yet).

6 Titia Loenen has recently argued that this problem has to do with the legal terminology of 'parenthood': the invisibility of care is constitutive for parenthood and the rights and duties related to it under family law. Only by ignoring relationships and the social relations of care and responsibility is it possible to construct a legal concept such as 'parenthood', which can serve as the locus for legal regulation. In this sense Loenen finds the central concepts of family law to be thoroughly gendered (Loenen 1994b). In fact, change is slowly taking place in this state of affairs: under the influence of the discussion about 'living arrangements', more attention is now being paid to the specific contexts in which people live and bring up children. See, for example, Emancipatieraad 1991; Ministerie van Justitie 1995. Discussion of this issue is far from being fully crystallized yet, in part because the discussion is kept strictly within the parameters of European law and the hegemony of biological descent.

7 This selectivity on the basis of gender can be seen in the fact that women are provided with much less opportunity of forcing men to do things than vice versa: for example, they have few legal resources for implementing an access arrangement which is not working well. Another example of this selectivity is that the Supreme Court has continuously ruled out lesbians from sharing parental authority over their partner's child. This would intervene too much in the principle of biological descent.

8 For this see, among others, Sevenhuijsen 1986, 1989, 1991a; Smart 1987; Smart and Sevenhuijsen 1989; Holtrust 1992, 1993; Eekelaar 1993; Collier 1995; Loenen 1995a, 1995b. The Dutch developments are documented in detail in the Dutch journal on women and the law, *Nemesis*, and in the Dutch legal journal *Nederlands Juristen Blad*.

9 This also emerges in research on legal history in which the recent past is glowingly described in terms of an ever-growing legal equality between men and women. Deviations from this, from whatever background, are nearly always presented in negative terms. See, for example, Von Boné and Combrink-Kuiters (1995). Such an image of linear progress is easy to maintain if only episodes from internal legal history are included, and not the political tensions, debates and discourses in which these are embedded, and in which issues of gender and power emerge in many ways. This means that the great diversity in the meanings of equality and the normative intentions behind the pleas for its application are also lost from the annals of history.

10 See Smart (1989, 1995) for a detailed critique of legal instrumentalism and ill-considered rights reasoning in feminist legal politics.

11 This political trend was also evident in the reform of the law on maintenance and alimony. During the 1970s, liberal feminists also tended to agree with a dismantling of alimony, with an appeal to equality, emancipation and the desirability of economic independence. Only when older divorced women organized themselves politically, and were listened to by the women's movement, were these political strategies revised.

12 The same association is echoed in the inaugural lecture given by former Minister of Justice, Job de Ruiter in 1990 as Professor of Personal, Family and Youth Law at the University of Utrecht. In my plea for an ethics of care, he hears an 'emphasis on the caring function of women', which 'sends a shiver down his spine'. If this is coupled with rights – and thus obligations – 'women will once more be chained to the kitchen sink' (De Ruiter 1990: 15). Equality remains the norm for him: taking account of gender differences would only be possible, he finds, on the basis of equal rights. Thus, not only does he remain trapped within the parameters of the equality–difference dilemma, but he is also unable to conceive of care and responsibility implying a different moral perspective than that contained in the ethics of rights. However, his ambivalence is evident at the end of his speech, where he states that care, responsibility and recognition of others as fully valued human beings are basic values of human existence. This ambivalence can in my view only be resolved when care is freed from its automatic association with 'femininity', 'nature' and 'tradition' and when gender is used as a multi-layered concept, as argued in Chapters 2 and 3 of this volume.

13 This problem is reflected in the 'equal' versus 'special rights' controversies, which have haunted American feminism in connection to the issue of maternity benefits and protective legislation. Ideological controversies such as this can flourish under a social and legal system where discussion starts from arguments about rights, rather than about needs and welfare. In the Netherlands there was less political controversy surrounding the difference–equality issue than in the United States, where there is a clearer tradition of contract law and a weaker welfare state. Nevertheless, similar arguments are also put forward in the Netherlands by feminist legal theorists. For the American situation see Scott 1988; Fraser 1989; Bacchi 1990, 1991; Minow 1990; Bower 1991. For a comparison between the Netherlands and the United States see Loenen 1992, 1995a.

14 Carol Smart and Bren Neale, in their analysis of the English Children Act of 1989 (implemented in 1992), which is similar to the recently introduced rule of joint parental authority in the Netherlands, show how the image of the 'implacably hostile' mother has informed case law and legal discourse. They also show how difficult this supposition makes it for women who have suffered domestic violence or harassment to convince the courts of the - often continuing - misbehaviour of their former spouses. Since there is such a powerful presumption of contact, based on a specific rhetoric of children's welfare and rights, the image of the 'implacably hostile' mother, according to Smart and Neale's analysis, is so powerful because 'she is seen to be not only hostile but selfish. She is seen to be in possession of an asset (the child) which she should be willing to share with the father. By refusing to do so she is obstructing the new ideal of the post-divorce family' (Smart and Neale 1997a: 335). This effect is strengthened, they say, because legal proceedings are invoked only where mothers contest contact, not where fathers refuse it.

15 This image harks back to the late nineteenth-century debates about evolution inspired by social Darwinism, in which the transition from matriarchy to patriarchy and its possible reversibility was a recurring point of discussion. In Sevenhuijsen (1987: Chapter 6) I argued that this expressed a fear of the potential power of mothers, which many felt would emerge if women were freed from the

patriarchal legal order. The matriarchy myth has played many different roles in the intellectual culture of the past century, also though in a more positive mode for example in feminist utopias.

16 See further Chapters 2 and 3 of this volume.

17 Hypothetical reasoning fits admirably into a Rawlsian line of reasoning: in this sense the idea of a thought experiment makes quite good sense. However, as argued in the rest of this volume, I believe that hypothetical reasoning is unsuitable as an approach to moral deliberation, among other things because it implies an inattentiveness to actually existing moral dilemmas. I use a thought experiment here to show the limitations of contractarian and redistributive thinking, not to recommend the results as an example of a good method of normative argument.

18 Liberal feminists have criticized Rawls's patriarchal view of the family and his limited attention to children to argue that Rawlsian principles should be extended to the private sphere and to the entire problem of gender. Only then could society genuinely be considered egalitarian and democratic (Okin 1987, 1989; Pessers 1994). However justified this criticism may seem, it is another example of early feminist criticism of sexism, in which social, political and legal theories were criticized for their exclusion of women, without the effects of their 'inclusion' being considered. For the different phases in legal women's studies and their normative implications see Smart 1995: Chapter 11.

19 In my opinion, a normative political theory should be able to express a critical perspective on both power relations in society as well as social processes and structures in a concrete, historical context. The question of what constitutes a good (i.e., accurate and responsible) description of the situation thus forms part of the normative deliberations, something in which different perspectives should be taken into account. If this is not done, it is easy to fall back on liberal philosophy's individualistic image of human nature. My approach does not exclude the use of liberal categories such as 'rights' and 'justice', rather it demands that these are embedded in a situated moral epistemology. For more on this position, see among others: Fraser 1989; Frazer and Lacey 1993; Young 1995. See also note 7 to this chapter.

20 This observation, or objective, itself implies a position based on the ethics of care, because it starts from the normative claim that caring values, such as continuity, trust and clarity, are also important values in children's lives, and that it is not in a child's interest to become a bone of contention between parents or to be saddled with the responsibility of having to choose between parents in situations of conflict. I do not take this to mean, as I shall argue later on, that the government should be more restrained in granting divorce, but rather that there should be clear, legal rules protecting children from prolonged conflicts.

21 According to the American political scientist Lisa Bower, feminist legal theory in the 1980s was too inclined to translate sexual difference into a juridified concept of motherhood and care, which meant that 'woman' was continually interpreted as 'mother' (Bower 1991). The reason for this, according to Bower, is that American feminism has been too heavily influenced by a sociological version of the object-relations theory, which allows too little space for symbolic and unconscious fantasies about mothers. The result is that an unproblematical and one-sided conception of motherhood and care has been able to enter into legal politics, so that the 'goodness' of the mother has become normative for thinking about law and politics. A poststructuralist theory in which symbolic theory has a place would, she argues, provide a greater opportunity for seeing the law as an arena in which psychic conflicts are reproduced and fought out through conflicts over images and representations. I can, without any hesitation, agree with this critical perspective, but I do not consider it an argument against the possibility of a feminist ethics of

care. It supports the plea, put forward in Chapter 1, that the epistemological basis of the ethics of care should not be founded in motherhood, but rather in a diversity of social practices and in the images and representations contained in these. Bower shows that the feminist version of 'maternal thinking' can lead to a 'strong state' in the tradition of contractarian theory. A postmodern vision of the ethics of care puts this 'strong state' into perspective and lays more emphasis on social responsibility as well as the importance of social policies and social citizenship. Thus, in short, it is important to bear in mind in which political context and in which conception of citizenship the ethics of care is placed. See also Yeatman 1994; Smart 1995: Chapters 10 and 12; Young 1995; and Chapter 3 of this volume.

22 See also Duindam 1996, 1997. The feminist ethics of care thus draws a radically different political conclusion from the existential fact of dependency than that drawn by patriarchal logic, where the dependency argument was continually used to justify patriarchal marriage and its gendered division of labour and power difference; it often appealed to a natural and functional order as well. In this way men and women were linked to each other through law. This also fitted in with the idea of making divorce more difficult or forbidding it, because it would damage the quality of care for children (Sevenhuijsen 1987, 1992b; on the genealogy of gender and dependency see Fraser and Gordon 1994a). The argument for this is frequently supported by an appeal to a supposed public interest in virtuous and independent citizens. See, for a critical perspective on such normative reasoning in modern liberalism, Young 1995. The patriarchal logic is also, from a historical viewpoint, linked to a marginalization of homosexuality through the regulation of parenthood, in part because it takes for granted an ordering principle based on a 'natural sexual identity' and bodies distinguished by their reproductive functions. Family law is thus a means of maintaining the heterosexual norm. See, among others on this, Orobio de Castro 1993; Collier 1995; Holtrust and De Hondt 1996.

23 This is also a theme in Carol Gilligan's findings. The women she interviewed saw the breaking of human connections as a form of violence, while men tended to interpret connectedness as a threat to their feeling of being a self (Gilligan 1982: 43).

24 Hannah Arendt herself was strongly against compassion as a political value, because she felt it would encourage too strong an identification with suffering and thus with all kinds of false loyalties and dangerous forms of patriotism. In her view, the public sphere guarantees the interpersonal space which is necessary for good judgement: compassion is a sentiment which should remain private. A number of authors believe that the feminist ethics of care is incompatible with republican citizenship. Others, among them Kathleen Jones, argue that a transformed concept of care can certainly function as a public virtue; Jones finds that Arendt's separation of the public and private spheres demonstrates the hidden marks of gender. See for this debate, among others, Arendt 1958; Komter 1990, 1995; Jones 1993; Honig 1995; Sevenhuijsen 1997a.

25 This is why it is complicated to ground an ethics of care in motherhood, at least as long as the image of maternal love is so heavily marked by self-abnegating dedication to the other/the child. An alternative view on maternity and love, ethics and politics can be found in the work of the French philosopher Julia Kristeva. She argues for an ethics that is not a question of morals or submission to the law, but rather of the transgression of the boundaries of the law, and the free play of negativity, need, desire and *jouissance*. Sexuality should in her view be grounded in feminine *jouissance*, as well as in the hitherto inarticulated experiences of semiotics; the ethical subject is not a fixed and self-contained substance but rather a subject-in-process, who recognizes the death-drive and eros. Kristeva finds her models for

this ethical subjectivity in poetry, maternity and psychoanalysis. As Kelly Oliver has stated, this subject does not need an external authority which ensures social relation. The social relation is inherent in the subject. This subject does not have to sympathize with others who are similar to the self, nor

> does he have to impose a Kantian imperative or golden rule in order to insure that he will be treated justly or kindly by others. Rather than love the other as himself, the ethical subject-in-process will love the other in herself. She will love what is different. She will love alterity, because it is within but not because it is homogeneous.
>
> (Oliver 1993: 16–17)

On the connections between ethics and politics implied in this vision see Edelstein 1993; Graybeal 1993. I have no space here to elaborate on the implications of this approach for a feminist ethics of care. Nevertheless, I want to stress the fact that a comparable approach informs the version of the care ethics outlined in this book.

26 See for example the way in which the Dutch social theorist Pim Fortuyn in his recent book *De verweesde samenleving* (The Orphaned Society) argues for a return to community values. In his view, the chief social problem lies in the lack of a symbolic father-figure, both in private life and in politics (Fortuyn 1995). He argues, it is true, that the father-figure is 'only' a metaphor (women too can exercise authority since their emancipation); but still his treatment is permeated with gender-laden dualisms and patriarchal symbols, and his text shows on a symbolic level an enormous nostalgia for traditional sexual difference. This also emerges in the fact that, for him, community values serve to dispel the 'bleakness' of contractarian thinking.

27 In divorce, there is often negotiation about who gets what. The decision about who the children live with and who has legal authority over them can thus become confused with material issues as well as emotions, fears and feelings of guilt. From research into conflicts on access, it appears that, for example, visiting agreements more often go wrong when the father is the guardian and the mother is dependent on him to see the children than in the reverse situation. In many situations, women are less inclined to fight back or are more sensitive to the conflict of loyalty which children can feel in a clash between their parents. They are also quicker to feel guilty if they deny the other parent rights over the children. For more on this see Wegelin 1988, 1990. If this dynamics occurs there is a great chance that, under the new regulations, women, even if they fully care for their children, will experience moral problems in refusing shared authority from an anxiety at not fulfilling the norms of good motherhood, even if this would be a better solution to protect their living conditions and the interest of their children in other respects.

28 The Dutch government indeed justifies its recent proposal for a presumption of equal parental authority by stating that the goal of this legal change is that both parents remain responsible for their children after divorce and to convince them that they 'both remain parents' after divorce. This is a rather mystifying statement when we realize what is the most frequent reality after divorce, namely, a situation in which one parent, mostly the mother, has the main responsibility for raising the child(ren). This injunction boils down to a moralizing statement about 'good parenting' after divorce, teaching mothers that they should involve their former husbands in the upbringing of their children as much as possible, while on the other hand telling fathers that they should remain involved as equally as possible. It is thus an example of what I have called earlier in this chapter a strategy of moral reform and a discourse of ascribed rather than achieved responsibility. This

mystification is strengthened by the fact that the Dutch legislator has chosen to conflate authority, care and responsibility under the umbrella term 'parental authority'. Through this conflation and by setting up extremely loose and vague norms, the state in fact abnegates its responsibility to protect the vulnerable and instead shifts this responsibility towards institutionalized forms of counselling and mediation. Mediation was indeed the compromise offered by the Dutch State Secretary of Justice in response to a critique of the recent Bill made by the Dutch Institute for Women and the Law. Mediation might be positively valued from the perspective of care, if it led to liveable compromises instead of continued antagonisms. In practice, however, it often amounts to no more than convincing parents of the norms of shared custody that underly the legal regulations.

29 In relation to this, it is striking that Von Boné and Combrink-Kuiters, in their recent article in which they pose equality in parental authority as the norm, talk so lightly about alcoholism, abuse, threatening behaviour and incest as 'arguments and accusations against which fathers have to defend themselves' if they are denied access (Von Boné and Combrink-Kuiters 1995: 424).

30 This makes it clear, yet again, that arguments in which the ethics of care is limited to intimate relations and the ethics of rights to public or impersonal relations fall short from a feminist perspective. These arguments can often be traced back to a romanticized view of intimate relations, in which care functions as a moral tenet defining how everyone should behave in the intimate sphere. For an example of such a view see Hardwig 1990. In my view, it is exactly because of the vulnerability of intimate relations that a certain amount of legal protection is necessary.

31 Martha Fineman has written a most insightful historical study about how the issue of mothers' rights has been continuously marginalized in the discourse of American family law (Fineman 1995). See also Sevenhuijsen 1992b.

32 In 1995 the Dutch Ministry issued a memo in which it tried to steer a course between the principle of biological descent and the imperative derived from liberal equality of rights which states that the government should refrain from unjust unequal treatment of homosexual relationships. This has resulted in the latest Bill about parental authority. This not only introduced the presumption of shared parental authority after divorce. In fact the main part of the Bill was the introduction of 'co-custody' for unmarried partners. This applies, according to its text, to the 'female partner of the mother of a child whose father is absent' (an unsurpassable euphemism for the apparently unspeakable term 'lesbian mother, who has become pregnant by artificial insemination'), as well as to the new partner of a divorced mother. The legislator has chosen the term 'co-custody' in these cases (and not shared parental authority) because it concerns the regulation of the relation with a 'third party' and not a biological parent. The biological mother remains the primary parent, and is thus accorded parental authority in these cases. The rationale behind this is the statement that biological descent should, in the name of 'the interest of the child', remain the guiding principle of family law: indeed many rules are aimed at protecting biological ties. The proposal also demands several guarantees that co-custody can only be granted in situations of steady relationships and responsibilities. This is in strange contrast to the refusal to demand comparable conditions in situations of shared parental authority after divorce. Apparently, it is easier to presume care in situations of steady family life than when family life has broken down. In fact, it testifies to the inability of present family law to deal in an innovative manner with care. However important a breakthrough this change may be for lesbian women, it also testifies to the fact that legal discourse is more receptive towards liberal norms of equal treatment than towards a feminist ethics of care.

5 FEMINIST ETHICS AND PUBLIC HEALTH-CARE POLICIES

1 For an accessible explanation of the Dutch health-care system see Schrijvers 1997.

2 The report exists in three different versions. The most well-known in the Netherlands is an abbreviated version (*Choices in Health Care* 1991), which was brought out to provide a framework for public discussion. The original report is more extended. It contains more examples and is more nuanced in its argumentation, although the basic arguments are similar to the shortened version. I will refer as much as possible to the English translation of the report (1992), which is closer to the extended version.

3 I am indebted to the many women who have contributed to this project, and especially to Claar Parlevliet, Annemiek Meinen and other contributors to the books we produced as a result of these campaigns (Parlevliet and Sevenhuijsen 1993; Meinen *et al.* 1994). Bart Lammers and Karin Schaafsma performed an unparalleled role through their part in the public debates on *Choices in Health Care*, which took place in the Balie in Amsterdam, and through the way they have stimulated me to express my ideas. Several of the ideas in this chapter took shape in close conversation with Joan Tronto. Anna Yeatman made comments on an earlier version which set my thinking on a new track. Finally I want to thank Iris Young, as well as Joan Tronto, for their thoughtful comments on an earlier version of this chapter. This chapter also appears in Patrice DiQuinzio and Iris Young (eds), *Feminist Ethics and Social Policy* (1997).

4 I think this is relevant not only from the point of view of Dutch politics or the feminist input in Dutch public discussion. I hope my approach has a broader relevance than the Netherlands, not least because the Dutch government has offered the policy document *Choices in Health Care* and its procedure of decision-making as a model for public policy-making in other countries, such as the United States and South Africa. For example, in 1992 the report was brought out in English under the title *Choices in Health Care, A Report by the Government Committee on Choices in Health Care*. (The Hague: Ministry of Welfare, Health and Cultural Affairs.) The model of the report and the campaign was presented in the United States by several Dutch policy-makers as an example for Hillary Clinton's project to reform the American health-care system. After the publication of the report, the chairman of the committee, the cardiologist Professor A.J. Dunning, was appointed as a member of a committee of the World Bank that is advising the South African government on the future of its health policies.

5 See for this the committee's charter (*Choices in Health Care* 1992: 7–8). An interesting detail for American readers is that the American Oregon experiment was put forward as an example in this charter. In this, the population was asked to list the treatments which they felt should be covered by obligatory basic insurance. The committee decided, however, not to pursue this model but to develop instead a more explicitly normative framework to structure the processes of choice.

6 At this point there are substantial differences between the two versions of the report. While the shorter version clearly argues for the community approach and against the other approaches, the longer version argues for a hierarchy in application of the approaches. It states that the community approach should be applicable to discussions on a macro-level, the medical–professional approach on the meso-level, while the individual approach could guide the choices made by individuals. This division also led to the design of the 'funnel'.

7 In this part of the report the committee also questions whether solidarity should be limited by several other principles. It concludes that there are no convincing arguments for limits of age and lifestyle, while favouring a limited possibility of weighing up the costs and benefits of certain provisions, and the possibility of allowing for individual preferences in insurance schemes, like, for example, the possibility of arranging a policy that excludes abortion for those who have moral objections against it, the so-called 'pro-life' contract.

8 Examples of proposals made in the report are: stimulating discussion about standardization of diagnoses and treatments and medical protocols, better management of the availability of medicines, stimulating the use of simpler medicines, standardized research about effectiveness of treatments such as psychotherapy, and new systems of accountability for the medical professions involving the setting up of platforms for negotiations between organizations in the health-care sector.

9 The report's main source of reference at this point is the work of the American philosopher Daniel Callahan (Callahan 1987, 1990).

10 The importance of recognizing informal care and the designing of just provisions in this field was indeed brought forward by a great majority of the women who participated in the discussion projects following *Choices in Health Care*. In that respect the campaign led by the women's organizations has had considerable influence on the public debate and on the awareness among policy-makers of the importance of informal care as a policy issue, also from the perspective of emancipation.

11 It could thus be seen as an example of what the Australian philosopher Val Plumwood has, in her analysis of the workings of dualisms, recently denoted as 'backgrounding': the more powerful party in a power relationship makes use of the other, by calling on his or her services, relying on and benefiting from the other's services, but at the same time denying the dependency which this creates (Plumwood 1993: 48; see also Jones 1988b; Pateman 1989; Caverero 1992).

12 This approach is to be found, for example, in Susan Moller Okin's work on distributive justice and the family (Okin 1989). I have commented on this in Chapter 3.

13 Several political philosophers have tried to position the ethics of care on the communitarian side of the liberalism–communitarianism controversy. In my view, this is a pointless endeavour, since it denies the possibility that the ethics of care is a moral perspective in its own right, while it also assumes a split between politics and ethics. The many points of epistemological and political divergence between communitarianism and the ethics of care are overlooked. It also tends to block the possibility of using the ethics of care for developing renewed concepts of justice. *Choices in Health Care* is to my mind a good example of how the liberalism–communitarianism divide is a fruitless path to pursue for feminist ethics. For a well-developed feminist critique of the liberalism–communitarianism opposition in political theory, see Frazer and Lacey 1993.

14 The course of political decision-making after the publication of the report proves this point in several respects. Because the concept of 'necessary care' is left open, it is subject to conflicting interpretations. This leads policy-makers to resort to the more familiar concepts of effectiveness and efficiency, thus confirming an economic–financial point of view.

15 For further discussion of this point, see Chapter 1 of this volume.

16 In this way, it might also be possible to avoid the recurring tendency towards foundationalism in ethical frameworks and thus in thinking on an ethics of care too. See further Chapters 1 and 3 on this point.

17 This points, for example, to the necessity of flexible parental leave and provisions for temporary leave for caring for sick relatives and friends.

18 In this respect, Iris Young's proposal is important in distinguishing between autonomy as the capacity for self-determination, on the one hand, and the normative view of human nature on the other. The former should remain an important
political goal for feminists while the latter should be critically examined (Young
1995).

19 Joan Tronto has argued recently that care as a virtue has the potential of mediating
between justice and democracy, concepts that are seldom linked in the great
canons of political theory (Tronto 1995b).

BIBLIOGRAPHY

Abel, E.K. (1990) 'Family Care of the Frail Elderly', in E.K. Abel and M. Nelson (eds): 65–91.

Abel, E.K. and Nelson, M. (eds) (1990) *Circles of Care: Work and Identity in Women's Lives*, Albany: State University of New York Press.

Addelson, K. Pyne (1991) *Impure Thoughts: Essays on Philosophy, Feminism and Ethics*, Philadelphia: Temple University Press.

—— (1993) 'Knowers/Doers and Their Moral Problems', in L. Alcoff and E. Potter (eds): 265–294.

—— (1994) *Moral Passages: Toward a Collectivist Moral Theory*, New York and London: Routledge.

Ainley, A. (1990) 'The Ethics of Sexual Difference', in J. Fletcher and A. Benjamin (eds) *Abjection, Melancholia and Love: The Work of Julia Kristeva*, New York and London: Routledge: 53–62.

Alcoff, L. (1988) 'Cultural Feminism versus Post-Structuralism: The Identity Crisis in Feminist Theory', *Signs: Journal of Women in Culture and Society* 13, 3: 405–436.

Alcoff, L. and Potter, E. (eds) (1993) *Feminist Epistemologies*, New York and London: Routledge.

Allen, A.L. (1983) 'Women and their Privacy: What is at Stake?', in C.C. Gould (ed.) *New Perspectives on Women and Philosophy*, Totowa: Rowman and Allenheld: 233–249.

Almond, B. (1988) 'Women's Right: Reflections on Ethics and Gender', in M. Griffiths and M. Whitford (eds): 42–58.

Antony, L.M. and Witt, C. (eds) (1993) *A Mind of One's Own: Feminist Essays on Reason and Objectivity*, Boulder, CO, San Francisco and Oxford: Westview.

Arendt, H. (1958) *The Human Condition*, Chicago: University of Chicago Press.

Arnault, L.S. (1989) 'The Radical Future of a Classical Moral Theory', in A.M. Jaggar and S.R. Bordo (eds): 188–206.

Assiter, A. (1988) 'Autonomy and Pornography', in M. Griffiths and M. Whitford (eds): 58–72.

Bacchi, C. (1990) *Same Difference: Feminism and Sexual Difference*, St Leonards: Allen and Unwin.

—— (1991) 'Pregnancy, the Law and the Meaning of Equality', in E. Meehan and S.L. Sevenhuijsen (eds): 71–87.

Badinter, E. (1988) *De een is de ander. De relatie tussen mannen en vrouwen*, Amsterdam: Uitgeverij Contact/Pandora Pockets.

169

Baier, A.C. (1987) 'Hume, the Woman's Moral Theorist?', in E. Feder Kittay and D.T. Meyers (eds): 37–55.

—— (1989) 'Trust and Antitrust', *Ethics* 96: 231–260.

—— (1991) 'Whom Can Women Trust?', in C. Card (ed.): 233–245.

—— (1993) 'Hume: The Reflective Women's Epistemologist', in L.M. Antony and C. Witt (eds): 35–48.

Bar On, B. (ed.) (1994) *Modern Engendering: Critical Feminist Readings in Modern Western Philosophy*, New York: State University of New York Press.

Bauman, Z. (1992) *Postmodern Ethics*, Oxford: Blackwell.

Benhabib, S. (1987) 'The Generalized and the Concrete Other. The Kohlberg–Gilligan Controversy and Feminist Theory', in S. Benhabib and D. Cornell (eds): 77–95.

—— (1992) *Situating the Self: Gender, Community and Postmodernism in Contemporary Ethics*, Bloomington: Indiana University Press.

—— (1996) *The Reluctant Modernism of Hannah Arendt*, Thousand Oaks and London: Sage.

Benhabib, S. and Cornell, D. (eds) (1987) *Feminism as Critique: Essays on the Politics of Gender in Late Capitalist Societies*, Oxford: Polity Press.

Benjamin, J. (1988) *The Bonds of Love: Psycho-analysis, Feminism and the Problem of Domination*, London: Virago.

Benner, P. and Wrubel, J. (1989) *The Primacy of Caring*, Reading, MA: Addison-Wesley.

Berkel, D. van (1994) 'Kiezen voor minder voortplantingstechnologie?', in A. Meinen *et al.* (eds): 138–155.

Bickford, S. (1995) 'In the Presence of Others: Arendt and Anzaldúa on the Paradox of Public Appearance', in B. Honig (ed.): 313–336.

—— (1996) *The Dissonance of Democracy: Listening, Conflict and Citizenship*, Ithaca, NY and London: Cornell University Press.

Billig, M., Condor, S. and Edwards, D. (1988) *Ideological Dilemmas: A Social Psychology of Everyday Thinking*, London: Sage.

Blustein, J. (1991) *Care and Commitment: Taking the Personal Point of View*, New York and Oxford: Oxford University Press.

Bock, G. and James, S. (eds) (1992) *Beyond Equality and Difference: Citizenship, Feminist Politics, Female Subjectivity*, New York and London: Routledge.

Boné, E. von and Combrink-Kuiters, L. (1995) 'Het juridisch gezag van vrouwen over hun minderjarige kinderen in historisch perspectief', *Tijdschrift voor Vrouwenstudies* 16, 4: 413–427.

Boor, E. (1995) 'Traditioneel gezag in een "moderne" wet', *Nemesis. Tijdschrift over vrouwen en recht* 11, 4: 103–107.

Bordo, S. (1986) 'The Cartesian Masculinization of Thought', *Signs: Journal of Women in Culture and Society* 11, 3: 439–456.

Bosch, M. (1994) *Het geslacht van de wetenschap. Vrouwen en hoger onderwijs in Nederland 1878–1948*, Amsterdam: SUA.

Bower, L.C. (1991) '"Mother" in Law: Conceptions of Mother and the Maternal in Feminist Legal Theory', *Differences: A Journal of Feminist Cultural Studies* 3, 1: 20–38.

Brabeck, M. (1993) 'Moral Judgement: Theory and Research on Differences between Males and Females', in M.J. Larrabee (ed.): 33–48.

Braidotti, R. (1986) 'Ethics Revisited: Women and/in Philosophy', in C. Pateman and E. Gross (eds): 44–60.
—— (1991) *Beelden van de leegte. Vrouwen in de hedendaagse filosofie*, Kampen: Kok Agora.
—— (1994) *Nomadic Subjects. Embodiment and Sexual Difference in Contemporary Feminist Theory*, New York: Columbia University Press.
Bransen, E. and Baart, I. (1994) *Net even anders. Sekse-specifieke aspecten van chronisch ziek-zijn*, Utrecht: Aletta, Centrum voor Vrouwengezondheidszorg.
Braun, M. (1992) *De prijs van de liefde. De eerste feministische golf, het huwelijksrecht en de vaderlandse geschiedenis*, Amsterdam: Het Spinhuis.
Bruijn, J. de (1991) *Omstreden kwaliteit; omtrent vrouwenarbeid en beleid*, Amsterdam: Vrije Universiteit.
Burg, W. van den (1993) 'Rechten van kinderen: enkele filosofische kanttekeningen', in C.H.C.J. van Nijnatten (ed.): 64–80.
Bussemaker, J. (1991a) 'Verlicht Eigenbelang of Verplicht Altruïsme? Literatuur over sekse en verzorgingsstaat', *Tijdschrift voor Vrouwenstudies* 12, 1: 515–531.
—— (1991b) 'Equality, Autonomy and Feminist Politics', in E. Meehan and S.L. Sevenhuijsen (eds): 52–70.
—— (1993) *Betwiste zelfstandigheid. Individualisering, sekse en verzorgingsstaat*, Amsterdam: SUA.
Butler, J. (1990) *Gender Trouble: Feminism and the Subversion of Identity*, New York and London: Cornell University Press.
Butler, J. and Scott, J.W. (eds) (1992) *Feminists Theorize the Political*, New York and London: Routledge.
Calhoun, C. (1988) 'Justice, Care, Gender Bias', *The Journal of Philosophy* 85, 9: 451–463.
Callahan, D. (1987) *Setting Limits: Medical Goals in an Ageing Society*, New York: Simon and Schuster.
—— (1990) *What Kind of Life: The Limits of Medical Progress*, New York: Simon and Schuster.
—— (1994) 'What Kind of Patients Ought We to Be?', Utrecht: Universiteit voor Humanistiek (unpublished paper).
Card, C. (ed.) (1991) *Feminist Ethics*, Lawrence: University Press of Kansas.
Cavarero, A. (1992) 'Equality and Sexual Difference: Amnesia in Political Thought', in G. Bock and S. James (eds): 32–47.
Chodorow, N.J. (1978) *The Reproduction of Mothering: Psychoanalysis and the Sociology of Gender*, Berkeley: University of California Press.
—— (1995) 'Gender as a Personal and Cultural Construction', *Signs: Journal of Women in Culture and Society* 20, 3: 516–544.
Choices in Health Care (1991) *Kiezen en delen. Advies in hoofdzaken*, Den Haag: Ministerie van WVC.
—— (1992) *A Report by the Government Committee on Choices in Health Care*, The Hague: Ministry of Welfare, Health and Cultural Affairs.
Clark, A. (1993) 'The Quest for Certainty in Feminist Thought', *Hypatia: A Journal for Feminist Philosophy* 8, 3: 84–93.
Clark, L.M.G. and Lange, L. (eds) (1979) *The Sexism of Social and Political Theory: Women and Reproduction from Plato to Nietzsche*, Toronto: University of Toronto Press.

Clement, G. (1996) *Care, Autonomy and Justice: Feminism and the Ethic of Care*, Boulder and Oxford: Westview Press.

Code, L. (1987) *Epistemic Responsibility*, Hanover: University Press of New England/ Brown University Press.

—— (1988a) 'Experience, Knowledge and Responsibility', in M. Griffiths and M. Whitford (eds): 187–205.

—— (1988b) 'Credibility, a Double Standard', in L. Code (ed.) (1988c): 64–88.

—— (ed.) (1988c) *Feminist Perspectives: Philosophical Essays on Method and Morals*, Toronto: Toronto University Press.

—— (1991) *What Can She Know? Feminist Theory and the Construction of Knowledge*, Ithaca, NY and London: Cornell University Press.

—— (1992) 'Must a Feminist be a Relativist After All?', in M. Pellikaan-Engel (ed.): 141–148.

—— (1995) *Rhetorical Spaces: Essays on Gendered Locations*, New York and London: Routledge.

Cohen, C.H. (1986) 'The Feminist Sexuality Debate: Ethics and Politics', *Hypatia: A Journal for Feminist Philosophy* 1, 2: 71–86.

Collier, R. (1995) *Masculinity, Law and the Family*, New York and London: Routledge.

Collins, P. Hill (1991) *Black Feminist Thought: Knowledge, Consciousness and the Politics of Empowerment*, Boston: Unwin Hyman.

Coltheart, L. (1986) 'Desire, Consent and Liberal Theory', in C. Pateman and E. Gross (eds): 112–122.

Commissie Toekomstscenario's Herverdeling Onbetaalde Arbeid (1995) *Onbetaalde zorg gelijk verdeeld. Toekomstscenario's voor herverdeling van onbetaalde zorgarbeid*, Den Haag: VUGA/Ministerie van Sociale Zaken en Werkgelegenheid.

Conley, J.M. and O'Barr, W.M. (1990) *Rules versus Relationships: The Ethnography of Legal Discourse*, Chicago and London: University of Chicago Press.

Coole, D. (1988) *Women in Political Theory: From Ancient Misogyny to Contemporary Feminism*, Brighton: Wheatsheaf.

Corea, G. (1985) *The Mother Machine: Reproductive Technologies from Artificial Insemination to Artificial Wombs*, New York: Harper and Row.

Cott, N.F. (1986) 'Feminist Theory and Feminist Movements: The Past Before Us', in J. Mitchell and A. Oakley (eds) *What is Feminism?*, Oxford: Blackwell: 49–62.

Cuppen, A. (1995) 'Vroedvrouw met visie. Protest tegen prenatale screening', *Tijdschrift voor Gezondheid en Politiek* 13, 5: 11–12.

Dalley, G. (1988) *Ideologies of Caring: Rethinking Community and Collectivism*, Basingstoke and London: Macmillan.

Dam, G. ten and Volman, M. (1995) 'Zorg voor feministisch burgerschap', *Tijdschrift voor Vrouwenstudies* 16, 3: 270–284.

Davis, K. (1989) 'Het geslachtsprobleem. Inleiding op Carol Hagemann-White', in S.L. Sevenhuijsen *et al.* (eds) *Socialistes-Feministiese Teksten 11*, Baarn: Ambo: 27–32.

—— (1990) 'Het probleem van de macht in de feministische common sense', *Psychologie en Maatschappij* 14, 2: 3–13.

—— (1991) 'Gender Dilemmas', in S.L. Sevenhuijsen (ed.) (1991c): 45–50.

—— (1992) 'Towards a Feminist Rethoric: The Gilligan Debate Revisited', *Women's Studies International Forum* 15, 2: 219–231.

—— (1994) 'De schoonheidsmythe voorbij', in A. Meinen *et al.* (ed.): 156–169.

—— (1995) *Re-shaping the Female Body: The Dilemma of Cosmetic Surgery*, New York and London: Routledge.

Deech, R. (1993) 'The Rights of Fathers: Social and Biological Concepts of Parenthood', in J. Eekelaar and P. Sarcevic (eds): 19–34.

Diamond, I. and Quinby, L. (1988) *Feminism and Foucault: Reflections on Resistance*, Boston: Northeastern University Press.

Dietz, M.G. (1995) 'Feminist Receptions of Hannah Arendt', in B. Honig (ed.): 17–50.

—— (1996) *Working in Half-Truth: Some Premodern Reflections on the Partisanship of Political Speech*, San Francisco: APSA.

Dimen, M. (1987) 'Interrupting Patriarchy: Toward the Deconstruction of the Father', in T. Knijn and A. Mulder (eds): 143–164.

Diprose, R. (1994) *The Bodies of Women: Ethics, Embodiment and Sexual Difference*, New York and London: Routledge.

DiQuinzio, P. (1993) 'Exclusion and Essentialism in Feminist Theory: The Problem of Mothering', *Hypatia: A Journal for Feminist Philosophy* 8, 3: 1–20.

DiQuinzio, P. and Young, I. (eds) (1997) *Feminist Ethics and Social Policy*, Bloomington: Indiana University Press.

DiStefano, C. (1991) *Configurations of Masculinity: A Feminist Perspective on Modern Political Theory*, Ithaca, NY and London: Cornell University Press.

Drenth, A. van (1991) *De zorg om het Philipsmeisje. Fabrieksmeisjes in de electrotechnische industrie in Eindhoven 1900–1960*, Zutphen: Walburg Pers.

—— (1994) 'Zorg-en-de-macht: over de sociale constructie van gender identiteit', *Psychologie en Maatschappij* 18, 3: 141–155.

—— (1995) 'De groote verantwoordelijkheid van haar vrouwzijn. Woningopzichteressen en de professionalisering van sociale zorg in Nederland (1880–1940)', in A. van Drenth *et al.* (eds) *Sekse als pedagogisch motief. Historische en actuele perspectieven op opvoeding, onderwijs, vorming en hulpverlening*, Baarn: Uitgeverij Intro: 171–186.

Dreyfuss, H.L. and Rabinow, P. (1982) *Michel Foucault: Beyond Structuralism and Hermeneutics*, Chicago: University of Chicago Press.

Duijnstee, M. (1992) *De belasting van familieleden van dementerenden*, Nijkerk: Uitgeverij Intro.

Duijnstee, M. *et al.* (1994) *Mantelzorg voor mensen met een chronische ziekte*, Zoetermeer: Nationale Commissie Chronisch Zieken.

Duindam, V. (1996) 'Zorgende vaders: een tevreden groep koplopers', *Opzij. Feministisch maandblad* 24, 1: 28–33.

—— (1997) *Zorgende vaders. Over mannen, ouderschap, zorg, werk en hulpverlening*. Amsterdam, Van Gennep.

Duindam, V. and Vroon, M. (1995) 'Zorgende vaders. Resultaten van een onderzoek', in L. Thooft and E. van der Molen (eds): 99–131.

Dupuis, H. (1995) 'Feminisme en medische ethiek', *Bulletin van de Vereniging voor Filosofie en Geneeskunde* 3, 1: 5–7.

Edelstein, M. (1993) 'Toward a Feminist Postmodern *Poléthique*: Kristeva on Ethics and Politics', in K. Oliver (ed.): 196–215.

Eekelaar, J. (1993) 'Are Parents Morally Obliged to Care for their Children?', in J. Eekelaar and P. Sarcevic (eds): 51–64.

Eekelaar, J. and Sarcevic, P. (eds) (1993) *Parenthood in Modern Society: Legal and Social Issues for the Twenty-first Century*, Dordrecht, Boston and London: Martinus Nijhoff.

Ehrenreich, B. and English, D. (1979) *For Her Own Good: 150 Years of the Experts' Advice to Women*, New York: Anchor Press.

Eisenstein, H. and Jardine, A. (eds) (1980) *The Future of Difference*, New Brunswick, NJ and London: Rutgers University Press.

Eisenstein, Z.R. (1981) *The Radical Future of Liberal Feminism*, New York: Longman.

—— (1988) *The Female Body and the Law*, Berkeley, CA, Los Angeles and London: University of California Press.

Elshtain, J.B. (1981) *Public Man, Private Woman: Women in Social and Political Thought*, Princeton, NJ: Princeton University Press.

—— (ed.) (1982) *The Family in Political Thought*, Brighton: Harvester.

—— (1986) *Meditations on Modern Political Thought: Masculine and Feminine Themes from Luther to Arendt*, New York: Praeger.

—— (1992) 'The Power and Powerlessness of Women', in G. Bock and S. James (eds): 110–125.

Emancipatieraad (1991) *Het afstammingsrecht en sociale ouders*, Den Haag: Ministerie van Sociale Zaken.

—— (1993) *Advies vrouwenmantel en mannentrouw in de thuiszorg*, Den Haag: Emancipatieraad.

English, J. (1977) 'Justice between Generations', *Philosophical Studies: An International Journal for Philosophy in the Analytical Tradition* 31: 91–104.

Everingham, C. (1994) *Motherhood and Modernity: An Investigation into the Rational Dimension of Mothering*, Buckingham and Philadelphia: Open University Press.

Everts, S. (1993) *Visie vanuit de zij-kant. Naar een feministische technologie-ethiek*, Delft: Eburon.

Fairclough, N. (1992) *Discourse and Social Change*, Cambridge: Polity.

Ferguson, K. (1984) *The Feminist Case Against Bureaucracy*, Philadelphia: Temple University Press.

Finch, J. and Groves, D. (eds) (1983) *A Labour of Love: Women, Work and Caring*, London: Routledge and Kegan Paul.

Finch, J. and Mason, J. (1993) *Negotiating Family Responsibilities*, New York and London: Tavistock/Routledge.

Fineman, M. (1989) 'The Politics of Custody and Gender: Child Advocacy and the Transformation of Custody Decision Making in the USA', in C. Smart and S.L. Sevenhuijsen (eds): 27–50.

—— (1995) *The Neutered Mother: The Sexual Family and other Twentieth Century Tragedies*, New York and London: Routledge.

Fisher, B. (1990) *Alice in the Human Services: A Feminist Analysis of Women in the Caring Professions*, in E.K. Abel and M. Nelson (eds): 108–131.

Fisher, B. and Tronto, J.C. (1990) 'Towards a Feminist Theory of Caring', in E.K. Abel and M. Nelson (eds): 35–62.

Flax, J. (1993) *Disputed Subjects: Essays on Psychoanalysis, Politics and Philosophy*, New York and London: Routledge.

Fletcher, J. and Benjamin, A. (eds) (1990) *Abjection, Melancholia and Love: The Work of Julia Kristeva*, New York and London: Routledge.

Folbre, N. (1995) 'Holding Hands at Midnight: The Paradox of Caring Labour', *Feminist Economics* 1, 1: 73–92.

Fortuyn, P. (1995) *De verweesde samenleving. Achtergrond van en oplossingen voor de huidige normen- en waardenproblemen*, Utrecht: A.W. Bruna Uitgevers.

Foucault, M. (1988) *De orde van het spreken*, Meppel: Boom.

Franks, H. (1990) *Mummy Doesn't Live Here Anymore*, London: Doubleday.

Fraser, N. (1987) 'What's Critical about Critical Theory? The Case of Habermas and Gender', in S. Benhabib and D. Cornell (eds): 31–56.

—— (1989) *Unruly Practices. Power, Discourse and Gender in Contemporary Social Theory*, Minneapolis: University of Minneapolis Press.

Fraser, N. and Gordon, L. (1994a) 'A Genealogy of Dependency: Tracing a Keyword of the U.S. Welfare State', *Signs: Journal of Women in Culture and Society* 19, 1: 1–29.

—— (1994b) 'Civil Citizenship against Social Citizenship? On the Ideology of Contract-versus-Charity', in B. van Steenbergen (ed.): 90–107.

Fraser, N. and Nicholson, L. (1988) 'Social Criticism without Philosophy: An Encounter between Feminism and Postmodernism', *Theory, Culture and Society* 5, 2/3: 373–394.

Frazer, E. and Lacey, N. (1993) *The Politics of Community: A Feminist Critique of the Liberal–Communitarian Debate*, New York and London: Harvester Wheatsheaf.

Friedman, M. (1993) 'Beyond Caring: The De-Moralization of Gender', in M.J. Larrabee (ed.): 258–273.

Gatens, M. (1991) 'A Critique of the Sex/Gender Distinction', in S. Gunew (ed.): 139–160.

—— (1996) *Imaginary Bodies: Ethics, Power and Corporeality*, New York and London: Routledge.

Gender en Zorg (1991) *Gender en zorg: identiteit, arbeid, moraal. Programma voor een aandachtsgebied NWO/WVEO 1992–1997*, Utrecht: Werkgroep Vrouwenstudies FSW, Universiteit Utrecht.

Gilligan, C. (1980) 'In a Different Voice: Women's Conceptions of Self and Morality', in Z. Eisenstein and A. Jardine (eds): 274–316.

—— (1982) *In a Different Voice: Psychological Theory and Women's Development*, Cambridge, MA: Harvard University Press.

—— (1987) 'Moral Orientation and Moral Development', in E. Feder Kittay and D.T. Meyers (eds): 19–33.

Glendon, M.A. (1977) *State, Law and Family*, London: North-Holland.

Goldschmidt, J.E. (1993) *We Need Different Stories: Een ander verhaal in het recht. Verhalen van verschil*, Zwolle: W.E.J. Tjeenk Willink.

Gordon, L. (ed.) (1990) *Women, the State and Welfare*, Madison: University of Wisconsin Press.

Govier, T. (1992) 'Trust, Distrust and Feminist Theory', *Hypatia: A Journal for Feminist Philosophy* 7, 1: 10–33.

—— (1993) 'Self-Trust, Autonomy and Self-Esteem', *Hypatia: A Journal for Feminist Philosophy* 8, 1: 99–120.

Graham, H. (1983) 'A Labour of Love', in J. Finch and D. Groves (eds): 13–30.

Graybeal, J. (1993) 'Kristeva's Delphic Proposal: Practice Encompasses the Ethical', in K. Oliver (ed.): 32–40.

Graycar, R. (1989) 'Equal Rights Versus Fathers' Rights: The Child Custody Debate in Australia', in C. Smart and S.L. Sevenhuijsen (eds): 158–189.

Gremmen, I. (1991) 'Gender, Power and Home Health Care', in S.L. Sevenhuijsen (ed.) (1991c): 56–72.

—— (1995) *Ethiek in de gezinsverzorging. Gender en de macht van zorg*, Utrecht: Jan van Arkel.

Griffiths, M. (1988) 'Feminism, Feelings and Philosophy', in M. Griffiths and M. Whitford (eds): 131–152.

Griffiths, M. and Whitford, M. (eds) (1988) *Feminist Perspectives in Philosophy*, Houndsmill and London: Macmillan.

Grimshaw, J. (1986) *Feminist Philosophers. Women's Perspectives on Philosophical Traditions.* Brighton: Wheatsheaf Books

—— (1988) 'Autonomy and Identity in Feminist Thinking', in M. Griffiths and M. Whitford (eds): 90–108.

Gunew, S. (ed.) (1991) *A Reader in Feminist Knowledge*, London and New York: Routledge.

Gunning-Schepers, L.J. (1994) 'Wat zijn de klemmende vragen in de gezondheidszorg?', in *Congresverslag Vrouwen Kiezen met Zorg*, Utrecht: Metis: 11–13.

Haan, F. de (1995) '"Niet langer cellulair, nog steeds Elizabeth Fry!" Elizabeth Fry: grondlegster van de zorg voor vrouwelijke gevangenen', *Nemesis. Tijdschrift over vrouwen en recht* 11, 2: 58–75.

Haber, H.F. (1994) *Beyond Postmodern Politics*, New York and London: Routledge.

Haegen, R. van der (1989) *In het spoor van seksuele differentie*, Nijmegen: SUN.

Hagemann-White, C. (1989) 'Geslacht and gedrag', in S.L. Sevenhuijsen *et al.* (eds) *Socialisties-Feministiese Teksten 11*, Baarn: Ambo: 33–48.

Hall, E. van (1994) 'Hormonale mythologie rond de overgang', in A. Meinen *et al.* (ed.): 124–137.

Halsema, L. (1994) 'Een gender-subtekst van beleid: een analyse van "Een werkend perspectief" van de Wetenschappelijke Raad voor het Regeringsbeleid', *Tijdschrift voor Vrouwenstudies* 15, 2: 212–224.

Haraway, D.J. (1988) 'Situated Knowledges: The Science Question in Feminism and the Privilege of Partial Perspective', *Feminist Studies* 14, 3: 575–599.

—— (1991) *Simians, Cyborgs and Women: The Reinvention of Nature*, London: Free Association Press.

Harding, S. (1986) *The Science Question in Feminism*, Ithaca, NY and London: Cornell University Press.

Hardwig, J. (1990) 'Should Women Think in Terms of Rights?', in C.R. Sunstein (ed.) *Feminism and Political Theory*, Chicago and London: The University of Chicago Press: 53–68.

Hartogh, G. den (1995) 'Het motief der barmhartigheid. Co-referaat bij de lezing van Cornelis Verhoeven', *Rekenschap. Humanistisch Tijdschrift voor Wetenschap en Cultuur* 42, 1: 76–80.

Heijst, A. van (1992) *Verlangen naar de val. Zelfverlies en autonomie in hermeneutiek en ethiek*, Kampen: Kok Agora.

Hekman, S.J. (1990) *Gender and Knowledge: Elements of a Postmodern Feminism*, Cambridge: Polity Press.

—— (1995) *Moral Voices, Moral Selves: Carol Gilligan and Feminist Moral Theory*, Cambridge: Polity Press.

Held, V. (1987a) 'Feminism and Moral Theory', in E. Feder Kittay and D.T. Meyers (eds): 111–129.

—— (1987b) 'Non-Contractual Society: A Feminist View', *Canadian Journal of Philosophy* 13: 111–137.

—— (1989a) 'Liberty and Equality from a Feminist Perspective', in N. MacCormick and Z. Bankowski (eds): 214–228.

—— (1989b) 'Birth and Death', *Ethics* 99: 362–388.

—— (1990) 'Feminist Transformations of Moral Theory', *Philosophy and Phenomenological Research* 50, 1: 321–343.

—— (1993) *Feminist Morality: Transforming Culture, Society, and Politics*, Chicago: University of Chicago Press.

Hennik, L. van (1996) *Ik ga. Moeders die hun gezin verlaten*, Utrecht: Scheffers.

Hermsen, J.J. (1993) *Nomadisch narcisme. Sekse, liefde en kunst in het werk van Lou Andreas-Salomé, Belle van Zuylen en Ingeborg Bachmann*, Kampen: Kok Agora.

—— (1994) 'Mannelijke moraal en vrouwelijke onbeschaafdheid?', in R. Braidotti and S. Haakma (eds) *Ik denk, dus zij is. Vrouwelijke intellectuelen in een historisch perspectief*, Kampen: Kok Agora: 115–143.

Himmelweit, S. (1988) 'More than "A Woman's Right to Choose"?', *Feminist Review* 29, 38–55.

Hirschmann, N.J. (1992) *Rethinking Obligation: A Feminist Method for Political Theory*, Ithaca, NY and London: Cornell University Press.

Hoagland, S.L. (1991) 'Some Thoughts about "Caring"', in C. Card (ed.): 246–286.

Hodge, J. (1988) 'Subject, Body and the Exclusion of Women from Philosophy', in M. Griffiths and M. Whitford (eds): 152–169.

Hoek, M. (1994) *Zorg kan niet wachten tot zondag. Een oriëntatie op een economische theorie van zorg*, Amsterdam: Universiteit van Amsterdam.

Holtmaat, R. (1992) *Met zorg een recht? Een analyse van het politiek-juridisch vertoog over bijstandsrecht*, Zwolle: W.E.J. Tjeenk Willink.

—— (1996) 'Deeltijdwerk, gelijkheid en gender', *Nemesis. Tijdschrift over vrouwen en recht* 12, 1: 4–7.

Holtrust, N. (1988) 'Het nieuwe afstammingsrecht: van onwettige kinderen naar opgedrongen vaders', in P. de Vries (ed.): 55–72.

—— (1992) *Rechtspraak Vrouwen en Recht*, Nijmegen: Ars Aequi.

—— (1993) *Aan moeders knie. De juridische afstammingsrelatie tussen moeder en kind*, Nijmegen: Ars Aequi Libri.

—— (1995) 'De geschiedenis van de afstandsmoeder. Dikke bult, eigen schuld', *Nemesis. Tijdschrift over vrouwen en recht* 11, 1: 45–59.

Holtrust, N. and Hondt, I. de (1986) 'Het effect van het Marckx-arrest', *Nemesis. Tijdschrift over vrouwen en recht* 2, 3: 98–105.

—— (1991) 'Gezin, geweld en recht', in E. Singer and M. Wegelin (eds) *De familieband verbroken? Opstellen over gezinsgeweld, autonomie en loyaliteit*, Utrecht: Jan van Arkel: 144–164.

—— (1996) 'Gezinsleven, transsexualiteit, sociaal ouderschap', *Nemesis. Tijdschrift over vrouwen en recht* 12, 1: 8–10.

Holtrust, N., Sevenhuijsen, S.L. and Verbraken, A. (1989) 'Rights for Fathers and the State: Recent Developments in Custody Politics in the Netherlands', in C. Smart and S.L. Sevenhuijsen (eds): 51–77.

Honig, B. (1993) *Political Theory and the Displacement of Politics*, Ithaca, NY and London: Cornell University Press.

—— (ed.) (1995) *Feminist Interpretations of Hannah Arendt*, Pennsylvania: The Pennsylvania State University Press.

Honneth, A. (1994) 'Das Andere der Gerechtigkeit. Habermas und die Ethische Herausforderung der Postmoderne', *Deutsche Zeitschrift für Philosophie* 42, 2: 195–218.

hooks, b. (1981) *Ain't I a Woman: Black Women and Feminism*, Boston: South End Press.

—— (1990) *Yearning: Race, Gender and Cultural Politics*, Boston: South End Press.

Houston, B. (1988) 'Gilligan and the Politics of a Distinctive Women's Morality', in C. Code (ed.) (1988c): 168–189.

Howe, A. (1987) '"Social Injury" Revisited: Towards a Feminist Theory of Social Justice', *International Journal of the Sociology of Law* 15, 4: 423–438.

Hulst, L. van der (1993) *Attitude-onderzoek onder verloskundigen in de relatie tot de plaats van de bevalling: thuis of in het ziekenhuis*, Utrecht: Werkgroep Vrouwenstudies Sociale Wetenschappen.

Hursthouse, R. (1987) *Beginning Lives*, New York: Basil Blackwell.

Irigaray, L. (1989) *Le temps de la différence. Pour une révolution pacifique*, Paris: Le livre de poche.

Jackson, K. (1989) 'And Justice for All? Human Nature and the Feminist Critique of Liberalism', in J. O'Barr (ed.): 122–139.

Jacobus, M., Keller, E. Fox and Shuttleworth, S. (1990) *Body/Politics: Women and the Discourses of Science*, New York and London: Routledge.

Jaggar, A.M. (1983) *Feminist Politics and Human Nature*, Totowa: Rowman and Alanheld.

—— (1989) 'Love and Knowledge: Emotion in Feminist Epistemology', in A.M. Jaggar and S.R. Bordo (eds): 145–171.

—— (1991) 'Feminist Ethics: Projects, Problems, Prospects', in C. Card (ed.): 78–104.

Jaggar, A.M. and Bordo, S.R. (eds) (1989) *Gender/Body/Knowledge: Feminist Reconstructions of Being and Knowing*, New Brunswick, NJ and London: Rutgers University Press.

James, S. (1992) 'The Good-enough Citizen: Citizenship and Independence', in G. Bock and S. James (eds): 48–65.

Jansz, U. (1990) *Denken over sekse in de eerste feministische golf*, Amsterdam: Sara/Van Gennep.

Jay, N. (1991) 'Gender and Dichotomy', in S. Gunew (ed.): 89–106.

Jones, K.B. (1988a) 'On Authority: Or, Why Women are not Entitled to Speak', in I. Diamond and L. Quinby (eds): 119–134.

—— (1988b) 'Towards the Revision of Politics', in K.B. Jones and A. Jonasdottir (eds) *The Political Interest of Gender*, London: Sage: 11–32.

—— (1993) *Compassionate Authority: Democracy and the Representation of Women*, New York and London: Routledge.

Kanter, R. de (1987) 'A Father is a Bag Full of Money: The Person, the Position and the Symbol of the Father', in T. Knijn and A. Mulder (eds): 6–26.

Kearns, D. (1983) 'A Theory of Justice – and Love: Rawls on the Family', *Politics: Journal of the Australasian Political Studies Association*: 36–42.

Keizer, M. (1997) *De dokter spreekt. Professionaliteit, gender en uitsluiting in medische specialismen*, Delft: Eburon.

Keller, C. (1986) *From a Broken Web: Separation, Sexism and Self*, Boston: Beacon Press.

Keller, E. Fox (1983) *A Feeling for the Organism: The Life and Work of Barbara McClintock*, New York: W.H. Freeman.

Kessler, J. and McKenna, W. (1978) *Gender: An Ethnomethodological Approach*, New York: Wiley and Sons.

Keuzenkamp, S. and Teunissen, A. (1990) *Emancipatie ten halve geregeld: continuïteit en inenging in het emancipatiebeleid*, Den Haag: Ministerie van Sociale Zaken en Werkgelegenheid.

Kittay, E. Feder (1995) 'Taking Dependency Seriously: The Family and Medical Leave Act Considered in the Light of the Social Organization of Dependency Work and Gender Equality', *Hypatia: A Journal for Feminist Philosophy* 10, 1: 8–29.

Kittay, E. Feder and Meyers, D.T. (1987) *Women and Moral Theory*, Totowa: Rowman and Littlefield.

Knijn, T. (1994) 'Zorg met mondjesmaat: paradoxen rond de dagelijkse zorg', in A. Meinen *et al.* (eds): 56–73.

Knijn, T. and Kremer, M. (1997) 'Gender and the Caring Dimensions of Welfare States: Towards Inclusive Citizenship', *Social Politics: International Studies in Gender, State and Society*, 4, 3: 328–361.

Knijn, T. and Mulder, A. (eds) (1987) *Unraveling Fatherhood*, Dordrecht: Foris Publications.

Knijn, T., Nunen, A. van and Avort, A. van der (1994) 'Zorgend vaderschap', *Amsterdams Sociologisch Tijdschrift* 20, 3: 70–97.

Komter, A.E. (1989a) 'Onder omstandigheden zelfs met geweld. Oude and nieuwe denkbeelden over "zedelijkheid" in de context van de machtsrelatie tussen vrouwen en mannen', in I. de Vries (ed.): 17–28.

—— (1989b) 'Lof der zorgzaamheid. Carol Gilligan en de "ethic of care"', *Psychologie en Maatschappij* 13, 2: 316–321.

—— (1990) *De macht van de dubbele moraal. Verschil en gelijkheid in de verhouding tussen de seksen*, Amsterdam: Van Gennep.

—— (1991) 'The Justice of Caring in Politics', in S.L. Sevenhuijsen (ed.) (1991c): 51–55.

—— (1995) 'Justice, Friendship and Care: Aristotle and Gilligan – Two of a Kind?', *The European Journal of Women's Studies* 2, 2: 151–169.

Krieger, L.J. (1987) 'Through a Glass Darkly: Paradigms of Equality and the Search for a Woman's Jurisprudence', *Hypatia: A Journal for Feminist Philosophy* 2, 1: 45–61.

Kristeva, J. (1991) *Strangers to Ourselves*, New York: Columbia University Press.

Krol, S. (1992) 'Feminisme, kennis en moraal. Lorraine Code en een epistemologie van verantwoordelijkheid', *Tijdschrift voor Vrouwenstudies* 13, 1: 71–79.

Krol, S. and Sevenhuijsen, S.L. (1992) *Ethics and Morality in Feminism: An Interdisciplinary Bibliography*, Utrecht: Anna Maria van Schuurman Centrum.

Landes, J. (1988) *Women and the Public Sphere in the Age of the French Revolution*, Ithaca, NY and London: Cornell University Press.

Larrabee, M.J. (ed.) (1993) *An Ethic of Care. Feminist and Interdisciplinary Perspectives*, New York and London: Routledge.

Lieshout, P. van (1995) 'Een sociaal democratische worsteling. De politieke urgentie van een zorg-beleid', *Socialisme en Democratie* 52, 6: 251–262.

Lloyd, G. (1984) *The Man of Reason: 'Male' and 'Female' in Western Philosophy*, London: Methuen.

—— (1991) 'Reason as Attainment', in S. Gunew (ed.): 166–180.

—— (1993) 'Maleness, Metaphor and the "Crisis" of Reason', in L.M. Antony and C. Witt (eds): 69–84.

Loenen, T. (1992) *Verschil in Gelijkheid. De conceptualisering van het juridische gelijkheids-beginsel met betrekking tot vrouwen en mannen in Nederland en de Verenigde Staten*, Zwolle: W.E.J. Tjeenk Willink.

—— (1994a) 'Mensenrechtelijke aspecten van de leefvormenproblematiek I: Familie-recht', *NJCM Bulletin* 19, 3: 207–219.

—— (1994b) 'De machtige taal van het recht: de onzichtbaarheid van zorg in de juri-dische constructie van het ouderschap', *Tijdschrift voor Vrouwenstudies* 16, 1: 18–32.

—— (1995a) 'Comparative legal feminist scholarship and the importance of a contex-tual approach to concepts and strategies. The case of the equality debate', *Feminist Legal Studies* 3, 1: 71–87.

—— (1995b) 'Echte of onechte ouders', *Nemesis. Tijdschrift over vrouwen en recht* 11, 4: 92–96.

Lugones, M.C. (1991) 'On the Logic of Pluralist Feminism', in C. Card (ed.): 35–44.

Lyotard, J.F. (1987) *Het postmoderne weten*, Kampen: Kok Agora.

McAfee, N. (1993) 'Abject Strangers: Towards an Ethics of Respect', in K. Oliver (ed.): 116–134.

MacCormick, N. and Bankowski, Z. (eds) (1989) *Enlightenment, Rights and Revolution*, Aberdeen: Aberdeen University Press.

MacGregor Davies, P. (1988) 'Pornographic Harms', in C. Code (ed.) (1988c): 127–145.

MacIntyre, A. (1981) *After Virtue: A Study in Moral Theory*, London: Duckworth.

MacKinnon, C.A. (1989) *Toward a Feminist Theory of the State*, Cambridge, MA: Harvard University Press.

McLure, K. (1992) 'The Issue of Foundations: Scientized Politics, Politicized Science, and Feminist Critical Practice', in J. Butler and J.W. Scott (eds): 341–368.

Macpherson, C.B. (1962) *The Political Theory of Possessive Individualism: Hobbes to Locke*, Oxford: Clarendon Press.

Maihofer, A. (1988) 'Ansätze zur Kritik des moralischen Universalismus. Zur moraltheoretischen Diskussion um Gilligans Thesen zu einer "weiblichen" Mora-lauffassung', *Feministische Studien* 6, 1: 33–52.

Mann, P.S. (1994) *Micro-politics: Agency in a Postfeminist Era*, Minneapolis and London: University of Minnesota Press.

Manning, R.C. (1992) *Speaking from the Heart: A Feminist Perspective on Ethics*, Lanham, MD: Rowman and Littlefield.

Manschot, H. (1994) 'Kwetsbare autonomie: Over afhankelijkheid and onafhanke-lijkheid in de ethiek van de zorg', in H. Manschot and M. Verkerk (eds): 97–118.

Manschot, H. and Verkerk, M. (eds) (1994) *Ethiek van de zorg. Een discussie*, Amsterdam and Meppel: Boom.

Martin, E. (1987) *The Woman in the Body: A Cultural Analysis of Reproduction*, Boston: Beacon Press.

Meehan J. (ed.) (1995) *Feminists Read Habermas: Gendering the Subject of Discourse*, London and New York: Routledge.

Meehan, E. and Sevenhuijsen, S.L. (eds) (1991) *Equality Politics and Gender*, London: Sage.

Meinen, A. *et al.* (eds) (1994) *Op haar recept. Vrouwen in politiek debat over de gezondheidszorg*, Amsterdam: De Balie.

Mendus, S. (1987) 'Kant: An Honest but Narrow-minded Bourgeois?', in E. Kennedy and S. Mendus (eds) *Women in Western Political Philosophy. Kant to Nietzsche*, Brighton: Wheatsheaf: 21–43.

—— (1993) 'Eve and the Poisoned Chalice: Feminist Morality and the Claims of Politics', in M. Brügmann, *et al.* (eds) *Who's Afraid of Femininity? Questions of Identity*, Amsterdam: Rodopi: 95–104.

Mens-Verhulst, J. van (1996) *Vrouwenhulpverlening: diversiteit als bron van zorg*, Utrecht: Universiteit voor Humanistiek.

Mens-Verhulst, J. van and Mesch, H. (1993) *Vrouwenhulpverlening op het transculturele pad*, Utrecht: Universiteit Utrecht/ISOR.

Mens-Verhulst, J. van and Schilder, L. (eds) (1994) *Debatten in de vrouwenhulpverlening*, Amsterdam: Babylon-De Geus.

Mens-Verhulst, J. van, Schreurs, K. and Woertman, L. (eds) (1993) *Daughtering and Mothering: Female Subjectivity Reanalyzed*, New York and London: Routledge.

Merill, S.A. Bishop (1994) 'A Feminist Use for Hume's Moral Ontology', in B. Bar On (ed.): 69–91.

Meyers, D.T. (1987) 'The Socialized Individual and Individual Autonomy: An Intersection between Philosophy and Psychology', in E. Feder Kittay and D.T. Meyers (eds): 139–153.

—— (1989) *Self, Society and Personal Choice*, New York and Oxford: Columbia University Press.

—— (1993) 'Moral Reflection: Beyond Impartial Reason', *Hypatia: A Journal for Feminist Philosophy* 8, 3: 21–47.

—— (1994) *Subjection and Subjectivity: Psychoanalytic Feminism and Moral Philosophy*, New York and London: Routledge.

Miller, B. (1990) 'Gender Differences in Spouse Management of the Caregiver Role', in E.K. Abel and M. Nelson (eds): 92–104.

Ministerie van Justitie (1995) *Leefvormen in het familierecht*, Den Haag: Ministerie van Justitie.

Minow, M. (1990) *Making All the Difference: Inclusion, Exclusion and American Law*, Ithaca, NY and London: Cornell University Press.

Mol, A. (1991) 'De publieke patiënt', *Tijdschrift voor Gezondheid en Politiek* 9, 1: 18–19.

Morée, M. and Oldersma, J. (1991) 'Gezinsverzorging. De onderkant van de zorgverlening', *Tijdschrift voor Gezondheid en Politiek* 9, 1: 10–13.

Morgan, K.P. (1988) 'Women and Moral Madness', in L. Code (ed.) (1988c): 146–168.

Mossink, M. and Nederland, T. (1993) *Beeldvorming in beleid. Een analyse van vrouwelijkheid en mannelijkheid in beleidsstukken van de rijksoverheid*, Den Haag: VUGA.

Mossman, M.J. (1986) 'Feminism and Legal Method: The Difference it Makes', *Australian Journal of Law and Society* 3: 30–52.

—— (1993) '"Running Hard to Stand Still": The Paradox of Family Law Reform', *Dalhousie Law Journal* 17: 1–34.

Mouffe, C. (1992) 'Feminism, Citizenship and Radical Democratic Politics', in J. Butler and J.W. Scott (eds): 369–385.

Mulder, A. (1987) 'Deconstructing God the Father', in T. Knijn and A. Mulder (eds): 116–128.

—— (1988) 'Het bouwwerk God de Vader: niet renoveren maar slopen', in P. de Vries (ed.): 100–115.

Mullet, S. (1988) 'Shifting Perspectives: A New Feminist Approach to Ethics', in L. Code (ed.) (1988c): 109–126.

Mullin, A. (1995) 'Selves, Diverse and Divided: Can Feminists Have Diversity Without Multiplicity?', *Hypatia: A Journal for Feminist Philosophy* 10, 4: 1–31.

Naffine, N. (1990) *Law and the Sexes*, Sydney: Allen and Unwin.

Nagl-Docekal, H. (1992) 'Feminist Ethics: The Controversy Between Contextualism and Universalism Revisited', in M. Pellikaan-Engel (ed.): 163–172.

Narayan, U. (1995) 'Colonialism and Its Others: Considerations On Rights and Care Discourses', *Hypatia: A Journal for Feminist Philosophy* 10, 2: 133–140.

Nedelsky, J. (1988) 'Reconceiving Autonomy: Sources, Thought and Possibilities', *Yale Journal of Law and Feminism* 1: 7–36.

—— (1990) 'Law, Boundaries and the Bounded Self', *Representations* 30: 162–189.

Nederland, T. (1995) *En nu ik . . . Vrouwen over ouder worden*, Utrecht and Antwerp: Kosmos.

Nelissen, H. (1994) 'Denkt Dunning wel aan Sjaan?', in A. Meinen *et al.* (eds): 74–85.

Nijnatten, C.H.C.J. van (ed.) (1993) *Kinderrechten in discussie*, Amsterdam and Meppel: Boom.

Noddings, N. (1984) *Caring: A Feminine Approach to Ethics and Moral Education*, Berkeley, CA: University of California Press.

NOV (Nederlandse Onderzoekschool Vrouwenstudies) (1994) *Aanvraag tot erkenning*, Utrecht: Universiteit Utrecht.

Nussbaum, M.C. (1986) *The Fragility of Goodness: Luck and Ethics in Greek Tragedy and Philosophy*, Cambridge: Cambridge University Press.

—— (1990) *Love's Knowledge: Essays on Philosophy and Literature*, New York and Oxford: Oxford University Press.

—— (1992) 'Human Functioning and Social Justice: In Defence of Aristotelian Essentialism', *Political Theory* 20, 2: 202–246.

—— (1995) 'Emotions and Women's Capabilities', in M. Nussbaum and J. Glover (eds) *Women, Culture and Development: A Study of Human Capabilities*, Oxford: Clarendon Press: 360–395.

O'Barr, J. (ed.) (1989) *Women and a New Academy. Gender and Cultural Contexts*, Madison: University of Wisconsin Press.

O'Brian, M. (1981) *The Politics of Reproduction*, London and Boston: Routledge and Kegan Paul.

O'Donovan, K. (1985) *Sexual Divisions in Law*, London: Weidenfeld and Nicolson.

O'Neill, O. (1986) *Faces of Hunger: An Essay on Poverty, Justice and Development*, London: Allen and Unwin.

—— (1988) 'Children's Rights and Children's Lives', *Ethics* 98: 445–463.

—— (1989) 'The Great Maxims of Justice and Charity', in N. MacCormick and Z. Bankowski (eds): 297–312.

Okin, S. Moller (1979) *Women in Western Political Thought*, Princeton, NJ: Princeton University Press.

—— (1982) 'Women and the Making of Sentimental Family', *Philosophy and Public Affairs* 11, 1: 65–88.

—— (1987) 'Justice and Gender', *Philosophy and Public Affairs* 16, 1: 42–72.

—— (1989) *Justice, Gender and the Family*, Princeton, NJ: Princeton University Press.

Oliver, K. (ed.) (1993) *Ethics, Politics, and Difference in Julia Kristeva's Writing*, New York and London: Routledge.

Oord, J.W.J. van den (1994) *Verdaagde rechten. Een visie op rechtsgelijkheid van vrouwen en mannen vanuit Derrida's filosofie van sexuele differenties*, Arnhem: Gouda Quint.

Orobio de Castro, I. (1993) *Made to Order: Sex/Gender in a Transsexual Perspective*, Amsterdam: Het Spinhuis.

Oudshoorn, N. (1991) 'Sekse als natuur of cultuur', *Tijdschrift voor Gezondheid en Politiek* 9, 2: 21–24.

—— (1994) *Beyond the Natural Body: An Archeology of the Origins of the Hormonal Body*, New York and London: Routledge.

Outshoorn, J. (1989) *Een irriterend onderwerp. Verschuivende conceptualiseringen van het sekseverschil*, Nijmegen: SUN.

—— (1991) 'Is This What We Wanted? Positive Action as Issue Perversion', in E. Meehan and S.L. Sevenhuijsen (eds): 104–121.

Özçelik, S. (1994) 'Geef migrantenvrouwen de ruimte om Nederlandse zorg te leren kennen', in A. Meinen *et al.* (eds): 86–95.

Parlevliet, C. (1995) *Zorg(e)loos ouder worden? Analyse van de begrippen ouderen en ouderenzorg in het rapport 'Ouderenzorg met Toekomst' van de commissie Welschen*, Utrecht: Universiteit Utrecht

Parlevliet, C. and Sevenhuijsen, S.L. (1993) *Zorg bekeken door een andere bril. Vrouwen en het debat over 'Keuzen in de zorg'*, Utrecht: Metis/Werkgroep Vrouwenstudies Sociale Wetenschappen.

Partij van de Arbeid (1995) *Familierecht bij de tijd*, Den Haag: PvdA.

Passerin D'Entrèves, M. (1994) *The Political Philosophy of Hannah Arendt*, New York and London: Routledge.

Pateman, C. (1988) *The Sexual Contract*, Cambridge: Polity Press.

—— (1989) *The Disorder of Woman*, Cambridge: Polity Press.

—— (1992) 'Equality, Difference, Subordination: The Politics of Motherhood and Women's Citizenship', in G. Bock and S. James (eds): 17–31.

Pateman, C. and Gross, E. (eds) (1986) *Feminist Challenges: Social and Political Theory*, Sydney, London and Boston: Allen and Unwin.

Pellikaan-Engel, M. (ed.) (1992) *Against Patriarchal Thinking: A Future Without Discrimination?*, Amsterdam: VU University Press.

Pessers, D. (1994) *De wet van het hart*, Amsterdam: Balans.

Plumwood, V. (1993) *Feminism and the Mastery of Nature*, New York and London: Routledge.

Poldervaart, S. (1991) 'Vrouwelijke kwaliteit voor alle mensen? Discussies over vrouwelijkheid aan de hand van het Franse utopisch-socialistisch feminisme 1830–1850', in M. Schwegman *et al.* (ed.) *Op het strijdtoneel van de politiek. Twaalfde jaarboek voor vrouwengeschiedenis*, Nijmegen: SUN: 131–152.

Porter, E. (1991) *Women and Moral Identity*, Sydney: Allen and Unwin.

Pott, H. (1992) *De liefde van Alcibiades. Over de rationaliteit van emoties*, Amsterdam: Boom.

Prins, B. (1988) 'Moeten vrouwen volwassen worden? Feministische ethiek en vrouwelijke moraal', *Lover. Tijdschrift over feminisme, cultuur en wetenschap* 16, 4: 278–285.

—— (1989) *Ethiek als tekstuele praktijk. Over vrouwen, moraal en uitsluiting*, Amsterdam: Werkgroep Krisis-onderzoek.

Rawls, J. (1971) *A Theory of Justice*, Cambridge, MA: Harvard University Press.

Reinders, H. (1994) 'De grenzen van het rechtendiscours', in H. Manschot and M. Verkerk (eds): 74–96.

Reverby, S. (1987) *Ordered to Care: The Dilemma of American Nursing, 1850–1945*, Cambridge: Cambridge University Press.

Rich, A. (1976) *Of Woman Born: Motherhood as Experience and Institution*, London: Virago.

—— (1985) 'Een politiek van plaats/aantekeningen', in A. Rich (1985) *Bloed, brood en poëzie. Essays 1971–1984*, Amsterdam: Feministische Uitgeverij Sara: 313–333.

Römkens, R. (1991) 'Het onbehagen over geweld tegen vrouwen, projectie en internalisering van verantwoordelijkheid en schuld', in P.B. Defares and J.D.van der Ploeg (eds) *Agressie. Determinanten, signalering en interventie*, Assen and Maastricht: Van Gorcum: 211–227.

—— (1992) *Gewoon geweld? Omvang, aard, gevolgen en achtergronden van geweld tegen vrouwen in heteroseksuele relaties*, Amsterdam and Lisse: Swets and Zeitlinger.

—— (1995) 'De partnerdoodster als statistische rariteit. Veroordelingen van vrouwen wegens moord en doodslag in Nederland', *Nemesis. Tijdschrift over vrouwen en recht* 11, 2: 44–57.

—— (1996) '"Zwei Seelen in einer Brust". Representaties van vrouwen die de partner doden', in R. Römkens and S. Dijkstra (eds): 77–100.

Römkens, R. and Dijkstra, S. (eds) (1996) *Het omstreden slachtoffer. Geweld van vrouwen en mannen*, Baarn: Ambo.

Rooney, P. (1991) 'A Different Different Voice: On the Feminist Challenge in Moral Theory', *The Philosophical Forum*, 22, 4: 335–361.

Rose, H. (1994) *Power and Knowledge: Towards a Feminist Transformation of Science*, Cambridge: Polity Press.

Ruddick, S. (1989) *Maternal Thinking: Towards a Politics of Peace*, Boston: Beacon Press.

Ruiter, J. de (1990) *Een vat vol tegenstrijdigheden*, Zwolle: W.E.J. Tjeenk Willink.

Sainsbury, D. (ed.) (1994) *Gendering Welfare States*, London: Sage.

—— (1996) *Gender, Equality and Welfare States*, Cambridge: Cambridge University Press.

Sandberg, K. (1989) 'Best Interests and Justice', in C. Smart and S.L. Sevenhuijsen (eds): 100–125.

Sandel, M. (1982) *Liberalism and the Limits of Justice*, New York: Cambridge University Press.

Sawicki, J. (1988) 'Identity Politics and Sexual Freedom: Foucault and Feminism', in I. Diamond and L. Quinby (eds): 177–192.

Scheman, N. (1993) 'Though This Be Method, Yet There Is Madness In It: Paranoia and Liberal Epistemology', in L.M. Antony and C. Witt (eds): 145–170.

Schiebinger, L. (1989) *The Mind Has No Sex? Women in the Origins of Modern Science*, Cambridge, MA and London: Harvard University Press.

Schoon, L. (1995) *De gynaecologie als belichaming van vrouwen. Verloskunde en gynaecologie 1840–1920*, Zutphen: Walburg Pers.

Schott, R.M. (1993) 'Resurrecting Embodiment: Toward a Feminist Materialism', in L.M. Antony and C. Witt (eds): 171–184.

—— (1994) 'Rereading the Canon: Kantian Purity and the Suppression of Eros', in B. Bar On (ed.): 127–140.

Schrijvers, A. (1997) *Health and Health Care in the Netherlands*, Utrecht: De Tijdstroom.

Scott, J.W. (1986) 'Gender: A Useful Category of Historical Analysis', *American Historical Review* 91, 5: 1035–1075.

—— (1988) 'Deconstructing Equality versus Difference: Or, the Uses of Poststructuralist Theory for Feminism', *Feminist Studies* 14, 1: 33–50.

Sennet, R. (1981) *Authority*, New York: Knopf.

Sevenhuijsen, S.L. (1978) 'Vadertje staat, moedertje thuis?', in S.L.Sevenhuijsen *et al.* (eds) *Socialisties-Feministiese Teksten* 1, Amsterdam: Feministische Uitgeverij Sara, 18–66.

—— (1986) 'Fatherhood and the Political Theory of Rights: Theoretical Perspectives of Feminism', *International Journal of the Sociology of Law* 14, 3/4: 329–340.

—— (1987) *De orde van het vaderschap. Politieke debatten over huwelijk, ongehuwd moederschap en afstamming in Nederland 1870–1900*, Amsterdam: IISG-Beheer.

—— (1988a) 'Vrouwelijkheid als bron van politieke wijsheid. Amerikaanse politieke filosofen over het moederschap', *Amsterdams Sociologisch Tijdschrift* 15, 2: 208–234.

—— (1988b) 'Vaderrecht als historisch-politiek concept', in P. de Vries (ed.): 34–54.

—— (1989) 'Gelijkheid en rechtvaardigheid. Feminisme en de politieke theorie van John Rawls', *Recht en Kritiek* 15, 2: 137–160.

—— (1991a) 'The Morality of Feminism', *Hypatia: A Journal for Feminist Philosophy* 6, 2: 173–191.

—— (1991b) 'Justice, Moral Reasoning and the Politics of Child Custody', in E. Meehan and S.L. Sevenhuijsen (eds): 88–103.

—— (ed.) (1991c) *Gender, Care and Justice in Feminist Political Theory*, Utrecht: Anna Maria van Schuurman Centrum.

—— (1992a) 'The Gendered Jurification of Parenthood', *Social and Legal Studies: An International Journal* 1, 1: 71–84.

—— (1992b) 'Mothers as Citizens. Feminism, Evolutionary Theory and the Reform of Dutch Family Law 1870–1910', in C. Smart (ed.) *Regulating Womanhood. Historical Essays on Marriage, Motherhood and Sexuality*, New York and London: Routledge: 166–186.

—— (1993a) 'Paradoxes of Gender. Ethical and Epistemological Perspectives on Care in Feminist Political Theory', *Acta Politica* 28, 2: 131–149.

—— (1993b) 'Hoe krijgen we de onderkant van de zorg weer boven?', *Tijdschrift voor Gezondheid en Politiek* 11, 3: 11–14.

—— (1993c) 'Feministische ethiek en rechten van kinderen', in C.H.C.J. van Nijnatten (ed.): 42–63.

—— (1993d) 'Mantelzorg hoeft niet strijdig te zijn met emancipatie'. *Tijdschrift voor Gezondheid en Politiek* 11, 1: 27–30.

—— (1995) 'De dubbelzinnigheid van autonomie. Reflecties over een feministische bio-ethiek', *Filosofie & Praktijk* 16, 1: 2–20.

—— (1997a) 'Feministische Überlegungen zum Thema Care und Staatsbügerschaft', in H. Braun and D. Jung (eds) *Globale Gerechtigkeit? Feministische Debatte zur Krise des Sozialstaats*, Hamburg: Konkret Literatur Verlag: 75–95.

185

—— (1997b) 'De ondraaglijke lichtheid van het bestaan. Over burgerschap en zorg in het emancipatiebeleid' in M. Van den Brink *et al.* (eds) *Een stuk zeep in de badkuip. Hoe zorg tot haar recht komt*, Deventer: Kluwer: 43–68.

Sevenhuijsen, S.L. and Vries, P. de (1980) 'Vrouwenbeweging en moederschap', in S.L. Sevenhuijsen, *et al.* (eds) *Socialisties-Feministiese Teksten 4*, Amsterdam: Feministische Uitgeverij Sara: 154–174.

Sevenhuijsen, S.L., *et al.* (eds) (1986) *Socialisties-Feministiese Teksten 9*, Baarn: Ambo.

—— (1989) *Socialisties-Feministiese Teksten 11*, Baarn: Ambo.

Shanley, M.L. (1982) 'Marriage Contract and Social Contract in Seventeenth-century English Political Thought', in J.B. Elshtain (ed.): 80–96.

—— (1995) 'Father's Rights, Mother's Wrongs? Reflections on Unwed Father's Rights and Sex Equality', *Hypatia: A Journal for Feminist Philosophy* 10, 1: 74–103.

Shklar, J. (1990) *The Faces of Injustice*, New York and London: Yale University Press.

Showstack Sassoon, A. (ed.) (1987) *Women and the State*, London: Hutchinson.

Shrage, L. (1994) *Moral Dilemmas of Feminism: Prostitution, Adultery and Abortion*, New York and London: Routledge.

Simonen, L. (1990) *Contradictions of the Welfare State, Women and Caring: Municipal Home-making in Finland*, Tampere: University of Tampere.

Simons, E.C. (1913) *De rechtstoestand van het natuurlijke kind*, Utrecht: Universiteit Utrecht.

Slotboom, H. (1994) 'Veilig in de armen van de Staat, of: wat heeft het strafrecht slachtoffers van vrouwenmishandeling te bieden?', *Nemesis. Tijdschrift over vrouwen en recht* 10, 3: 62–74.

Smart, C. (1987) '"There is of course the Distinction Dictated by Nature": Law and the Problem of Paternity', in M. Stanworth (ed.): 98–117.

—— (1989) *Feminism and the Power of the Law*, New York and London: Routledge.

—— (1992) 'The Woman of Legal Discourse', *Social and Legal Studies: An International Journal*, 1: 29-44.

—— (1994) 'Law, Feminism and Sexuality: From Essence to Ethics', *Canadian Journal of Law and Society* 9, 1: 1–23.

—— (1995) *Law, Crime and Sexuality: Essays in Feminism*, London: Sage.

—— (1997) 'Wishful Thinking and Harmful Tinkering? Sociological Reflections on Family Policy', *Journal of Social Policy* 26, 3: 121.

Smart, C. and B. Neale (1997a) 'Arguments against Virtue – Must Contact be Enforced?', *Family Law* 27: 332–336.

—— (1997b) 'Good Enough Morality: Divorce and Postmodernity', *Critical Social Policy* 17, 4: 3–28.

Smart, C. and Sevenhuijsen, S.L. (eds) (1989) *Child Custody and the Politics of Gender*, New York and London: Routledge.

Smith, D.E. (1990) *Texts, Facts and Femininity: Exploring the Relations of Ruling*, London and New York: Routledge.

Smith, J. Farell (1984) 'Parenting and Property', in J. Trebilcot (ed.): 199–212.

Spelman, E.V. (1989) *Inessential Woman. Problems of Exclusion in Feminist Thought*, Boston: Beacon Press.

—— (1991) 'The Virtue of Feeling and the Feeling of Virtue', in C. Card (ed.): 213–233.

Stanworth, M. (ed.) (1987) *Reproductive Technologies: Gender, Motherhood and Medicine*, Cambridge: Polity Press.

Steenbergen, B. van (ed.) (1994) *The Condition of Citizenship*, London: Sage.

Suurmond, J. (1992) 'Het tere punt: mannelijke en vrouwelijke moraal in het debat over vrouwenbesnijdenis', *Lover. Tijdschrift over feminisme, cultuur en wetenschap* 20, 3: 156–161.

Taylor, C. (1989) *Sources of the Self: The Making of Modern Identity*, Cambridge, MA: Harvard University Press.

Thooft, L. (1992) 'Kiezen voor jezelf of voor het moederschap. Vrouwen die hun kinderen bij de scheiding afstaan aan de vader', *Opzij. Feministisch maandblad* 20, 5: 32–35.

Thooft, L. and Molen, E. van der (eds) (1995) *Werk en moederschap: moederen op de derde golf*, Baarn: Bigot and van Rossum.

Thornton, M. (1986) 'Sex Equality is not Enough for Feminism', in C. Pateman and E. Gross (eds): 77–99.

Tong, R. (1993) *Feminine and Feminist Ethics*, Belmont: Wadsworth.

Trebilcot, J. (ed.) (1984) *Mothering. Essays in Feminist Theory*, Totowa: Rowman and Allanheld.

Treichler, S.A. (1990) 'Feminism, Medicine and the Meaning of Childbirth', in M. Jacobus *et al.* (eds) *Body/Politics: Women and the Discourses of Science*. New York and London: Routledge: 113–138.

Tronto, J.C. (1987) 'Beyond Gender Difference to a Theory of Care', *Signs: Journal of Women in Culture and Society* 12, 4: 644–662.

—— (1989) 'Women and Caring: What Can Feminists Learn about Morality from Caring?', in A.M. Jaggar and S.R. Bordo (eds): 172–187.

—— (1991) 'Reflections on Gender, Morality and Power: Caring and the Moral Problem of Otherness', in S.L. Sevenhuijsen (ed.) (1991c): 1–19.

—— (1993) *Moral Boundaries. A Political Argument for an Ethic of Care*, New York and London: Routledge.

—— (1995a) 'Care as a Basis for Radical Political Judgements', *Hypatia: A Journal for Feminist Philosophy* 10, 2: 141–149.

—— (1995b) *Caring for Democracy: A Feminist Vision*, Utrecht: Universiteit voor Humanistiek.

—— (1995c) 'Van produkt naar praktijk: gezondheidszorg als zorg', *Rekenschap. Humanistisch Tijdschrift voor Wetenschap en Cultuur* 42, 3: 148–157.

—— (1996) *Caring as Democratic Practice*. Unpublished paper.

Tronto, J. and Fisher, B. (1990) 'Toward a Feminist Theory of Caring', in E.K. Abel and M. Nelson (eds): 35–62.

Udovicki, J. (1993) 'Justice and Care in Close Associations', *Hypatia: A Journal for Feminist Philosophy* 8, 3: 48–60.

Ungerson, C. (1987) *Policy is Personal: Sex, Gender and Informal Care*, New York and London: Tavistock.

—— (ed.) (1990a) *Gender and Caring: Work and Welfare in Britain and Scandinavia*, New York and London: Harvester Wheatsheaf.

—— (1990b) 'The Language of Care', in C. Ungerson (ed.): 8–34.

Vega, J. (1986) 'Dwang en instemming: klassiek liberale koncepten in teksten over seksueel geweld', *Tijdschrift voor Vrouwenstudies* 7, 2: 179–195.

Vegetti Finzi, S. (1992) 'Female Identity Between Sexuality and Maternity', in G. Bock and S. James (eds): 126–145.

Verkerk, M. (1994) 'Zorg of contract: een andere ethiek', in H. Manschot and M.Verkerk (eds): 53–74.

—— (1995) 'How Politics Saved the Life of Ethics', Rekenschap. Humanistisch Tijdschrift voor Wetenschap en Cultuur 42, 3: 158–164.

—— (1996) Mijnheer, heb ik met u een zorgrelatie? Over ethiek, over zorg en over een ethiek van de zorg. Utrecht: Stichting Socrates.

Verloo, M. and Roggeband, C. (1994) Emancipatie-effectrapportage: theoretisch kader, methodiek en voorbeeldrapportages, Den Haag: Ministerie van Sociale Zaken en Werkgelegenheid/VUGA.

Voet, R. (1988) 'Republikeins Feminisme', Krisis 8, 31: 65–79.

—— (1994) 'Groepsidentiteit en groepspolitiek', Tijdschrift voor Vrouwenstudies 15, 1: 139–148.

—— (1995) Feminism and Citizenship: Feminist Critiques of the Concepts of Social-Liberal Citizenship, Leiden: Rijksuniversiteit Leiden.

Vogel, U. (1994) 'Marriage and the Boundaries of Citizenship', in B.van Steenbergen (ed.): 76–89.

Vries, P. de (ed.) (1988) Aan het hoofd van de tafel. Feministische artikelen over vaderlijk gezag, Amsterdam: Sara/Van Gennep.

—— (ed.) (1989) Ongewenste intimiteiten, gewenste rechten, Alphen aan den Rijn: Samson/ W.E.J. Tjeenk Willink.

—— (1997) Kusheid voor mannen, vrijheid voor vrouwen, Amsterdam: Het Spinhuis.

Waaldijk, B. (1996) Het Amerika der vrouw. Sekse en geschiedenis van maatschappelijk werk in Nederland en de Verenigde Staten, Groningen: Wolters-Noordhoff.

Waals, F. van der (1994) 'Mother's Little Helpers', in A. Meinen et al. (eds): 110–123.

Waerness, K (1987) 'On the Rationality of Caring', in A. Showstack Sassoon (ed.): 207–234.

Walker, M. Urban (1989) 'Moral Understandings: Alternative "Epistemology" for a Feminist Ethics', Hypatia: A Journal for Feminist Philosophy 4, 2: 15–28.

Wallace, K. (1993) 'Reconstructing Judgment: Emotion and Moral Judgment', Hypatia: A Journal for Feminist Philosophy 8, 3: 61–83.

Warnke, G. (1993) 'Feminism and Hermeneutics', Hypatia: A Journal for Feminist Philosophy 8, 1: 81–98.

—— (1995) 'Discourse Ethics and Feminist Dilemmas of Difference', in J. Meehan (ed.) Feminists Read Habermas. Gendering the Subject of Discourse, New York and London: Routledge: 247–261.

Waters, K. (1994) 'Women in Kantian Ethics: A Failure at Universality', in B. Bar On (ed.): 117–126.

Wegelin, M. (1988) 'Vaderschap na echtscheiding. Over ideologie en praktijk van "eerlijk delen"', in P. de Vries (ed.): 73–86.

—— (1990) 'Moeders en vaders, scheiden en delen. Constructies van gelijkheid in de verdeling van het ouderschap na echtscheiding', Amsterdam: Thesis.

Werkman, L. (1993) Recht doen aan vrouwen in de kerken. De feministische discussie over rechtvaardigheid en zorgzaamheid als bijdrage aan een visie op kerk-zijn, Kampen: Kok.

—— (1994) 'Zorg and emancipatie: een schijnbare tegenstelling?', in H. Manschot and M. Verkerk (eds): 38–52.

West, C. and Zimmerman, D.H. (1991) 'Doing Gender', in J. Lorber, J. and S. Farrel (eds) *The Social Construction of Gender*, London and New Delhi: Sage: 13–37.

West, R. (1988) 'Jurisprudence and Gender', *University of Chicago Law Review* 55, 1: 1–72.

Whitbeck, C. (1984) 'A Different Reality: Feminist Ontology', in C.C. Gould (ed.) *Beyond Domination: New Perspectives on Women and Philosophy*, Totowa: Rowman and Allenfeld: 64–88.

White, S.K. (1991) *Political Theory and Postmodernism*, Cambridge: Cambridge University Press.

Widdershoven, G.A.M. (1995) *Principe of praktijk? Een hermeneutische visie op gezondheid en zorg*, Maastricht: Rijksuniversiteit Limburg.

Wiel, I. van de (1985) *De adoptiewet: strijdtoneel van godsverbod en psychologenverbod. Een onderzoek naar veranderende concepties van moederschap, vaderschap en afstamming in de katholieke zuil in de jaren vijftig*, Amsterdam: Universiteit van Amsterdam.

Wingerden, I. van (1994) 'Vrouwen en de overgang. Valkuilen, verleiding en feministische variatie', *Gezondheid en politiek* 12, 3: 21–24.

Withuis, J. (1990) *Opoffering en heroïek. De mentale wereld van een communistische vrouwenorganisatie in naoorlogs Nederland 1946–1976*, Amsterdam and Meppel: Boom.

—— (1995) *De jurk van de kosmonaute. Over politiek, cultuur en psyche*, Amsterdam and Meppel: Boom.

Woodhull, W. (1988) 'Sexuality, Power and the Question of Rape', in I. Diamond and L. Quinby (eds): 167–176.

Woolf, V. (1938) *Three Guineas*, London: The Hogarth Press.

Yeatman, A. (1994) *Postmodern Revisionings of the Political*, New York and London: Routledge.

Young, I.M. (1983) 'Rights to Intimacy in a Complex Society', *Journal of Social Philosophy* 14: 47–52.

—— (1987) 'Impartiality and the Civic Public: Some Implications of Feminist Critiques of Moral and Political Theory', in S. Benhabib and D. Cornell (eds): 56–77.

—— (1989) 'Polity and Group Difference: A Critique of the Ideal of Universal Citizenship', *Ethics* 99, 2: 250–274.

—— (1990a) *Justice and the Politics of Difference*, Princeton, NJ: Princeton University Press.

—— (1990b) *Throwing Like a Girl and Other Essays in Feminist Philosophy and Social Theory*, Bloomington: Indiana University Press.

—— (1992) *Equality, Empowerment, and Social Services: Some Questions and Problems*, Utrecht: the Netherlands Institute for Care and Welfare.

—— (1994) 'Punishment, Treatment, Empowerment: Three Approaches to Policy for Pregnant Addicts', *Feminist Studies* 20, 1: 33–57.

—— (1995) 'Mothers, Citizenship and Independence: A Critique of Pure Family Values', *Ethics*, 105, 3: 535–556.

Zeegers, N. (1996) 'Feministisch denken over geweld in de jaren zeventig en tachtig. De politiek van het persoonlijke', in R. Römkens and S. Dijkstra (eds): 123–138.

Zipper, J. (1988) 'Vaders bij de buis. Reproductieve technologie en vaderschap', in P. de Vries (ed.): 87–99.

—— (1989) 'What Else Is New? Reproductive Technologies and Custody Politics', in C. Smart and S.L. Sevenhuijsen (eds): 243–269.

Zipper, J. and Sevenhuijsen, S.L. (1987) 'Surrogacy: Feminist Notions of Motherhood Reconsidered', in M. Stanworth (ed.): 118–138.

Zwaard, J. van der (1993) *El Mizan. Wijkverpleegkundigen over de opvoeding in allochtone huishoudens*, Amsterdam: SUA.

Zwinkels, M. (1990) 'Zorgen als ballast', *Tijdschrift voor Vrouwenstudies* 11, 3: 247–260.

INDEX